Soul
and
Silicon

Spirits in a High-Tech World

Carl A. Goldman

Rising Star Press
Los Altos, California

Soul
and
Silicon

Spirits in a High-Tech World

Carl A. Goldman

Rising Star Press
Los Altos, California

Rising Star Press
Los Altos, California

Library of Congress Catalog Card Number: 97-69777

Interior design by Joanne Shwed, Backspace Ink
Jacket design by Detta Penna
Jacket photos by Ginger Smith Bate

Manufactured in the United States of America

Publisher's Cataloging-in-Publication
(Provided by Quality Books, Inc.)

Goldman, Carl A.
    Soul and silicon : spirits in a high-tech world / by Carl A. Goldman. -- 1st ed.
    p. cm.
    Includes bibliographical references.
    ISBN: 0-933670-01-X

    1. Santa Clara County (Calif.)--Religious life and customs.
2. Santa Clara County (Calif.)--Religion--20th century. 3. Technology--Religious aspects. I. Title.

BL2527.C2G65 1998   291'.09794'73
                                              QBI97-41033

For *M*
Path starter, life partner

Contents

Acknowledgements

Spiritual matters are deeply personal, and people are understandably hesitant to bare their souls for public review. Those who agreed to be interviewed for this book earned my profound admiration and respect as well as my gratitude. I hope that readers will find them good companions for their own journeys.

My sincere thanks also to those who contributed to the mind- and eyeball-taxing task of reading drafts and providing editorial feedback: Ginger Bate, Kit Goldman, Joan Passarelli, Joanne Shwed, Jackie Vaccarello, and Michole Nicholson, Editorial Director of Rising Star Press.

And finally, thanks to Diane Wood Middlebrook for her many helpful suggestions and comments throughout the project.

Interviewees' names and other identifying details in this book have been changed to protect privacy.

iii

❧

Introduction

This book is about spiritual journeys in the computer technology capital of the world: Silicon Valley, California. It's about people here, and how the unique local culture—future-oriented, engineering-driven, fast-moving, intensely competitive—interacts with and influences the search for meaning in life.

The Valley has been a particularly fertile environment for the growth of independent, iconoclastic minds. It hums to the energy of people pushing the boundary of what *is* in search of what is even better—faster, more powerful, more ingenious. Stakes are high, both in money and ego, fueling the passion to create something new. In this environment, "conventional wisdom" is an oxymoron. All ideas must be tested. New information is constantly being gathered and examined to find some new wrinkle, some new piece of data from which the next "killer app" will be developed.

These traits are not confined to practical matters; they carry over to the philosophical. For those who have participated, even indirectly, in the creation of technological wonders inconceivable 10 years ago, it is a short leap to ask what truths elsewhere in life are yet to be fully understood. Inquirers into this conceptual realm

often find themselves questioning, in the true Valley style, the va-
lidity of old assumptions and traditional approaches.

This is largely a book of stories about individuals' paths and
the adventures behind them. It is an anecdotal account, not a sociological or theological study.

At its heart are the voices of the people who shared with me
their experiences and thoughts about the human spirit and life in
the Valley. For research, I conducted over 80 formal interviews and
a like number of informal ones. The people in these pages represent widely diverse beliefs, backgrounds, ages and professions—
corporate CEOs and community volunteers; homemakers and engineers; clergy and laity; believers, agnostics and confirmed atheists; all emerging from a multiplicity of ethnic and religious backgrounds. Some have chosen spiritual paths, some haven't. Some
have given names to their life philosophy, some haven't. Practically
everyone has strong opinions, even when those opinions are in
transition. All shared the sense that their view of life has been influenced by Valley culture.

Interview questions were open-ended, designed to encourage
free association. I asked people:

❖ about the events and processes they felt had shaped their spiritual lives and beliefs

❖ how spiritual life in Silicon Valley compared with spiritual
   life where they came from (and practically everyone comes
   from somewhere else)

❖ what changes they've experienced in their spiritual life or views
   since coming here

❖ whether or not they had done any exploration of alternative
   belief systems and, if so, whether they had found anything of
   value

❖ what they want from their spiritual lives, and how that compares to what they actually get

Next, I asked them to define what some of the core concepts of religion and spirituality mean to them. Questions included:

❖ what their vision of God was, how they communicate with God, and how or whether they get communication back

❖ whether one can be spiritual, even if one does not believe in a defined deity or practice a religion

❖ how they think about the soul, and whether they believe everyone has one, even those who never experience any spiritual awakening

Then we turned to the dynamics of spiritual life in a material, high-tech world. I asked people:

❖ what conflicts, dilemmas or problems they've had to deal with in living their beliefs in the real world

❖ if any specific job-related experiences caused them spiritual conflict

❖ whether their code of morals and ethics comes primarily from their spiritual beliefs, or from some other source—their upbringing, or just being a law-abiding citizen

❖ whether they thought that those with spiritual lives or beliefs were likely to hold different moral and ethical codes from those without a spiritual life

Then I asked interviewees to think about those who reject any spiritual life or beliefs:

❖   what factors lead to that rejection

❖   do people stay with that decision once made, or do they re-
    visit it

I also asked them to describe situations they knew where one person in a marriage or relationship had a spiritual life but the other did not, and how that tended to work out.

Then I switched the focus from where they started and where they are to where they're going: the trends and future directions they see for their personal spiritual lives, and for the Valley in general.

Clergy were asked to provide a somewhat different perspective, commenting on their observations about their parishioners' views more than their own. However, I did ask clergy to talk about how their role as a spiritual leader in Silicon Valley differed from being a spiritual leader elsewhere.

The interview process itself produced unexpected reactions. Many interviewees remarked that this was the first time they had occasion to talk about these matters to anyone—even the people closest to them. It was striking to hear the comment repeated, "I wish I could be a fly on the wall when you interview my _____ [spouse, adult child, colleague, friend, neighbor, pastor]."

Some found the process of answering the questions to be an act of self-discovery: they had not previously put their beliefs into words. They came away intrigued, and considered their answers to be the starting point for further reflection.

Many expressed surprised appreciation at being listened to by an interested, nonjudgmental party. It is often said that there is a great spiritual hunger in the world today. Based on the experience of writing this book, I would add that part of that hunger is a great need to be *heard*.

Many of the dynamics and characteristics of modern times reflected in these pages are found elsewhere. But Silicon Valley culture is unique. It is a primordial soup out of which the new and unpredictable constantly emerge. Questions about the meaning of life are ingredients in the soup pot, and the fire is lit. Spiritual life in the next millenium will be influenced by the forces already at work in the lives presented here.

CHAPTER ONE

൦

Silicon Valley Overture

*In the past decade, the dynamic work environments of
so-called baby boomer companies, most notably the
high-stakes, high-tech firms of Silicon Valley and
Route 128 outside of Boston, provided a perfect
breeding ground for such ("every man for himself")
attitudes. ...Each new success generated more work
and more of a sense that the pace of the job had taken
on a life of its own.*

Amy Saltzman, *Downshifting—
Reinventing Success on a Slower Track*

There is no formal "Silicon Valley" designation on
most maps.

Driving in from the south along U.S. Highway 101, you pass
the lettuce and artichoke farms of Salinas, the garlic fields of Gilroy,
and the low, rolling, summer-brown, winter-green hills of south
San Jose.

1

Coming in from the east, terrain is spare and dusty along Highway 580 from Tracy to Pleasanton. A few cows and the wind farms of the Altamont Pass, reaping stored energy to be sold to PG&E, provide landscape variety. On one flank grow the affluent bedroom communities of east Contra Costa County.

Heading in from the north takes you through the area's heavy civilization: Marin County, The City (San Francisco), the suburban upper Peninsula communities.

Finally, you can vector in from the west: here are the beaches, funk, college ambience and '60s counterculture remnants of Santa Cruz; and the more prosaic settings of Half Moon Bay, fog-shrouded Aptos, and the blue-collar-and-folk-arts persona of Pacifica.

Wherever your trip started, when you get here you've arrived at one of the world's most unconventional locations. Think of it as one-third geography, one-third history, and one-third state of mind.

❖ The geography includes, roughly, the northern two-thirds of Santa Clara County, the southern half of San Mateo County and the southwestern quadrant of Alameda County.

The two million people within this 30-mile radius have played a part in crafting a lifestyle richly, if hotly, spiced by the area's unique culture and economy.

❖ The history is an amalgam of top-notch educational institutions, inspired inventors, entrepreneurial energy and a synergistic business climate.

Seeds dropped into this soil have produced blooms beyond anyone's expectation. The stories of the fabled founders—Hewlett and Packard, Noyce and Moore, Jobs and Wozniak, Treybig and Perkins, and many, many others—are the warp and woof of the Valley fabric. They helped create a singular, ongoing success story. Some of the new generation of Valley companies have attained billion-dollar market valuations and revenue levels in incredibly short periods.

They also pioneered innovative views of how business organizations ought to work. Maximize employee creativity. Minimize bureaucracy. Simplify decision making. Put authority where the knowledge is. Ability outranks seniority. Speed is essential. Growth is king. Missions are stated. Involvement should be high. Profits should be shared.

Most of this was not unique in a rhetorical sense: these buzzwords were afloat elsewhere. The difference was that in Silicon Valley they passed the talk stage and became reality. Not in every company, not in all situations and departments, not all the time. But enough to say a new industrial culture had been born.

That culture was a magnet. People wanted to be where the action was, where they could push back technical frontiers, move up fast, make big money. The bright, the creative, the aggressive, the impatient, the first nerds flocked to the area. The race was on.

❖ The state of mind revolves around the predominant economic activity: producing the tools of information technology that will shape much of 21st century life.

Some people are directly involved with this effort because they're the ones making the technology happen. Others are close, but not directly involved. Still others are neither involved nor close, but they know it's going on. It's in the air, the water, the wires. Osmosis happens. Everyone gets affected by the technology chase, one way or another.

OPTIONS AND STARTUPS

Valley companies have trailblazed some radical compensation notions. These notions helped define the economy, and the economy has helped define the culture. One notion was dramatic expansion of the use of stock options. Traditionally, in American industry, options were an executive perk. Many companies in the Valley have had a policy of awarding options to *every* employee. Some haven't gone quite that far, but use guidelines which include the majority of employees. Most companies grant additional options to eligible employees every year.

"Stock options" and "incentive compensation" have become part of the working vocabulary of most Silicon Valley professionals. Companies which don't offer them may have a hard time keeping their work force in place. Annual turnover rates of 30 to 40 percent are a fact of life for many organizations in any case. A substantial portion of this turnover consists of people leaving established companies for the wilderness of a new, small company: either a startup, or one still in its formative stages.

The lure is not just financial. There's an excitement and an involvement level in new companies that established companies just can't match.

Rules are nonexistent.

Everyone gets into everything.

Jeans and tennies are OK every day, not just on dress-down Fridays.

Massive amounts of pizza get ordered in for 10 PM debugging sessions which run until 3 AM or until everyone is too loony to continue.

Cots for overnighters populate the cubicles.

To keep costs down and avoid running through the venture capital too fast, computer parts and office supplies are bought with personal credit cards.

Offices leased to house 20 people now contain 56.

Fascinating, cryptic notes fill the whiteboards: thoughts of ultimate profoundness when first written; now smudged, incomprehensible scrawls.

Hobbies, families and love lives are put on hold until FCS (first customer shipment) of whatever the new product is.

People *commit*: to the schedule, to the success, to the team.

Listen to someone who's done this talk about it. Watch the eyes glow. Many who have been there regard the new-company experience as the high point of their career, and wonder if they'll ever match it for exhilaration and sheer fun.

There is, however, another side to the dynamics of fast wealth and new-company romance. The area is rife with stories of three years of 80-hour weeks poured into startups which didn't make it, leaving behind exhausted, deprived shells instead of new millionaires. It's part of the drama.

No, the money's not the only thing. But it is by no means a rare story for employees of technology companies to find that their stock options have vested with a value that exceeds a year's salary. Some strike it big: early option grants (particularly "pre-IPO"—grants awarded prior to a company's initial public stock offering) from a successful company might catapult even nonmanagerial recipients into full financial independence. It's not unusual. This potential carrot helps keep many people working very long and very hard.

RESIDENCE ROULETTE

When a substantial increase in personal net worth arrives, what happens next is often a real estate tradeup. Micro-moves (15 miles or so) to larger houses as salaries increase or options vest keep the ambience transitory in many neighborhoods. They contribute to the pervasive atmosphere of restless rootlessness. The concept of the generation-to-generation family home is not well known in the Valley. The concept of the amazing runup in property values is.

Forty years ago, the out-of-the-ordinary demographics and economics of Silicon Valley were nascent; no more than a hazy outline, visible only to the most farsighted among the fruit tree orchards, Eichler tract homes, suburban shopping strips ... and the first electronics facilities. A typical middle-class house sold for $16,000.

Real estate agents who have been in the business long enough still recall the profession's disbelief when a typical ranch-style home in the area was first listed for over $100,000 in the '70s—and sold. Now, a 1,200-square-foot bungalow in a prime spot might cost half a million, and might sell within 24 hours with several backup offers waiting in the wings in case the first buyer can't swing the mortgage.

Absent a stock option windfall, these high-overhead households often run on two high-tech incomes, both with 70-hour work weeks. A few years of hard work might permit the luxury of migrating to one salary and one 70-hour week. It can't be counted on. Predictability isn't one of the Valley's strong points.

OUT WITH THE OLD

Deep local roots are rare: most residents are from somewhere else.

Tradition is even rarer, unless it is redefined to mean one-tenth the time span "tradition" implies elsewhere. The contrast with other parts of the country is stark. People in most areas develop affection, respect, even reverence for time-honored ways and things. In Silicon Valley, the frantic pursuit of the latest feature in the newest product seems to osmose through individual nervous systems and collective consciousness, and generate a ceaseless whirl of change. Anything tagged as tradition is a ripe target for suspicion of obsolescence, assumption it needs an update, or the same flavor of contempt given to "down-rev" software.

This pace is driven by the fact that product life cycles in the technology business are often only three to five years from "womb to tomb." The products making up an entire revenue stream today may not be generating a nickel in 36 months, and this puts enormous pressure on the tempo at which companies operate and change.

Product death tends to reverberate. People know this. The tension keeps them focused. That focus does not make it easy to find time to participate in the community. It does not make it easy to pursue intangible, nonmortgage-payment-related esoterica such as spiritual paths.

New work paradigms are emerging, and some of the historic fellowship, contact, and community offered by the office is fading:

❖ Telecommuting allows workers to get the job done from home via electronic communication.

❖ "Virtual" work groups are formed to accomplish a task. When it's done, everyone is reassigned. Group members may never see each other's faces except via videoconference.

❖ Meet the project gypsy. This person carries a laptop computer and a portfolio of technical skills from project to project, company to company, location to location. He or she is the Information Age Lone Ranger—a contractor, not an employee, galloping into the sunset once the new system successfully boots up. Life for this gypsy is a one-task stand, with no commitments or promises on either side, and no time to make friends.

THE 'HOOD

Silicon Valley is a working definition of the term "multiculturally diverse." The emphasis on technological achievement and business success has meant open doors for anyone from anywhere who can perform. People with these skills have come to the Valley from every part of the world. Cultural differences are not just tolerated, they are welcomed. This is not to say that culture clashes don't happen in the Valley, but the insatiable demand for highly competent workers makes intolerance a liability no organization can afford.

Many towns face the challenge and opportunity of building a cohesive and functional community from a widely diverse population. Neighborhoods change rapidly, and people can suddenly feel like outsiders, nonmembers of the community, when they step outside their doors. A few years ago California schools, which routinely offer classes in English as a second language, reported that they were faced with the challenge of teaching students who speak 74 different first languages. A recent *San Jose Mercury News* article reported that the number is now over 100.

STRESSES AND STRAINS

A substantial price tag comes with the affluence and sense of achievement that shaping technology and pushing back its frontiers have brought to the area. The price includes several varieties of stress, difficult or impossible time demands, conflicting priorities, family identity crises, career triumphs turning to heartbreak (and vice versa), and recurring "who am I really?" angst.

Some people end up concluding that the price is too high, and depart for Oregon, Washington, New Mexico, or "back home," wherever that might be. Others find soothing relief just thinking they might split some day. A few can thrive in this stew indefinitely. Most stay put and cope, and eventually have to deal with some form of burnout or emotional fatigue.

These secular dynamics add up to a fine formula for relegating thoughts of spiritual values or quests to a very low spot on the priority list—if for no other reason than personal energy stores are sucked dry by the pace and demands of daily life. They are also, arguably, a fine formula for molding people who may need a spiritual life more than most.

In much of the country, places of worship over a hundred years old are common, and families have been attending them for generations. It's a hard-coded part of life, a given. There's comfort to the continuity, to the certainty of community, to the existence of some spiritual component in life's pattern, even for those who experience it mostly on automatic pilot. They can be effective parts of a strategy for coping with tough times. Transplants to the Valley often find that structure difficult to duplicate.

DUELING DYNAMICS

A January 12, 1996 *Wall Street Journal* article entitled "The Spirit in Technology," by Tom Mahon, starts by saying, "Coincidentally or not, our nation's spiritual crisis has paralleled a remarkable explosion in technological prowess." Part of this book's thesis is that Mahon's observation is no coincidence, and it's clear he doesn't think so either. Since the technological explosion booms loudest in Silicon Valley, here is where we would expect to see its impact strongest. Why is there any inherent incompatibility between technology and spirituality?

The reasons fall into two categories. Let's call them the *cultural* and the *intellectual*.

Some of the factors relating to the cultural category have been alluded to above. Getting in touch with the inner person requires time for reflection, energy for exploration. Serious pursuit of answers to meaning-of-life questions needs space in which to take form. Consideration of matters spiritual benefits from having a foundation on which to build. Structuring a lifestyle which includes active participation in the community flows most easily when that tradition exists and the community is known.

Spare time, energy, space, foundations and traditions are not in long supply in the Valley.

The intellectual category contains the orientation that must, by nature, accompany technological endeavors. It requires a focus on analysis, not faith. Unlike pure science, it's not heavy on theory, demanding instead expedient pragmatism. Demonstrability often buries the conceptual when they collide. "Vaporware," a term referring to a software product which is not yet ready to use, is one of the Valley's most scathing pejoratives.

The dictum of constant change and short product life cycles creates a mindset that does not often encourage—or more importantly, reward—ongoing contemplation of recurring themes. These terms are chosen advisedly. This is not a *contemplative* environment. And it's generally considered better for thoughts to keep moving rather than recur.

Being regarded as a traditional thinker, or one whose rate of mental change doesn't keep up with the Valley beat, can equal the playing of taps to a career.

But it's not human nature to turn on a dime, or slip into different mindsets and personae two or three times a day as if they were clean shirts. The person at work is pretty much the person who comes home, the same one who makes decisions about whether or not there's room and support and need for philosophical bricklaying.

When that person leaves for the office at 6:45 AM and comes home at 7:30 PM, the odds against engaging in metaphorical masonry are long. If the arrival typically includes a full briefcase and a terse comment that, for example, Microsoft announced a competing product today, the smart money drives the betting off the board.

There are those who are gifted with the ability to put it down at the end of the day, pick it up in the morning, and have a free mind in the interim. They are rare.

(Not) Getting Away

An indicative trend in the Valley is that many companies have had to establish a maximum number of accrued vacation hours employees can carry. You might ask why. It's particularly surprising since the combination of brisk turnover and relatively new companies means that few employees have been on the payroll long enough to get up to the hallowed realm of earning five weeks or more of annual vacation.

The answer is that people are taking fewer and shorter vacations. The job demand level and the business crisis frequency level make it difficult to get away. The two-job household has double the problem: when one can make it, the other can't. Even if they manage to schedule it, there's a good chance something will come up and one of them will be asked to reschedule. A vacation alone is not much fun, so they both cancel. By the time the dust has cleared, the end of another year is approaching. They've accrued another 80 hours of vacation apiece, which they have no idea when they'll be able to take.

So the vacation has mutated to bite size. A day here. A three-day weekend there. An extra day slipped in with a holiday. If the stars line up right and no one has been kicking the cat, things might come together to allow a full week. More than that can be tough.

It's particularly tough for those whose internal operating systems don't slip into relax mode quickly. If you've got a four-day vacation and it usually takes you three just to get unwound enough to be able to start to play, the actual relaxation you get from the break might fit in a thimble.

As if time pressure isn't enough of a roadblock to recreational intervals, a new round of technological invasion is in full force. Say howdy to your cellular phone, worldwide pager, notebook computer with extra-long-lasting lithium ion batteries, remote e-mail package, wireless modem, and car fax. You're IN TOUCH, and you can't get out.

That's fine most of the time. But it can certainly take a toll on the mood when you're lying on the beach with your main muffin, sipping long-awaited mai tais, letting the warmth of the sun and the gentle sound of the surf do their magic, fingertips ready to jolt each other with a megawatt of marvelous magnetism, and three of the above devices clatter into action.

More and more people are being issued these tools. And it's often considered bad form to leave them behind, no matter where you're heading.

AND YET ...

No, it's not a conducive environment for pursuing deeper meaning. And yet ...

Against the background of semiconductors, networks, bandwidth, peripherals, clock speed, baud rates, Web surfing, source code, motherboards, stress, rush and uncertainty, some people find themselves (sometimes to their surprise) on a reconnaissance mission to find spiritual significance or something akin to it. Let's meet some of them.

CHAPTER TWO

❧

Enter the Spirit

What we call "the spiritual life" and "the spiritual quest" are simply the ways we discover to transcend our delusions of our own separateness, superiority, or inferiority and gradually feel our identity with our fellow beings and compassion for them.

Sam Keen, *Hymns To An Unknown God*

What causes people to embark on a spiritual path and stay on it?

Sam Keen's view of spirituality as a manifestation of the inherent connection between humans is certainly not universal. But even the casual observer can't miss the fact that members of spiritual "search parties" often form powerful links.

TWO VIEWS

Justin and Walter are both ministers to vigorous, medium-sized Protestant churches in the heart of Silicon Valley. Their theological outlooks and personal observations have led them to different perspectives on the question of what gets people started on a path.

Walter sees the momentum to commence a spiritual journey stemming primarily from the life experiences and conditions of the individual. Some of the contributory variables he identifies are:

❖ curiosity (fed, in part, by the Valley's "inquiring minds" culture)

❖ success, money and power, once achieved, being a less filling dish than had been expected, leaving a puzzling, inner hunger for something else

❖ dissatisfaction with the obvious or pat answers offered to questions about deeper life meaning

❖ gratitude or appreciation for good things swelling past the ability of the usual mechanisms to adequately express it

❖ problems that can't be solved by attacking them with the usual tools—or at all

This last item captures an important part of Valley culture. A frequently used term here is "Silicon Valley cowboy" or "Silicon Valley maverick." These designate individuals who do life and business their own way; disregard rules or values established by others; make things happen through the force of their personalities; and characterize the high-tech version of the American rugged individualist. "Cowboy" and "maverick" are generally considered very complimentary appellations. To these hard-chargers, the idea of a problem that can't be solved is an alien concept, probably originating somewhere in the Centaurus cluster.

However, self-containment, nonconformity, and implacability of vision can add dangerous levels of mass and velocity to a single-minded steeplechase to success. A crash, even a serious bump, is magnified. The individual may be caught between the need for a new kind of intervention and a personal direction which rejects both the intervention, and the very idea that one might ever need it. Show weakness and the sharks will smell it, gather, and devour you: the maverick's ultimate nightmare.

At the very least, unsolvable problems can be good inner conversation starters.

Justin's view on spiritual birth is founded more on theology and less on the pragmatism of circumstances than Walter's. He believes that, ultimately, no external condition *decides* or *causes* the start of a journey. Rather, it is an "awakening," and the result of the work of the Holy Spirit. However, he does see high-impact events such as children, marriage, emergency, grief, economic loss or failure as having the capability to produce an opening in which the Spirit can do its work.

Justin has a guardedly optimistic view of increasing numbers of people finding their way onto spiritual paths. "Silicon Valley is not atheist, it's agnostic," he says. He sees the need for churches and spiritual leaders to take a strongly proactive approach in reaching out to the community, partly because wallflowers don't thrive in this climate, and partly because of the nature of the populace.

Justin's first church was in Pennsylvania. "Denomination was much more important there. Here, we have a lot of young people pursuing high-tech careers who are part of the 'post-Christian' generation. They're growing up without a church." He believes many will sense isolation in their lives, and initiate some kind of spiritual exploration. He does not believe denomination will be the key to their eventual choice. He sees them focusing on people, message, programs, responsiveness, "organizational personality." The free market competition for ideas and products may spill over into spirits.

BAR TALK

At this point, let me pose a question.

You're sitting in your favorite pub, enjoying a bracing mineral water with a twist of fresh lime. A person you know well and like joins you. It's a rare, laid-back moment. Neither of you has to run off at any particular time, so the conversation flows. Let's hypothesize that you have recently had some thoughts about spirituality, religion, God, or maybe just the deep-meaning-of-life brand of philosophy. Or perhaps you've been thinking about what you're reading in this book.

Do you discuss this with your companion?

Statistically, the answer is *probably not*.

Here are some numbers which appear to contain contradictory messages. Sixty percent of Americans are members of churches and synagogues, and 70 percent say they are involved with one even if they're not a member. Yet a recent Gallup poll reported that only 2 percent of men and women talk with even their best friends about religion. And it's reasonable to assume that we share deep issues more freely with best friends than just about anyone else.

So the bottom line appears to be that this is a rare discussion topic. In Silicon Valley, based on anecdotal evidence, it's rare to the point of disappearance. Maybe it's because there's a concern that introducing the topic might drive people away, and no one likes to be lonely. Maybe it's more complicated than that.

Olivia, who moved here from the South, described how spiritual lives in her home area were tightly intertwined with social

---

Spirituality is definitely not a cocktail party topic in this area. People will reveal their sexual orientation sooner than their religious orientation.

Jesse, a Bay Area journalist

activities. As a teenager, she joined a church partly because she enjoyed hanging out with members of their choir and youth group. In sharp contrast, the Valley tends to regard matters of the spirit as private and personal. Not everyone wants tight coupling of the social and the spiritual—but many aren't sure what takes its place.

QUICKENING

Marie and her husband Ray came to Silicon Valley from old-line neighborhoods in East Coast cities. He's chief executive officer of a high-tech services firm. She was a marketing analyst for an electronic communications company. The "gotta-go-whether-you-want-to-or-not" approach of her parents toward church had turned her off to anything smacking of religion: no way was she going to get snared again.

The hard-charging Valley environment kept her mind off spiritual matters until she became pregnant. Then, consciousness of the miracle of new life began to enwrap her. When their first child was born, they made the decision that she would become a full-time homemaker. As the corporate world receded she felt ready to begin an inner dialogue on spirituality, and how it might work for her and her family. "In Boston," she says, "you're either Catholic, Protestant, Goddess or weird. You can be so much more unconnected out here."

Indeed. "Connection," or its lack, is often central to the initial energy flow impelling people to search for meaning or spirit. A faint touch of emptiness appears. A vague sense of dissatisfaction crawls up to a noticeable level. A knock on an inner door behind which something valuable should be found is greeted with a hollow echo. This can be disconcerting enough to jump-start a new process or revive a comatose one.

This process might be subtle, even elusive. Discovering emptiness is one thing; figuring out what to fill it with is another. The time span from initial gnaw to defined direction can be lengthy and filled with numerous dialogues: internal, external, to the point, cloudy, uplifting, confusing. This is the nature of exploration, and it's not unusual for people dealing with exploration's ambiguity to envy those who have already made up their minds, one way or another.

Nagging feelings of missing community and missing pieces of self can be low level and intermittent in the midst of daily life demands. Some come onto a search path via more intense experience.

MIRIAM

Miriam is a well-qualified observer of the scene. In the early '80s she left a job at a large bank to join a hot Silicon Valley telecommunications company. They had decided to form a finance subsidiary to do in-house equipment leasing. As employee number two of the leasing sub, she experienced the dynamics of both an established Valley stress mill and a startup. The company was subsequently acquired by a larger corporation, leading her to a rotating set of assignments over the next few years.

Miriam had been raised Roman Catholic, but by age 16 she had concluded that she wasn't getting anything she needed or wanted from the Church: "I came to believe that religion was for people who were weak." She didn't regard herself as weak. For the next 20 years there was to be no spiritual practice in her life.

The Silicon Valley experience gave her inner person a roughing up it won't soon forget. As the pace and her perceived need to prove herself increased, she found less and less time for anything but work. Eventually, she was to separate from her long-time boyfriend, become almost inaccessible to friends and family, and discontinue all activities that didn't relate to work. "Work pressures drove me to my knees," she recounted.

Miriam never felt that her spirit had died; more that it was taking a long nap. She felt ungrounded, insecure, afloat. As her anxiety waxed, her dormant belief in a higher power kicked in. She began to do something she hadn't done for a long time, and hadn't expected to do again: pray for help. Her spirit stirred. She hoped it wasn't waking up just in time to be devoured.

On a muggy Wednesday night in a tacky hotel room in North Carolina, Miriam had an epiphany.

She was there on the most mundane of business purposes: a sales call the next day. It would be a tough presentation to a skeptical audience. The pressure was on. The company wanted this business. They expected her to get it. To do that she'd need to absolutely nail the presentation, then have crisp, flawless answers to an unpredictable set of questions.

A good night's sleep would help. But as she lay, apprehensive and alone, in the strange bed in the rundown hotel in the humid, sticky night 3,000 miles from home, she wondered if she'd be able to sleep at all. She drifted. Then, she sensed ... she was ... being tenderly held ... by "a being that I *knew* was the Holy Spirit." It offered her comfort, reassurance. It was "a transforming moment."

The next day she was calm and capable, and aced her sales presentation. Over time, the business transaction faded into the obscure wastebasket of industrial history which is the destiny of somewhere between 95 and 99 percent of all daily business activities. The transforming moment will live in her forever.

Miriam reclaimed her awakened spirit, and will never again leave home without it. Through that process, she came to realize that for her, the demands of the Silicon Valley business environment were inimical to her inner life. She did not have the bandwidth to commit the time, the emotional energy, the mindset required for business success and have anything left with which to sustain the spirit.

Circumstances gave her choices. She quit. She does not expect to return to the corporate world. She also does not expect to forget it.

Miriam now uses her business skills in local community and church work. She has become a certified spiritual director. She will be well qualified to direct those struggling to balance soul and silicon needs in the Valley corporate environment. She has become something she would never have predicted: a Silicon Valley success story. The definition may be new, but that's fine. The Valley likes new ideas.

Miriam found that her spiritual life and her high-pressure professional career could not peacefully coexist. Yet, perhaps she owes her fulfilling current path to the work-related strains. Her spirit may have gone into hibernation because it was not needed or appreciated. If she had not cooked in the Valley crucible for a while, she might never have tenderized up enough to welcome it back.

FRANK

Frank's centrally located, glass-wall office gives him a panoramic view of the bustling office activities around him. He's CEO of a community bank in the heart of the Valley. The bank's mission is to provide financing and business counsel to smaller, local enterprises.

It's a financial services version of the startup story. Frank competes with the giants of his industry. He's comfortable with this. He knows them well.

One of the things he knows is that the climate in large corporations has mutated in some unpleasant ways over the years. "People don't make friends in big companies anymore," he says. "There's the politics. Then, it's become like war. Chances are good friends will get killed off at some point. It's painful, and it's pervasive." He moved to the smaller organization because he wanted more relationships and closer ties to the community.

Frank's parents had no religion or spiritual practice, and neither did Frank for most of his life. He saw no particular need, felt no particular lack.

Seven years ago, in his late teens, Frank's younger son attempted suicide during a period of severe emotional problems. He survived. But the impact of the event caused Frank's wife, Yvonne, to restart her spiritual path. She joined a church and introduced Frank to her minister, Allen.

Over the next few months Allen became both friend and "conduit to spirituality" for Frank. The inner opening, the creation of a space in which a spiritual journey could take initial form, was the product of three things: his son's problems, Yvonne's bringing her journey into the home, and a high-impact realization about himself.

Despite his professional success, Frank saw that he did not have much in the way of meaningful, personal (as opposed to material) resources in his life. He had himself and his considerable abilities; he had his job; and he had his wife. "If any of these went away, I knew I'd be in trouble."

This was not just idle worry. Frank is solidly into midlife; health problems can happen. Today's economic uncertainties probably put anyone who doesn't think he or she can get canned smack-dab in the Pollyanna category. And, in fact, he and Yvonne had worked through a period where they discussed a separation.

Frank needed community: connection with others at a meaningful level, not the wary, let's-couch-all-our-conversation-in-company-clichés-and-accepted-business-code-so-neither-of-us-exposes-too-much-of-ourselves level. He was ready to *explore* spirituality. But he was ready to *commit* to community. He saw the church they were attending as a good place to do both. It proved to be not so simple.

Frank's experience and abilities, and his close relationship with Allen, led to an invitation to join the lay board responsible for church oversight. He accepted. Shortly thereafter, tragedy struck. Allen was diagnosed with cancer.

The original prognosis was that Allen would respond to treatment and enjoy at least partial recovery. He asked Frank to accept responsibility for chairing the lay board during his incapacitation. He felt Frank was the right person to hold the parish together during a tough time, and trusted him to maintain the church's course.

Frank took the responsibility. During this period he was also in the process of moving from a large bank to the top job in the community bank. This wasn't just a full plate. This was a heaping plate, with gravy sloshing over the sides.

Allen's illness meant that the parish had little pastoral support. The decision was made to bring in an interim minister. Frank quickly discovered that political wrangling is not unique to the corporate world.

The interim pastor was a disaster. She moved forcefully to further her own agenda: positioning herself to assume the ministerial mantle upon Allen's death. She was controlling and manipulative. She stimulated the formation of feuding factions. She drove a wedge between the younger and older members of the congregation. "Enemies lists" were drawn up. Machiavelli was alive and moving through the pews.

Frank had never anticipated that his newly started spiritual pursuit would entail such ugliness—or worse, that he would be the point person who had to deal with it. But he's a trained executive and used to taking charge. Allen had entrusted him with the health of the parish; he wasn't going to let his friend and spiritual guide down. "This was not going to happen on my watch," he recalled emphatically.

He threw himself into the muck. How he got things resolved is not the story here. Eventually, he did. But he paid a price.

"Much too early, I got to see the warts on the organizational side of religion," he says. His emerging spirituality was not yet past that critical stage where it could stand alone, unquestioned and strong, without a formal support structure. It had been fed the wrong nourishment at a critical time, and had been stunted.

The battle left dregs and doubts. He decided he couldn't stay there. Too much baggage would have to be carried forward and dealt with.

Spiritually, Frank is now doing what may be the hardest thing in the world for a take-charge executive: *waiting*. "I'm not good at just letting things flow," he says. But he's enough in touch with the inner process to realize that it took a body blow. The spirit entered. The spirit got roughed up. It hasn't left, but it needs an injury time-out.

Frank and Yvonne have acquired a 55-acre farm in Tennessee. ("To her, it's spiritual. To me, it's rural.") Visits there are a voyage to a land as far away from Silicon Valley as Kansas is from Oz. The multitude of contrasts includes the role of spiritual life.

"You're in Church of Christ and Baptist country," Frank says. "The interesting thing is the pervasiveness of the structure church creates in society there. Everyone goes to church. Then everyone goes to brunch. Don't even try to get a table in the local restaurants late Sunday morning.

"We intellectual types tend to look down our noses at the fundamentalist types. Our image of them is Bible-thumping. But there's a lot of positives that come out of that shared spirituality, a lot of community strength.

"I was standing in line at the water company outside Cedar Hill, Tennessee, to get our water turned on. I saw a guy I knew there, and after we talked a bit, he said, 'Let's go to church together sometime.' I was amazed. That just doesn't happen in Silicon Valley."

Frank places a high value on the Valley's dynamic qualities, its warm embrace of change. But he also believes that there are some absolutes and some eternal truths, some things that don't require a design update every two years.

Frank's high-octane personality would almost certainly miss the action if he spent much time in rural Tennessee. But his spirit might find a little rest, a little healing, and the assuring certainty of a community which believes it has found some things worth keeping.

COURSE CORRECTIONS

Over the past few years there has been increasing focus, research and writing on the dynamics of midlife. Not "midlife crisis," which is old hat. The new view might correctly be termed "midlife opportunity," or "it's midlife and the sky's the limit," or "let that pony run." In her book *Roads Home—Seven Pathways to Midlife Wisdom*, Kathryn Cramer offers this insight:

> *Many scholars believe that midlife offers the best*
> *opportunity for a deep conversion of the spirit because it*
> *is during this period that a person experiences a*
> *convergence of life skills, confidence, pain over the*

harsh realities and compelling necessities of life, and a
desire to rethink inconsistencies or untenable spiritual
beliefs.

OLIVIA

Olivia, the Southern transplant we met earlier, is in the process of sorting out her midlife beliefs. Rethinking inconsistencies is high on her list. The complexities of her journey started long ago. She's been in Silicon Valley for eight years, and this is where she'll try to resolve them. The good news: the Valley is a fine place for asking questions. The bad news: sometimes it's a tough place to find answers.

Olivia was born into a fundamentalist family. "Religion gave no comfort," she says. "It was a behavioral system. God was a watchbird and a rule maker."

Her first spiritual feelings emerged at a campfire service with some friends from another church. She responded to the quiet and the darkness, and felt a touch of something sacred. Their minister "talked thoughtfully," while her minister "harangued." She didn't like harangues. Also, the other church had a better choir and youth group. She joined.

During college she felt increasingly uncertain about religion. She questioned her beliefs. One day, in the middle of a service, she realized it wasn't speaking to her. Olivia was forthright and decisive. She got up and walked out. She didn't go back.

Olivia's first husband practiced no religion when they were married. Five years down the pike, he experienced big-time personal change and joined a charismatic Christian church. She finally told him if he said "Praise the Lord" one more time, she'd leave. He did. And she did.

After her divorce, she wanted to restart her spiritual search, but via a different path. She found a church that had many things she liked: short, philosophical, commonsense sermons; liturgy that moved her; beautiful music. Her fundamentalist memories made her wary of highly emotional worship, and she enjoyed the restrained style of the new church. She joined.

Now she's in midlife, and the midlife mindset has enabled her—maybe *required* her—to gaze more deeply at her path. She's finding some disturbing things.

She feels there's a conservatism in the church that puts it out of touch.

She doesn't see people connecting with each other.

She has serious reservations about the quality of some of the spiritual leadership she's seen.

She doesn't see prayers being answered.

She's looking for a "system of kindness and comfort," and thinks church actions or teachings can sometimes be cruel.

She thinks the virgin birth doctrine is a sexist teaching.

In short, it's not working for her. Olivia is still forthright and decisive. She may walk out. She's done it before; she can do it again. But it will leave her with a problem to solve.

Olivia's spirit is alive and kicking, but it has not found the fulfillment it craves. It is not yet feeding on the peaceful energy which springs from inner truth.

She is not a solitary person. Her spirit wants to commune with others. But she is inherently a person of strong opinions, a person who judges, and it would be almost contrary to her nature to avoid observational criticism of any group to which she belongs.

The Valley's open-ended, freeform environment provides her no particular guidance. On the other hand, a more traditional setting could trigger an iconoclastic rejection of what she might see as presumptuous "ought-to's."

In the meantime she'll read, write, seek daily quiet time, and look for opportunities to do good works. She is attracted to the concept of small groups sharing spiritual quests. It may be that such a group, flexibly and undogmatically accommodating its members' needs, is her best bet for finding her true path.

ARI

An unseasonable warm spell made the early April air smooth and toasty, even though it was only 8:30 in the morning. Ari and I sat on well-seasoned wooden furniture in the beautifully landscaped garden in front of his house. Each shrub looked like it was born to be there. It made a perfect setting for discussing Silicon Valley spirituality with a former large-technology-company manager who had started life in an East Coast Jewish family, and was now a Buddhist monk.

Ari's entire career was spent with a household-word computer company. Early on he became interested in the power of meditation, and the possibility of what might now be called "new paradigms" for workplace interaction. He still remembers being amazed when his employer immediately granted his request for a three-month leave of absence to go to a Zen monastery. "It's an unproved premise," he says, "but on reflection, I think the managers who approved it probably felt the same way I did: that it was a good thing. I think it touched their sense of spirituality."

I started by asking about his parents' reaction to his pursuit of Zen. "I sensed that the formal observation of Judaism wasn't really a big part of their lives," he said. "But they were a little confused by my decision. They saw it as something of a threat. They associated Zen with hippies and drugs, and it wasn't easy for them to sort it out."

Ari's many years in the technology trenches were processed in parallel with his adventurous path of personal enlightenment. I asked him to reflect on the area's spiritual dynamics.

"What often starts people onto a spiritual path is suffering, in the broad sense. A feeling of isolation, aloneness, lack of community. That explains the fascination some people have with cults. It's not what the organization is preaching—it's that it's *an organization*, and fills a need for community.

"My wife's family is from Oklahoma. People there are less sophisticated, but more at peace, and friendlier. They smile. They're courteous. It's wonderful to go back there.

"In the Valley we have a lot of experimentation and exploration, and a willingness to try new things. The 'technology presence' goes with this. In smaller towns, people tend to just stay with the religion of their childhood, and don't seem to feel the same need to experiment.

"What takes people off their path is usually doubt, or alienation from the group, or a more realistic view of their leader. In fact, it's *usually* a leadership issue.

"People here are looking for their spiritual practice to show them how to find equanimity, peace, joy and wisdom in the frantic, stressful, uncertain events of their everyday life. These issues are not unique to Silicon Valley. We just have more stress, more uncertainty, more change.

"I truly believe that everybody recognizes the existence of something greater than themselves. And they recognize that they're a part of it. We give different names to the 'something greater.' Some say God. Some say 'Big Self.' We come up with a word, and because we assign a word, people mistake the word for the thing. Then, because our definitions differ, we fight or go to war. Needless to say, this has nothing to do with true understanding.

"The word is a 'pointing finger,' not the thing. The whole point of spiritual practice is to bring that into view. Spiritual practice should transcend religious strife, and the confusion people feel about God, and ideas relating to beliefs.

"Technological change happens so rapidly in this area. It puts pressure on companies and people. They live with a constant feeling that their survival is threatened. In the effort to feel safe, and cope with the stress, the tendency is to put aside matters of the spirit as not being useful to professional or economic survival. But at the extreme, stress can cause spiritual seeking.

"Work and spiritual pursuits can be integrated. But it's much easier if the spiritual practice is a contemplative one that enables us to explore and accept our own suffering. Having just a belief system, as opposed to a contemplative practice, may not lead to the compassionate, nonjudgmental viewpoint which helps us see ourselves in others.

"Meditation lowers our emotional defenses, and we're more easily touched."

RON

Ron has a goal: he wants to help the spirit grow in his neighbors.

He's been in Silicon Valley for six years. He grew up in a comfortably middle-class family in Connecticut. His "cradle religion" was agnostic: his family had no active religious affiliation.

After receiving a liberal arts degree from Dartmouth, Ron entered the Columbia University architecture program. He put his newly learned expertise about line and structure to good practical use by leaving to become a furniture maker. He got married, had four daughters, moved to Northern California.

Ron always had a gut feeling that there was something sacred, something to be held in awe, somewhere. When making furniture, he enjoyed thoughts of trying to connect the buyer's spirit with the piece. But he felt no drive whatever to take the thoughts further.

One day his wife told him she would like to put the kids in Sunday school. His response was, "Over my dead body." He didn't mind pursuing spiritual ideas, but not Christianity and, in fact, not any formal religion. Religion was hypocrisy. Christianity was a fairy tale. End of discussion.

About three months later he was standing in a doorway of his house. Suddenly, he felt reality blurring, melding into a dream-image hybrid. The air was still and he stood still and felt as if a wind were blowing through the house. He sensed a new presence, very deep inside him. And he *knew*. Improbably, with no thing, no event happening, unexpected, unrequested, Christ had come for him, and to him, in "a whisper and a thunder."

As a matter of fact, Ron knew very little about *Jesus* at the time, which didn't matter. What happened was what he calls "a profound mystical connection with *the Christ*"; a powerful life force to which he had to respond. He had not one shred of question about this.

Shortly thereafter, he began teaching Sunday school.

His new-found faith was not without its practical challenges. The first time he visited a Christian bookstore, he skulked furtively through the storefront shadows, and peered carefully down the street in both directions to make sure no one he knew would see him going in. "It would have been easier to go into a porn shop," he recalls.

Sadly, Ron's new path was not enough to keep his marriage together. After 15 years, the festering of old, unresolved problems and the entry of new problems brought separation. "My heart was split open, in both grief and attendance to spirit," he says.

During the year following his divorce, he walked five miles every day in the low hills near his house. He used these walks for deep contemplation, and maintained an extensive journal of his thoughts while walking. He kept life simple: "I cried, I wrote, I sweated."

One day he walked to the top of the hill and experienced "images of an abyss." He got home, booted up his computer, and keyed in journal entries to record the images. He finished and was ready to power the machine down. Suddenly he felt the pressure of one more paragraph waiting, needing to be written. His fingers hit the keys. On the screen, in italics, were the words:

You have been a stubborn child and you must be stripped naked. I can't promise you'll end up with everything you want, but I can give you the gift of love.

Ron believes he has received a clarion call which he must not deny. He will dedicate his life and professional pursuits to his own spiritual path, and to enabling others to follow theirs. The fact that he'll be trying to do this in Silicon Valley should probably daunt him somewhat. But he's up for the challenge.

He's been ordained as a minister in a mainstream Christian denomination and spent four years as a church pastor. Now he knows it's not the right setting for him. In fact, he doesn't think "mainstream church" is the right setting to make the right things happen in this environment at all. So he's doing the Valley thing. He's planning to establish a center to focus on spiritual formation and "helping people attend to God in their lives": a spiritual startup.

JOSH

I was fortunate to catch Josh. The day after our discussion he was heading out. His mission: a two-year pilgrimage in Syria.

Josh hails from Fort Worth, Texas, and arrived in the Valley before it was under a full head of steam. He sold computers in the prehistoric times when the industry was known as "IBM and the BUNCH," an acronym for IBM's competitors: Burroughs, Univac, NCR, Control Data and Honeywell. He sold these mysterious, new machines to "bare dirt," an affectionate expression for new accounts.

Josh's early entry into computers opened other doors, and he sailed through management positions in timesharing, product development, and application systems. His career was hot, but his inner life during this period was not. He had spent time in a Roman Catholic seminary, and was aware of the role spiritual beliefs can play in lending life meaning. He felt a low-level hunger. But he couldn't muster a commitment.

He thought the problem might be that traditional religion just didn't fit him anymore, so he took a long look at New Age spirituality. That didn't fit either. He decided he needed to change things around, shake them up, "for the sake of my family, myself, and our spiritual lives."

He left the big-company environment and bought a business that would give him more free time. Then he embarked on the search for an answer to a straightforward question: "What does God want from me?" His search included exploration of all the world's major religions, except Islam. "I had too many negative images of Islam," he recalls.

Five years ago, his business took him to a technical publications trade show in Atlanta. A young woman was seated next to

him on the plane. Josh regarded airplane time as a valuable opportunity for reading and reflection. He did not like to talk to seat
mates. Clearly, however, this woman wanted to talk. Josh relented.
"When the coffee and tea came, I reluctantly took my nose out of
my book."

She was having family troubles. She needed to unburden herself to a stranger. He listened. He noticed that references to God
were interleaved throughout her story. She seemed like a very spiritual person, he told her. They talked throughout the flight. Eventually she told him she was a Muslim.

The way she described Islam shocked him by being such a
good fit with what he was searching for, but hadn't found. He was
inspired to do research. He read the Koran. He boiled it down: "I
concluded this is what I believed."

During his religious exploration, he had come to feel that
"... Christianity today has been altered, and in many ways has
nothing to do with Jesus' message. I reread the New Testament.
Separating out what I read from what I had been told, I concluded
that Jesus hadn't said he was God, hadn't really preached the concept of the Trinity.

"I believe that God sends messengers to us from time to time
to help us sort things out. But clergy and church organization and
power structure, that stuff is human, not divine, and it gets in the
way.

"All religions say basically the same thing about God and ethics and walking humbly on the earth. We're here to use what we've
been given. We're here to be good to each other. That's what Islam
is about, and I discovered that I had inadvertently become a Muslim, and believed exactly what Mohammed preached.

"What I want to accomplish during my two years in Syria is
to get back to the sources. Translations don't do justice to sources.

Translators often have their own bias or agenda, and I think that's why there are some problems with the Bible.

"I'm going to study Arabic, then I'm going to dig into the source documents. I'm going to read the originals of the sacred, traditional Islamic texts. The Muslim world is fragmented and fractious because of the differences between sects, but of all the major religions, it has the most complete database."

Commenting on spirituality in the Valley, Josh says, "When I left big business, I got involved in a 12-step program because my son had an alcohol-addiction problem. I got a better understanding of addiction, and I believe Silicon Valley is addicted to its own success. People here seem to be saying, 'I'll do anything to get well except give up my addiction,' and the core addiction is to wealth and success.

"Maybe we won't have real, widespread spiritual life in the Valley until that addiction is cured. Success must flow from spirituality, not the other way around."

ALICIA

Alicia's journey to the Valley started in Arizona, with stops in Texas and the Midwest. She's been here for 12 years. Her household has been a well-entrenched member of the two-careers-in-high-tech bunch. She's the administrative assistant to the chief information officer for a networking company. Her husband, Sean, is a telecommunications engineer for a large semiconductor firm.

There has always been a spiritual component to Alicia's life, but it's taken some twists and turns. Her family was Roman Catholic. As a kid, she thought everyone in the world was Catholic.

When she started having her first serious thoughts about God, she was struck by how much was going on in the world, and the number of people who must be vying for His attention. She concluded that busy as He must be, she'd better plan on figuring life out for herself. This worked for a while.

Shortly after moving to the Valley, Alicia had her first child. The life pattern modifications mandated by the arrival of first children are not news. But during this period Sean was also dealing with increased demands at work, and one of the well-known Silicon Valley dynamics kicked in: families are number two. His employer and his boss were not particularly sensitive to or interested in his new parental role.

In addition to long work hours, it was part of the internal culture of Sean's work group to head out after work and spend time unwinding together at local watering holes. After a stressful day, this was often a more enjoyable prospect than going home to an equally tired spouse and a fretful child. He found himself joining the group more and staying later. His boss approved. His wife did not. She felt he wasn't doing his share at home. She said so, often. It didn't help.

After more than a year of deteriorating domestic relations, Alicia began to comprehend that her husband was dealing with inner demons with big-time fangs and claws. It was good to feel she understood more. But she didn't have a clue about what to do next.

Alicia is skilled at evading reality when she wants to, but she didn't want to in this case. She sensed both of them withdrawing, creating a web of miscommunications and unmet expectations, the

> *I know my family sometimes feels that work and church "outrank" them. In Silicon Valley it's easy to get caught up in the race for more, and you probably have enough already.*
>
> Trent, president of a Valley telecommunications company

marriage falling apart. They had serious disagreements about money. It would have been a good time to draw on her spiritual life. But the internal program that told her God was busy and she'd have to wait for an appointment was still running. Also, she's a strong person; she felt she should be able to fix the problems herself.

But she couldn't, and she didn't know where to go for help. "Living through this just hollowed me out," she says. "I was spiritually bankrupt."

Joining a support group composed of people dealing with similar problems was a major step for Alicia. It may have kept her off a disastrous path. Her inability to return her marriage to health was laying down a psychic topsoil in which the seeds of perceived failure were growing into riotous luxuriance. The group provided a desperately needed herbicide: *look how strong some of us are, and yet look how many of us can't solve these problems.*

After their second child arrived, Alicia felt that her spirit had been revived. Largely through her support group, she had come to terms with what she could and couldn't fix in her marriage. She attended a women's renewal retreat and felt ... renewed. Gratitude for her children had reopened her connection with God: she no longer felt she was waiting for the next available teller in a Friday afternoon bank line when she wanted a word.

Alicia also has all the requisite office automation skills an administrative assistant of the '90s needs. Such people are highly valued and well compensated in the Valley. She felt she was economically and internally ready to take a bold step.

She still loved her husband, still felt committed. But it wasn't going to fly without change. The drinking problem, the money issues, the time priorities had to be addressed. Parenting had to be a joint venture. So did household responsibilities.

Words hadn't worked, so she decided on a trial separation. It wouldn't have been her first choice, and she understood the risks. But the status quo had to be shattered if a new life was going to form. She felt guided and supported by rejuvenated faith. An anecdote which was powerful for her told of a circus performer pushing a wagon across a tightrope. Everyone enjoys it from the seats, but faith is being willing to get in the wagon. She felt ready to climb aboard.

Alicia and Sean were separated for a year. She developed the habit of getting up half an hour earlier each morning, while the children slept, "for meditation and quiet before hell breaks loose." She prayed about things that bothered her, and for the success of their marriage. She and Sean engaged in lengthy, meaningful dialogue about their problems, the kind of dialogue that never seemed to happen before.

Her program worked. They're back together, and she thinks they'll stay that way. They have been able to address the forces that were driving them apart.

The challenges in Alicia's journey have led her to frequent inner reflection. She's not sure what the precise relationship is between practice of a religion and true spiritual belief. Maybe not much.

But she is struck by the degree to which both were a greater part of the fabric of life in other places she's lived. Extra stitching, to stop things from tearing while their owners scrambled over sharp obstacles.

MARTY

Marty vividly remembers the morning he took a .357 Magnum to his failing T-shirt shop, and sat there for an hour and a half with the gun in his mouth.

His business was dying. His wife was planning to leave him—his second failed marriage. His electrical engineering degree and former job at a pioneering Valley electronics company had brought him no joy. He was struggling to think of a reason he would want his life to continue.

Suddenly, he heard a noise. The man who worked in the print shop next door had come in early. He was never there that early. Marty had expected complete privacy and solitude as he contemplated ending it all.

"I knew if I shot myself, he'd hear it," Marty recalled. "Then he'd be involved in finding me. It would be a terrible experience for him. It wouldn't have been fair to him. I didn't want that.

"I always wondered if God put that person there. Otherwise, I might have pulled the trigger. Instead, I found myself asking, 'OK, God, what do you want me to do?'

"Three months later I was in a seminary studying to become a minister."

He completed his theological education and became pastor of a large mainline Protestant church in the heart of the Valley. But after many years of ministry, he found himself squaring off with issues which made him question whether he should continue.

A big issue was the impending breakup of his third marriage. "We were married for 18 years," he said, "the last 12 of which we shouldn't have been. But our denomination doesn't really allow divorced ministers, and I agonized over this because I knew it would end my ministry. I finally decided to resign before the issue could cause divisiveness in our church."

So "minister" joined "engineer" and "T-shirt entrepreneur" in Marty's hats-worn collection, and he executed another career change. He now makes his living as a car salesman, adding to an unusually varied set of perspectives. I asked him to reflect on his personal path, and his views on spirituality in the Valley.

"I've only gone to church a few times since leaving the ministry," he said. "As a car salesman I only get every fifth Sunday off, but I don't know if I'd be going anyway. I have a hard time with organized religion now. A lot of people in this area do.

"Organized religion doesn't seem responsive to people's needs. If an engineer is working 70 or 80 hours a week, but the church wants him or her there every time the doors are open, that's a conflict. And often churches don't really want to hear people's problems. They're not showing the unconditional love they're supposed to. When I was going through my struggles, I got more support from the local Rotary Club than I did from my spiritual community.

"Even though I didn't live an exemplary life, my experiences made me a better minister. Some of my parishioners came to me *because* I had been divorced. They could relate. One woman came to me because her former pastor had told her to solve her marital problems by being obedient to her husband. Probably not good advice in the Valley.

"People here are looking for something that gives them hope beyond what they see in their daily lives. They need to feel someone cares for them. We have a lack of concern for each other in this area, a tendency not to care. Most churches fall short. With God in the equation, you would think we would be able to get past our tendencies and reach out to each other more. Churches should feed spirituality, but sometimes they drain it.

"Within every human, implanted by God, there is a spiritual need. But there are a lot of good, spiritual people here who can't or just don't want to go to church on Sunday. Organized religion equates sitting in the pews with spirituality too much. Sometimes one finds more spirituality in people who don't go to church much.

"The relationship most people have with God in Silicon Valley is not as personal as Christian theology would present it. People here have a hard time with heaven, hell, Christ's miracles, the idea of God excluding anyone. Turns people off, and makes them struggle with their vision of God.

"Another turn-off is the pressure people feel to share any spiritual life they might have, to be 'out there,' witnessing or evangelizing. For some people spirituality is too private and personal to do that, so they opt out. I think Christianity has missed the boat by making this an issue. What's important is the way people *live*, not being 'out there.' "

I asked Marty if he saw a difference in the moral and ethical codes of those who had spiritual lives and those who didn't. "Those with spiritual lives do have a different code—mostly toward others," he replied. "They're *less* tolerant! But other than that, there may not be much difference. Sometimes we forget that Christian belief says we get salvation by grace, and we go around judging others. If God were to judge us the way most of us judge others, we probably wouldn't do too well, and that's sad."

MISSION CONTROL

A May 24, 1996 *San Jose Mercury News* article was headlined "Workplace stress and the meaning of life," and subheadlined "Spirituality is a godsend for workers trying to cope." It's noteworthy that this was in the business section, and labeled as a "Management/ Leadership" focus article.

"There's a new trend developing in the workplace," the article starts off. "It's not teamwork, it's not layoffs and it's not retraining. It's spirituality." Author Laurie Beth Jones, interviewed in the article, has a recommendation: people should look inward and determine what their mission is in life. Not work, life. Then use the insight to go through the common business exercise of developing a personal mission statement. What do *you* really want to accomplish in this life?

Her point is that if you don't say it, you don't know it, and if you don't know it, you can't do it. Her conclusion: "You are either living your mission, or you are living someone else's."

Pat, a local pastor, has a similar observation. "You have to discover why you're here," he says. "If you don't, you live a compromised life. You're responsible, but you're not in charge." Many Valley residents would agree. They're pouring substantial energy into efforts to make the mission they're living their own.

CHAPTER THREE

❧

Discoveries Along the Path

*A friend ... showed his résumé to ... a corporate
headhunter ... who told him crisply that if he was
serious about moving ahead in the business world, he
should remove from the resume any mention of his
involvement with a social welfare organization that
was connected with a church, but not one of the
genteel mainstream denominations. Otherwise, she
explained, a potential employer might think him a
religious fanatic.*

Stephen L. Carter, *The Culture of Disbelief: How
American Law and Politics Trivialize Religious Devotion*

To call competition for technical talent in Silicon
Valley "fierce" is like referring to a Lamborghini as "a car": too
understated to convey the full picture. Therefore, I was delighted
to get the news from the human resources director of the company
I worked for that our difficult search for an engineering vice president
had finally been successful. She described the new member of

43

the executive team in detail, and concluded by mentioning that he was a serious, practicing Christian. She added that this should not be discussed with others: the new VP felt it would undermine his credibility and acceptance.

He may have been right.

"Technologist with religion" is tough enough contrast for one's image. But in a peculiarly Silicon Valley-flavored twist, the VP's baggage might have been heavier because he *did* belong to a "genteel mainstream denomination." Affiliation with a New Age cyberchurch could be viewed as commendably quirky, at least requiring some computer keystroking expertise to "attend." But mainstream church? Bending the knee to traditional authority is often felt to reflect a deficit in gumption, a lack of creativity, or a null individuality quotient.

There has always been an inherent tension between science and spirit. Much of what goes on in the Valley is more properly called "technology development" than "science." Whatever it's called, it has inherited much of the personality of science. It's from Missouri. It says "show me."

Nothing wrong with that. But some things are hard to show, and not everyone is comfortable doing head-on confrontations with skepticism. Journeys of the spirit, and discoveries along the path, are frequently held close to the vest.

But, sometimes, out they come.

PHIL

Phil is a seemingly rare breed: born and raised in Silicon Valley. As a successful real estate agent in the area's explosive property market, he has been close to the dynamics of "doing the deal," geographical change, and sudden wealth. He has also had to gaze into the mirror and confront a face on the road to hell.

Phil's life got off to a dicey start before he was old enough to recognize the fact. His parents got divorced when he was 3 months old. He was adopted by his paternal grandparents. His grandfather was an urban missionary, working primarily in African-American ghettos and helping black workers form labor unions. Phil went to Sunday school most weeks and liked it.

When Phil was 7 his grandfather had a severe stroke. Incapacitated, he and his wife could no longer care for a small child. Phil went to live with his father and his father's second wife. He did not have a good time.

His father and his stepmother were both alcoholics at the peak of their substance abuse. Phil's life was predictably unpleasant. They practiced no religion, and Phil found himself missing Sunday school. At age 9 he started bicycling himself to a neighborhood church school on Sundays. His father and stepmother were too fuzzy to know or care.

By the time he was 11, conditions at home were intolerable. Phil decided to start a new life for himself. He hopped on his trusty bicycle, vectored to the nearest on ramp, and began pedaling up the Bayshore Freeway. He headed for San Francisco. He had heard good things about the City, and figured it was the right place for a heads-up kid like himself.

There have been immense changes in my spiritual outlook since coming to Silicon Valley. From naiveté to blistering reality. From simplicity to complexity. From invincibility to vulnerability. From altruism to commercialism. We deal with an environment of overwhelming materialism, incredible avarice and self-indulgence, where everything has to have a value, and if you give, you have to get. The Valley has made me a realistic mystic.

Pat, a Valley pastor

He was sailing along at a good clip when the police picked him up. He ended up back with his grandparents, but it wasn't a homecoming. His grandfather had never completely recovered from the stroke, physically or mentally. His grandmother was becoming senile. It wasn't like the abuse he had experienced with his father and stepmother. It was more like being alone, made eerie by the presence of bodies with absentee landlords. He didn't like spending time there, so he didn't. The streets were better.

❧ "No Creator" ❧

Phil's early enjoyment of Sunday school, the initial touch of a spiritual component, faded. Circumstances didn't support it.

He remembers lying in bed one night at age 14 and having a rather advanced thought for a 14-year-old: "The universe is infinite and infinity implies no creator." Therefore, there was no God. He had felt relieved, somehow released from obligation.

He remembered how his father and stepmother had enjoyed drinking. He decided to give it a try. He found he had something in common with his dad: he enjoyed it, too.

One month after they both graduated from high school, when he was 17, Phil's girlfriend became pregnant. He found out on Thursday. On Monday he did what he felt was the responsible thing and married her. He stopped drinking, got a job. They had a baby girl.

When he was 21, the marriage went the way so many do when they start too fast and too young. He and his wife divorced. At that, he gave his daughter a better start than he got. She got three years of living with Mom and Dad.

The divorce gave Phil a feeling of release, somewhat similar to what he experienced from his revelation that there could be no God. He celebrated in a similar but expanded fashion, commencing the use of a panoply of recreational substances.

Phil started college at 22. He wasn't particularly motivated by a desire to learn; mostly he didn't want to carry a 1-A draft classification and get sent to Viet Nam. He did not lack for company. Draft avoidance was a widespread national phenomenon at the time, but in the Bay Area, home of Berkeley and Stanford, it was Unquestionable High Doctrinal Correctness.

His previous experience with illicit substances gave Phil a head start on college life of the late '60s. He settled on "LSD, peyote, grass and cheap red wine" as his mixture of choice. This put him into a receptive, exploratory frame of mind, and he became "New Age, drug-induced spiritual."

Phil did not make blazing progress through the higher educational system. By the time his daughter was 10 and wanted to come and live with Phil, he was still in his junior year. He agreed to take her, dropped out of college, and got a job. A few years later he remarried and had two more children.

∾ Bad to Worse ∾

He and his wife were compatible in that they both enjoyed copious quantities of alcohol and other substances. He started a property management company which quickly folded. Then he landed a job containing both good and bad news. The good news was that it had strong financial potential and involved a product he knew well. The bad news was that it wasn't helpful to his problem. He became a buyer and sales rep for a wine wholesaler.

Silicon Valley is less than a two-hour drive from the premium wine-making areas of Northern California, and wine is a very big part of the area's affluent ambience. Some of the capital invested in the cabernet vineyards of Napa, the chardonnay vineyards of Sonoma, the zinfandel vineyards of Monterey, and the boutique wineries throughout the region originated as technology money. "Palate wars" are a form of friendly competition. Restaurants vie for the most imaginative wine lists. Upscale liquor emporiums run allocations and waiting lists for high-demand vintages. Residential wine tasting parties are frequent fun. Wine-tasting weekends, staying at sumptuous bed-and-breakfast inns, are a signature mini-vacation for the area. Wine is in, and Phil was in with what's in.

It didn't work. "Eventually I couldn't stay sober long enough to make my sales calls," he says. No surprise, not even to Phil.

As he passed his 40th birthday with his life in tatters, Phil thought back to the relief he had felt when, at 14, he concluded there was not, could not be, a God. He had no remaining sense of relief. He did have, rising like a triage supplicant from a battlefield, an emerging sense of discovery: he was thirsty for something besides a big, oaky reserve chardonnay. He needed a connection, an anchor. To survive, he had to touch and revive his core of life, his spirit—if any of it was left.

❧ Making the Bed ❧

He knew what he needed to do; he just didn't know how to start. He didn't think he could go it alone. But since his teenage revelation, he had felt repulsed by discussions of God and thoughts of prayer. "It was like the cross to Dracula." Then he remembered some advice that gave him the boost he was looking for.

An acquaintance had said to him once, "Don't think of God, if that's threatening. Use the word as an acronym: Good, Orderly Direction." Not an earthshaking suggestion, but enough to allow Phil to bypass a long-standing psychic jam-up.

He used the acronym. To give it concrete form, he started making his bed every day. It became an important symbolic act. He got up. He made his bed. It was good. It was orderly. It was the beginning of a new direction.

"That's where my spiritual path started," he says. "Making my bed. It was a ray of light. It removed some darkness."

He got his real estate license and went to work. He stopped drinking. He was poised for good things to happen.

But the universe was not yet done testing Phil, not by a long shot. His wife filed for divorce. His father-in-law killed himself. And Phil was diagnosed with throat cancer.

During this time Phil's spiritual life had slowly, painstakingly inched forward. His good, orderly direction felt established. He did something he would never have expected to do a few years back: he joined a church. It was what might be called an alternative church, one that doesn't mention God, but focuses on inner spirit and harmony. But it was a church. He started saying one prayer, Reinhold Neibuhr's "Serenity Prayer":

> *God, grant me the serenity*
> *to accept the things I cannot change,*
> *the courage to change the things I can,*
> *and the wisdom to know the difference.*
> *Living one day at a time,*
> *enjoying one moment at a time;*
> *accepting hardship as a pathway to peace …*

It helped. He accepted that his cancer would probably leave him dead or seriously disabled. But he cranked his spirit up as high as it would go and started treatment. During treatment, he says, "I was a frightening apparition. I looked like an Auschwitz survivor."

"Survivor" it was to be. The treatment worked. He lived, and did not need disabling surgery. He met his current wife and reestablished relationships with his children. He sold lots of houses in the hot Silicon Valley market, and joined one of the prestigious real estate firms in the area.

A day came when his alternative church didn't seem quite enough. He needed something more. He saw an interesting article about a small, local church and went there for services a few times.

One Sunday, the associate pastor delivered a sermon in which she referred to God as "she."

"When she said that, I knew I was home," he recalls. He had never associated God with a gender identity. Removal of the masculine representation swept away a barrier.

Phil looks fit and affluent. He believes he is now a counselor of value to people in his life. He reflected on his walk through the valley of the shadow.

"There was a time when I had no ethics, no fidelity, no honor, no life. Somehow that evil went away, and the space feels filled with Good, Orderly Direction.

"I threw away a piece of my inner life puzzle at 14. Without that piece, the puzzle couldn't fit together."

MELIAN

In a way, Silicon Valley is the refuge that Melian has wanted for a long time. That's unusual. The Valley is many things, but rarely a refuge.

Melian was born to a Roman Catholic family and grew up on the East Coast. At 17, she entered a convent hoping it would be a refuge from years of vicious family abuse. "I needed to do the virgin-in-the-volcano thing," she remembers.

The convent ended up being a workable, interim escape mechanism. It was not a long-term refuge from memories, hormonal pressures, and the need to find out who she was. Also, as the youngest and healthiest nun in the convent, she saw her work assignments creep up to 18 hours a day, with no relief in sight. She left the convent at 28, to take her first shot at being an independent adult participating in the adventure of life.

She eventually left the Catholic Church completely, and became an ordained Protestant minister. It proved to be a frustration-filled pursuit, fraught with church politics, problematical acceptance of female clergy, and passive parishioners when she wanted passionate parishioners. "I tried to be flamboyant," she recalls, "and preach sermons that would stimulate energy, thought and challenge. Then people would come up to me and say, 'That was a lovely sermon,' and I wanted to say 'NO! It wasn't *lovely*!' "

Two religious environments having failed to deliver what she wanted, Melian is now adamant that organized religion is not right for her, and that it needs to fix some problems before it's right for others. She has discovered that the freedom to pursue her own spiritual path is a strong Silicon Valley feature, and she's doing that as a counselor and community volunteer. She's even managed to get some Valley maverick language into her vocabulary. "I never said the f-word before I came to California," she said with a mischievous grin.

I asked for her observations on spiritual life in this area.

"People here are less bound by theology and more bound by emotion," she believes. "They're less bound by liturgy, more bound by practice. I see much less denominational commitment here, particularly to what might be called middle-of-the-road denominations. The energy flow seems to be toward either agnostic beliefs and turning away from churches, or passionate involvement in charismatic or missionary activities.

"There's an openness here. More freedom, different ways of looking at things, less judgmental, more live and let live. That freeform environment is probably good, because I have very strong negative feelings about 'self-righteous Christians'—or self-righteous anything, for that matter.

"But there's an anonymity to spiritual life here. You don't see people talking about it in their neighborhoods the way you do back East. It's not part of being a citizen in the community.

"Most church denominations tend to have a legalistic approach, and I don't think that's where God is. To me, God is personal, a partner, not a thundering, Old Testament God of truth and law."

She paused, then concluded, "And it's God that people want a sign from, not a pastor. Ultimately, everyone's walk with God needs to be their own."

KAMAL

Kamal's route to Silicon Valley was roundabout: San Jose via Oklahoma, Pakistan and South Africa (where he was born), with other assorted stops. He is an engineer and technical training curriculum developer for a large, successful software company.

Kamal demonstrated strong multiplexing ability (the gift of doing several complex things at once) when we met at his house for our discussion. He and his family had just moved into their new home that day; his 3-year-old son was in hyperdrive and couldn't get enough of Dad's attention; an urgent computer problem which needed his expertise joined the party via telephone; and I was asking him questions about his journey and philosophy. He proved to be a first-rate juggler, able to keep his train of thought on track while 3-year-old elbows and knees mercilessly marauded his solar plexus.

Coming to the United States nine years ago gave Kamal a strong dose of culture shock. He is a devout Muslim, and understands fully the Islamic code of behavior. He was dismayed to find himself violating it.

"Muslims don't hear God's voice," he explained, "they see His signs. The Muslim is encouraged to look at and ponder what he has been given. What does this mean? What could it mean?" He was to have several experiences that he regards as signs meant to teach him during this period.

Two well-known American customs that he found he enjoyed were casual dates with women, and imbibing alcoholic beverages. These activities are not in accord with Muslim beliefs. One night he was enjoying a few drinks at a party when he met a Hindu woman.

She asked him about his roots, and he told her he was a Muslim from Pakistan. She said, "But Muslims aren't supposed to drink." He was humiliated. "I wanted the ground to swallow me up." But in the depth of the humiliation he felt he had received a sign.

On another occasion he decided to experience the American tradition known as "macho male." A friend wanted some marijuana. He agreed to go score it for him. As he was consummating the transaction, the dealer put a knife to his throat and robbed him. He felt certain that his life being spared, despite his wrong actions and bad judgment, was another sign.

Other signs emerged, and eventually Kamal changed friends, discontinued alcohol and macho, and got back to Islamic basics. His brother convinced him it was time to get married and start a family, which would short-circuit the dating issue. He married a woman he had met in Pakistan. They are spiritual partners, and their faith is the centerpiece of their marriage.

Kamal observes the Muslim practice of ritual prayer five times a day. He and a Muslim co-worker go behind the company tennis courts or onto a path on the company campus for noon prayer.

Occasionally he finds himself in a business meeting when it is time for prayer. He knows it raises questions when he excuses himself.

Kamal received threatening crank calls during the Gulf war. "The war was tough on Muslims living in the United States." However, he is very pleased with the strong response the U.S. Muslim community makes to what it considers unfair attacks. "In Europe, you see a lot of Muslims with their heads down, broken, from being called terrorists."

Comparing Muslim communities in other lands to those he has seen in Silicon Valley, Kamal observes, "Colonized countries tend to have an ongoing slave mentality even after being freed. The fact that many Muslims are well-to-do here gives them respect."

Kamal wants to play a significant role in helping to spread the Islamic faith and the word of Allah. He would particularly like to contribute by working in inner cities with gangs and at-risk youth. "I look up to most American converts to Islam because they have usually learned a lot," he says.

Technology has been harnessed to help do sacred work: Kamal has set up a site on the World Wide Web through which he offers books, tapes, CDs, and information relating to Muslim activities and publications. If this business becomes successful enough, he would love to devote himself full time to his spiritual path.

"I have to speak softly to hear myself thinking," he says, "and what I often think about is, 'what is a human?' The human is not just a seller or buyer in a consumer sense. He finds himself when he finds God. For me, that answers the question."

I asked interviewees and many Silicon Valley spiritual leaders to comment on discoveries along the path. What are people in the area searching for in their spiritual lives? How does this compare with what they need and what they find? Here are some of the answers.

From nonclergy:

I need to believe. *I don't want to go around again, not even in heaven. I just want to believe my spirit will become a part of a massive force for good. I want to spend my life feeling that I'm working in tandem with that force.*

I'm trying to reach the point where I'm just satisfied to know there's a higher power, and we don't need to live in existential loneliness. Even if the higher power was an abusive father, it would be good just to know *He's there.*

Peace. Direction.

A sense of having a place and a space which is neither work nor home, but a community I belong to.

A way of understanding life, death, and the way we're supposed to live together.

A feeling that I'm listened to, loved, cared for, and forgiven. To know that I can screw up and it's not a big deal, I can go back again and try not to screw up next time.

To banish fear.

Growth, strength and increased closeness to God.

I'm an engineer and I'm not good at expressing myself with words. I need music and the ritual of services to carry my spiritual emotion.

To connect to everyone I meet from the heart.

To set my inner compass on True North.

... and from clergy:

People want to have their hearts listened to. Every human being carries a deep longing. They want to match up the work and the value system with emerging spirituality. But they find it's tough to do, and the attempt can threaten their inner equilibrium.

For some, spirituality is their center; for others it's "icing on the cake." For some, what they want isn't what they need. Successful churches here need unique offerings for different "ages and stages."

They're looking for a sense of community and a place to belong. If you're spending hour after hour writing programs and starting companies, that's not enough. It's isolating. We try to fill a deep hunger people feel to know God.

People are aware they live in a rat race, and they get to a point where they say, "Let me have peace." But it's scary to go from a hundred miles an hour to a calm and quiet place. The speed gives people juice, and when they slow down they have to look closer.

What people long for is a Savior who will "do it for us."
What they need and what they get is a Messiah who comes
to show us the way. In my more judgmental days I might
have had more to say about what this difference tells us.

This is the cradle of high tech, computer science, and
workaholic creativity. People begin to ask bigger questions
because of that mixture. They want a sense of meaning and
purpose. They need a real connection with the spiritual
reality that's there. Some get what they need, but some try
to do their own thing and get a one-legged stool that has no
chance of providing balance to their lives.

Many want prosperity and a quick fix. The Valley is very
consumption-oriented, and the challenge to afford
everything they want causes people stress. They may embark
on meditation or a spiritual journey to get relief. Some
aren't looking for transcendence, they're looking for a
cosmic Valium.

WHAT IF

In her book, *Roads Home—Seven Pathways to Midlife Wisdom*, Kathryn Cramer says:

> *The trap of fatalism is quite compelling at midlife. By age forty, many of the men and women I counsel have seen, in their companies and their communities, a full range of self-serving, power-hungry, unethical and immoral behavior undertaken in the name of the organization, the city, the state and the nation. They have witnessed the destructive power of human frailty. It is natural for midlifers to become numb, disenfranchised, or themselves corrupted by the influence of evil.*

Let us speculate.

Let's suppose *everyone* stopped in the middle of every day, went out to the tennis courts (or wherever) and communed with their personal vision of a higher power. Let's suppose everyone had been doing that since their careers in their companies and communities began.

Might it be less likely that midlifers would be susceptible to becoming numb, disenfranchised, or themselves corrupted by the influence of evil?

Of course, the fact that Kathryn Cramer says they are doesn't mean they are.

MARJORIE

Perhaps Marjorie's professional destiny was molded by the size of her family. Her parents had 12 children—just the right number to staff a home-grown jury. Marjorie became an attorney.

When she was 23, her mother's death prompted her to begin exploring spiritual groups and philosophies. Ultimately she became a member of the Baha'i faith. "I regard my mother as a Baha'i, even though she never heard of it," Marjorie says. "She lived the kind of life a Baha'i should."

Marjorie has been in Silicon Valley 13 years. She came here from the Midwest to attend Stanford Law School. "When one becomes a Baha'i, one gets tested by difficulties," she says, and law school qualified. It was tough and stressful. Added stress arrived in the form of a setback for her husband, who is also an attorney. Hired by one of the Valley's well-known law firms, he didn't pass the California bar exam on his first try. "When you don't pass on your first attempt," she explained, "you get a dark cloud hanging over your head at the firm.

"These were soul-wrenching times, particularly in an environment where people are very image-conscious and achievement-oriented, and no one seems to be suffering—or lets you see it if they are. To walk around as if life is OK when you're really facing big challenges is very tough. But we regarded this period as a test of faith, an opportunity for what Bahai's call 'deepening.' "

Most evenings, as part of her spiritual practice, Marjorie "calls herself to account" for what she did that day, and reflects on what she wants to accomplish the next day. When she misses her prayer and meditation time, she becomes aware that her spiritual wants and needs are not being met. "This is the essence of the Silicon Valley challenge," she says. "To be calm, centered and spiritual in the midst of the time crunch and the work demands. To be steadfast, and maintain routines, is tangibly important.

"It's a hard row to hoe here. We've been given so much, but there are so many distractions and more is expected of us. Recently I flew into Montana, and immediately felt a sense of peace from the place. But I would not want to be elsewhere, wouldn't want to give up the excitement and diversity we have here.

"I'm very conscious of the Valley's diversity, because the area I grew up in was very racist. My school was almost all white, and as an African-American I would get called names as soon as I got on the bus. But I also got it from the black kids because I wasn't dark enough, so I was getting it from all sides. Just as I now call myself to account at the end of each day, I hope these folks will someday call themselves to account for their actions.

"The greatest challenge to my spiritual values comes from my work. Litigation is subject to so many variables that holding on to ethics can be difficult. I want to uphold standards, but I don't want to be taken advantage of. Spirituality is rewarding, but there are tempting times when one would just like to be selfish. I probably wouldn't struggle as much with this if I weren't a Baha'i. As a Baha'i, it would be tough for me to just suck in profits and not be concerned with where they came from.

"There has been a lot of change in the Valley in the last several years, and I'm very optimistic about the future of spiritual life here. It won't be easy, and there will be many challenges. But social insensitivity may fade, I hope without great social upheaval, and baby boomers are hungry for moral values. This is a very rich area, with tremendous spiritual potential."

THE VIEW FROM THE PULPIT

There is a great deal of commonality in spiritual professionals' view of the Silicon Valley culture. Their outlook is influenced by the makeup of their individual flocks, but key themes and challenges recur. One of them is that spiritual leadership in this high-dynamics arena is no walk in the park. Sam Keen's short recipe for a successful vision quest wasn't written for the Valley, but it captures some of the natural inclination of the collective psyche, and gives a fine hint regarding the challenges faced by local leadership:

> *The path to personal freedom involves two long and terrifying steps across the void. Step one: Question authority. Step two: Overthrow authority.*

Heck, that's not so terrifying for Silicon Valley stalwarts.

Roland, a local pastor, offered an ad hoc statistical analysis. "On the East Coast, most people who go to church either go 10 percent of the time or 90 percent of the time. Anyone midway between the two would be considered a flake. Here, most people who go to church probably go 50 to 60 percent of the time. That's considered normal, and it's the 10 percenters and the 90 percenters who are considered the oddballs."

Pat, also a Valley pastor, pointed out characteristics specific to each geographical region of the country. "In the Sunbelt, people attend church in far greater numbers than anywhere else. Churches are filled to capacity. In the Northeast, the religious experience tends to be *reserved:* smaller churches, more intellectual, less emotional. In the 'great middle plains,' you find the traditional institutional religious experience. Denominations are still important. When people cross the Rockies, they tend to drop their religion on the mountains, and discontinue their practice when they hit the West Coast. If they pick one back up, people here become very *intentional* about their religion."

Sam

The church secretary put me right through to Sam when I called to arrange an interview. He's pastor of a sizable, mainstream Protestant congregation. We shared immediate rapport: he couldn't confirm an appointment time until his computer finished a disk initialization and he could restart his calendar program.

He also mentioned that the office was fully automated, and had been for some time, thanks to a former church member who had been associated with a computer company and donated lots of equipment. He expected to head home shortly because he liked to prepare his sermons on his home computer. We discovered that we both used the same word processing software.

A little tech talk, to get an acquaintanceship off to a good start.

Our meeting took place at a coffee shop he called his "office East." He knew the staff by name. Over chicken Caesar salad and iced tea we discussed life experiences, spiritual paths, and his observations about Silicon Valley.

"My father came to the U.S. from Sweden. When I turned 21 he told me 'Make sure you vote, and make sure your vote counts.' He was a Socialist; he made his vote count for Eugene Debs.

"I was born and raised in Iowa. Our family had a strong belief in a Christianity more of deeds than of words.

"There's a solidity and a history in the heartland which we don't have here, so we experiment. People here want to try new things. It's fun. Matthew Fox would have died in Toledo.

"There's no community pressure here to belong to any spiritual institution. In other parts of the country, corporate officers are expected to belong to churches and community organizations. In the Valley, if you tell people you can't meet them on a Sunday morning because you're going to church, you're likely to get derided. It's close to what it must have been like when St. Paul first started out.

"If people who had never been involved in the community transferred from a job at Hewlett Packard in Silicon Valley to a job at an HP facility in, say, Boise, Idaho, within one year they'd be involved in the PTA.

"The hardest part of becoming a pastor out here is that people have no respect for office or institution. But if spiritual journeys stay purely individualistic, they'll die. You need the continuity of an institution."

❧ Friends and Acquaintances ❧

"A part of the Silicon Valley culture I find terribly sad is that people so often have no real friends. They think people they ski with or bowl with are their friends. But usually they're just doing things together. Doing things together isn't necessarily the same thing as being friends. People sometimes get quite offended if others they're doing activities with suddenly want to talk about personal stuff. That's not my idea of friendship.

"I know of a man who had been bowling with a group for 30 years. *Thirty years.* One night, after bowling, he went home and hung himself. The investigators asked his bowling group if they had noticed anything unusual that night. They said, 'No, he didn't seem any different.'

"I've noticed an interesting thing about weddings. Attendance is always about 20 percent less than confirmed RSVPs. People walk outside on the wedding day, and say, 'It's a nice day, let's go to the beach instead.' There's just not the respect for the importance of rituals and ceremonies. And no one's mother lives in the area to take them to task and tell them to do what's right."

❧ Technical Expertise ❧

"One thing that's great about this place is that a lot of my parish are engineers. They're used to working on projects and schedules. All my committees run well except one: buildings and grounds.

Everyone knows how to use a computer, but no one knows how to use their hands or what to do with tools.

"My prior parish, in another state, was largely doctors and lawyers. If I started a discussion about 'What is truth?' they'd talk and argue about it forever and probably have a great time, but not get anywhere, of course. If I started the discussion here, I wouldn't be surprised if four days later the group came back and said, 'Pastor, we have an interactive program to step you through the "What is truth?" issue. We're going to beta test it in Bakersfield next week, and once it's debugged, everyone can get it on the Internet at "TruthSearch.com."'

"Pastors in some areas may get stale after they've been with their churches awhile. With the speed at which things change in the Valley, there's not much risk of that here.

"The most secular institution in our society is the university, and this is a very university-oriented environment. More advanced degrees seem to lead to rejection of spiritual paths."

❧ Roots ❧

"Because so many people came here from somewhere else, they don't have the rhythmic involvement of an extended family in their daily lives. That can make them feel very lonely. If you have a fight with your spouse, you can't go blow off steam to your sister, and you don't have an uncle around to take you out for a drink, calm you down, and explain how he and your aunt used to fight the same way, and you really shouldn't go call that divorce lawyer just yet.

"As far as taking that first step onto a spiritual path, you either believe there's a God or you don't. There's probably nothing that clergy or anyone else can do if the belief hasn't been born yet. If you have to explain God, people won't get it.

"People need to relearn the art of *welcoming someone back*. Some may stop coming to a church for a while, for any reason, or for no reason. When they come back, they're likely to be greeted with accusatory questions about why they've been away so long, or find parishioners needling them about their absence. This makes it hard to come back, and just encourages people to find another church, or no church, and never return."

❧ Culture and Counselors ❧

"There's a lot of diversity in this area, and spiritual leaders have to have the flexibility and sensitivity to deal with that. Last week I married an Asian couple. I gave the groom my card and said, 'I am your pastor.' He said, 'But we're not Christian.' I said, 'That's OK, I'm your pastor anyway. And I want you to stay in touch, let me know how you and your family are doing, and let me know if there's anything I can do for you.'

"I don't do much counseling. Not because people don't need it, but because they get it elsewhere. They need it so much, and get it so much, that the secular counseling business is a thriving growth industry. There's a lot of counselors in this area.

"In most companies, it seems people have to work 12 hours a day or they're considered shirkers. I started up a class recently, and all but one of the people who attended were retired. You can't schedule anything on weeknights, because everyone works late. Maybe 5:00 AM would work, but I'm not going to get up at 5:00 AM to teach class.

"Eighty percent of the visitors to a church are there because someone in the parish invited them. Of the remaining 20 percent, most are there because of a family crisis, such as an illness. I call them 'foxhole Christians.' They're under fire, and somehow we have to get them through the battlefield safely.

"It's important for clergy to take doses of their own advice, and try the things they advise others to do to make sure they work. A story I like is about the pastor in a traffic jam. He peers around the cars, and sees the problem is a dump truck with a flat tire. The driver has a lane blocked. He's struggling to get the flat tire off, but it won't budge. The pastor pulls over and asks, 'Have you tried prayer?' The driver says, 'No, but at this point, I'll try anything.' He says a quick prayer, and the tire slides right off the wheel. The pastor says, 'Well, I'll be damned!'

"Getting caught up in making money causes many people in the Valley heavy conflict. They say they're doing it for their family. But the stress and the 16-hour days can end up destroying the family. Michael Milken was once asked, 'What do you need all that money for?' and he said, 'To keep score.' I think that applies to some people here. The carrot is always moving.

"There's a dynamic of noncontinuity we have to deal with in this area. People always have their résumé updated, and there's no real trust or commitment anymore between company and employee."

❧ Rejuvenation ❧

"The youth orientation in high-tech companies can be tough on midlifers. Lots of older tech whizzes feel they have to use Grecian Formula 16. In fact, there's even starting to be a youth movement in the clergy world, and most churches won't hire anyone over 50. How sad!

"Everyone needs to have quiet time, peaceful time, in their life pattern, to recharge and permit the spirit to rest and grow. Before I came here I interviewed at a church elsewhere. They asked how I maintained my spiritual life. My answer was, 'First, I take my days off.' I get exhausted from my work, from caring. I need to read and sleep late occasionally like anyone else. They were very uncomfortable with that answer. I think they wanted to hear me say I spend my leisure time memorizing the writings of 16th century clerics. I didn't get the job.

"It's great how the Holy Spirit works. I got turned down for a job in one of the least attractive places in the world, and ended up in Los Altos, one of the nicest."

Many of the people interviewed offered observations about the differences between spiritual life and pursuits in Silicon Valley and other places they knew. Here are some perspectives of local clergy:

In the Southeast, you're expected to belong to a church. It's a sense of duty. But here, people go to church based not so much on expectations, but because they're truly seeking a path. The numbers may be greater there, but perhaps there's more real dedication here. There's more tradition there. Here, we're willing to blend traditions to create something new.

There's an intensity about this area that sometimes I love and sometimes I hate. People here are used to making choices and being proactive. We're in Stanford Country. *There's a real tolerance for new ideas and open dialogue.*

Some people spend all this money to be in big houses on large, private grounds, and then feel disconnected. Before coming here I worked as an inner city urban minister. In a way, I feel as if I traded one homeless population for another.

Silicon Valley has more diversity, more freedom, more "soul liberty."

Other areas may have a much deeper sense of past and continuity.

This area seems to have a greater awareness of both the threat and the promise of other religious traditions.

People here ask more questions.

... And comparisons from some nonclergy observers:

Everything's bigger in Texas, including the size of churches and the percent of people who attend.

Where you have traditional values and a relatively stable population, you'll find churches playing the strongest roles. That describes the East Coast and the Southwest. It doesn't describe Silicon Valley.

Spiritual diversity here seems to match the cultural diversity. The exposure to different things helps keep my mind open.

When I talk to people from the Midwest, we're not communicating. I used to find much of my spirituality in nature, and spent a lot of time hugging trees. I'm sure they'd think I was nuts.

New Jersey was very homogeneous—lots of whites, Christians and pilots. This area is a melting pot, and the different beliefs require tolerance and bring challenges to conventional thinking. But the diversity, and the "careerism," can make it harder to build community.

Even in spiritual matters, people here are self-starters and wonder how technology can help their journey.

In other areas neighbors were more neighborly. If people are helping and volunteering, they're being spiritual even if they don't go to church.

Lots of New Age stuff here which isn't found elsewhere. There's a lack of the traditional rhythm of life. Spirituality here is a smorgasbord, and people pick whatever seems tasty.

When I was first asked to come out here, I wasn't sure I wanted to leave Illinois and raise my family on the "left coast." But although religion here may not be as "in vogue" as it is back there, many people here are just as committed.

We're an intellectual, science-driven area. Intellectuals often don't take religion seriously. The scientific mind has difficulty accepting the mysterious, and tends to be skeptical.

We have strong pockets of spirituality, but we also have spiritual vacuums where people have no fellowship.

My home area's spiritual practices are more structured, conservative, and punitive. Here, no one knows if you go to church, and no one talks about religion at work.

In Chicago I was in a homogeneous Southside Polish Catholic community. You saw everybody on the streets: friends, neighbors, priests. Community life and spiritual life continued when you went out. Here, you don't see anybody on the street. I've never seen a priest just walking through a neighborhood, and it's difficult to have spiritual continuity once you leave the church premises. People don't just "hang out" together here.

Back East, where you go to church is part of the social pecking order. In Silicon Valley, the social pecking order is one thing: money.

In Oregon and Indiana, spiritual thinking is much more "Western traditional." Here, you can make a religion out of anything. Maybe the intolerance in other areas comes from fear of having their belief systems proved wrong.

CHAPTER FOUR

❧

Visions of Higher Powers

It is ironic but appropriate that science should be the possible path back. Science probably did more than anything else to take away the wonder in nature that we associated with the divine ... In the present age, a religious believer may not want to agree that God has disappeared or that God has died; but he or she can acknowledge, albeit sadly, that the awe has disappeared, or at least diminished dramatically, both among religious and nonreligious persons.

Richard Elliott Friedman,
The Disappearance of God

"I wish you'd quit thinking of me as God," Joe said a bit irritably. *"The term is so outdated."*

Joan Brady, *God on A Harley—A Spiritual Fable*

What we're often looking for when we add the extra overhead of building a computer into our business and our lives is certainty. We want something to believe in, something that will take from our shoulders the burden of knowing when to reorder muffler clamps. In the twelfth century, before there even were muffler clamps, such certainty came in the form of a belief in God, made tangible through the building of cathedrals—places where God could be accessed. For lots of us today, the belief is more in the sanctity of those digital zeros and ones, and our cathedral is the personal computer. In a way, we're replacing God with Bill Gates.

Uh-oh.

Robert X. Cringely, *Accidental Empires—How The Boys Of Silicon Valley Make Their Millions, Battle Foreign Competition, and Still Can't Get A Date*

S top.

I want you to stop reading at your normal speed.

In a minute I'm going to ask you to stop reading, period. Not for long. Just for a bit. But in preparation for that, I'd like you to ... just ... slow ... the ... pace ... and ... ... let ... ...your ... ... mind ... ... feel ... ... peaceful ... ... and ... ... deep.

Now,

  get ready

    to think,

      to picture

        and to feel.

Put the picture

    before the words

       but don't let

     an unclear

    picture

   block

  the words.

Picture

   then emotions

      then words.

If you believe in a God, a Creator, a Higher Power, close your eyes for a moment. Let whatever *picture* you have of your Divinity take shape.

Trace the vision back. Has this always been the picture? Have there been others? Where did they start? What was the progression? What caused the picture to change?

Is He/She in one place? Or in the rocks and waves, trees and malls, people and cats?

Now the emotions.

Who or what *is* God to you? Parent? Teacher? Boss? Bully? Guardian?

Does She/He cause you to feel reverence? Joy? Anger? Resentment? Puzzlement? Unquestioning love?

Any fear in there anywhere?

Now the words.

How do you *think* of God? What role does the Divinity play in your daily life? How about in the world at large? Does He/She let the universe just tick along? Or are events and happenings micro-managed? Or something in between?

How do you communicate with the Higher Power? Do you ever hear His/Her voice coming back to you?

Take a few minutes. Or as long as you like.

If you do not believe in a God, a Creator, a Higher Power, close your eyes and transport your imagination back 15 billion years or so. Picture a point of infinite density and infinite temperature hanging suspended in a roiling bath of colorless, lightless probabilistic foam twisting and convulsing continuously into and out of existence in berserk, mutated obeisance to the Schwarzchild solution to the Einstein field equation, leaving a nebula of unknown and impossible particles performing unknown and impossible physical phenomena, dancing, trailing and contorting back into the 26-

---

I served as an evangelist and high school teacher in Kenya for 17 years. The natives call Mount Kenya "The Hill of Brightness." At its top, 17,000 feet, it's snow and glaciers, shining and radiant, inaccessible. The name and the vision of God many tribes use is "The Great Divider": He divides the heavens above from the earth below. When He comes down to visit the Earth, they believe He lives at the peak of the Hill of Brightness. The vision is part of a powerful metaphor. We want to climb the mountain and be with God. At first it's easy. But then we get to the snow, and then the glaciers, and we can't see how to go any farther.

From Kenya, I was transferred to Silicon Valley.

Michael, a Valley priest

dimensional multiverse where it was spawned a quadrillion years ago by its torturous protrusion from a 39-dimensional hyperverse, exploding outward, suddenly and finally, in a paroxysmal cataclysm of energy, death and birth.

Or, if that's too easy ...

The objective is just to get you thinking about whatever *your* vision is of Beginnings and Meanings. This can be a difficult, elusive track to follow. It's probably somewhat easier for those who do believe in a God. For one thing, the belief wraps a lot of complex variables into one entity. For another, there's been so much written, discussed, and sung about God, so much formal and informal religion developed, that there's a rather large set of jumping-off points available.

Of course, the jumping-off points often contradict each other. The advantage may be a little less than first meets the eye.

I asked you to consider the pictures, emotions and words which comprise your vision of Higher Powers and Beginnings and Meanings to give you a foundation for considering the visions of others. Part of the dialogue with people interviewed for this book focused on those visions. They are not the easiest visions to develop. They can be even harder to communicate.

Anna

Anna is a single parent. Her son is now 21, so in theory, most of the rough parenting spots are behind her. (On the other hand, it's the late '90s, and this particular theory is starting to develop some warts.) Her ex-husband dropped out of their life very soon after the birth of their son. He provided neither participation nor financial support for child rearing.

That was OK with Anna. It was still OK when several years went by and Mr. Right had not appeared. She didn't put much energy into looking for him, anyway. Work and child kept her very busy.

She did get to a point, however, where she was interested in putting energy into something else: her own house. She was tired of living in rented digs. She wanted her own piece of turf. She wanted to be able to have two dogs and a cat; or two cats and a dog; or two cats, three dogs, six hamsters and a macaw without checking in with the landlord. She wanted to plant flowers and tomatoes in her own soil, and paint the walls vermilion if she was in the mood. The basics.

The problem: this was Silicon Valley, with its bloated property values. Getting into a house, unless you've hit it big or inherited big, is often a two-income proposition. She only had one.

A second income was needed. A second job was the obvious solution.

However, she was not able to find another job like the one she had, or that paid as much, or that wouldn't have required her to clone herself so she could be in two different places during normal work hours. She cogitated. She did the logical thing: she took *two* more jobs.

Anna became a female, Silicon Valley version of Clark Kent. By day, she blended in as a mild-mannered customer service representative for a microwave subsystem manufacturer. On weekends,

> *Through prayer and meditation, one is often inspired. This is not a rational process, but more akin to the* Aha! *experience related by many mathematicians and scientists. Something spiritual is going on in these experiences.*
>
> Neil, a former Silicon Valley programmer

she checked in as an intrepid utility player for a department store chain, taking inventory, running cash registers, balancing accounts receivable payments, helping a customer find a size 8—whatever was needed. And every morning, seven mornings a week, she got up at 4:00 AM to metaphorically don her blue-and-red Superwoman togs, and toss copies of a local newspaper into the dark driveways of houses with still-sleeping occupants on a neighborhood paper delivery route.

That's what she needed to do to save the down payment. That's what she needed to do to meet the mortgage payments. That's what she did. She succeeded. She bought the house and kept it.

For a few years, sick days and vacations were purely theoretical abstractions. She knew they were things other people did. She couldn't. That was OK.

Eventually, raises and promotions happened, the furniture got paid for, and the son graduated from high school and got a job. Anna is now back to living a normally frenetic lifestyle, and working just one job. She's even found time for the pleasure of teaching country-and-western dance classes.

Anna derives a great deal of strength and centering from her spiritual life, which she practices in a totally institution-free manner. She regards herself as a "generic Christian." She is not associated with a church and doesn't expect to be. One reason is her vision of God. Another is her church experience.

> *Everyone defines their own God. Ask a group of 20 people how they think of the Creator and you'll get 25 answers. God loves us, looks out for us, and it's His job to throw curve balls at us. In the past, people saw God primarily as a bookkeeper, maintaining a ledger of what you did right and wrong. Very few think that way anymore, and that represents real growth in people's visions.*
>
> Edward, a Valley priest

Music is what first brought Anna to religion. She loved to sing, and started going to a neighborhood church to do it. The music and the singing brought out her spirituality.

Then she and her mother became involved with another church, and problems came up. Anna saw church leaders doing things she thought were wrong: things she felt were harmful, arbitrary, maybe even a little cruel. She got to a point where she could not continue to accept the spiritual leadership of these individuals, and by extension, the church which had placed them in authority. She left to pursue her own path.

Anna's communications with her God require no intermediary, and no formal faith community. God is with her at all times. She does not have regular prayer times set aside. She carries on an ongoing conversation. It's one-sided in the sense that she doesn't feel she has ever heard God's voice coming back to her—but she feels His presence.

"God is the closest thing I've ever had to a grandfather," she says. "It's a different vision from seeing Him as a father. A father image might be tied up with a very authoritarian relationship. I don't want to picture God as telling me 'do this or don't do that because I'm your father and I said so.' That wouldn't work for me.

"He might still be telling me the same things. But with the grandfather vision, one step removed from the parent, He's doing it as a loving mentor."

COLIN

Colin is a senior product manager for a leading-edge company making specialized computer equipment. He describes himself as cerebral and introverted. He's currently devoting a substantial amount of cerebral effort to developing his vision of a Higher Power.

About six years ago Colin went through a period of strong inner conflict. His introverted nature was acting as a barrier to understanding people he worked with. He couldn't figure out why they didn't think the same way he did. He frustrated others, and they frustrated him back. The barrier became too big to ignore. It had to be torn down, or at least diminished, if he was going to continue to be successful at his work. "I was desperate for personal change," he says. "Despite having a great life on the surface, I was miserable, and knew I had a problem."

He got a couple of unusual suggestions from his manager. The first was to try Vedanta meditation as a way of getting more in touch with his core. You can't share with others what you don't know yourself.

The second suggestion was to consult a psychic. The psychic emphasized the importance of finding solitary, self-awareness-increasing time on a daily basis.

Colin's father was Roman Catholic, his mother's father was a Presbyterian minister, and his parents compromised on Episcopalian. As the Vedanta meditation led him deeper into Hinduism, he pondered the direction his spiritual path had taken.

He realized that following the practices of his childhood had ceased to have any meaning. "I was a 'rote Christian.' My spirituality had no humility, no depth, no real thought."

Sometimes people ask, "Does God know what I'm going through? Doesn't He understand how hard this is?" Usually when this happens it means they've moved away from God, not vice versa. I almost always get an answer to my prayers, but few of the answers are "Damascus Road blinding light" responses.

Trent, president of a Valley telecommunications company

It is through Hinduism that Colin feels he has rediscovered Christianity. A major signpost of inner change has occurred for his cerebral self: he has gotten past being so highly judgmental.

During the season of Lent he banishes computer books from the bedroom and reads Christian mystics for an hour each night. His vision of God contains ingredients from each of the sources that has influenced him, blended together with the product of his personal reflections. A quote from a swami has stuck with him: "Belief in God is not necessary, but it's useful."

His God is unknowable, but close. There is the Trinity; above that is the Godhead, the Transcendent, the quiet-mind Presence, an integral part of everything. Hinduism offers multiple manifestations of God, and Christian mystics provide glimpses into an afterlife tantalizingly tinged with their own inner certainty: the beginnings of a rich, flowing, composite vision.

"We are knives, and life is a whetstone," Colin says. "You have to position yourself to get sharpened, not blunted."

MOLLY

Molly is human resources director for a Valley company that makes computer networking equipment. Her faith has always been unshakably bound to her life, but she described two circumstances in which she felt severely tested.

God is light. Light is healing, soothing, joyful. I have a problem with the "Father" image, and "light" gets me around that. I totally reject the Old Testament view of a vengeful God, although I could wake up one morning and find I'm wrong.

Kate, a Valley church office administrator

The first related to her husband's cancer. They had been married a relatively short time when it struck, and struck hard. They were very much in love. She prayed with everything in her for his healing. When he died after a valiant battle, she felt a surge of bitterness toward her God. "My first thought was, 'I don't have anything more to say to You,'" she recalls.

But she felt her bitterness fade into a realization: her prayer had been answered in a higher sense. Her husband had been freed from the cancer that was choking him. And she had been given the strength to be there for him. "Realizing his *soul* had been healed made me feel God was my counselor again."

The other challenge she described took place in the more prosaic surroundings of her company's offices. It happened in her first month on the job. During a conversation, the CEO, standing in the hall near her office, bellowed "Jesus F__ing Christ." Molly was shocked and dismayed. "I had a great salary and a great job, and I suddenly had to wonder if I was working in a vulgar hellpit."

She thought about it. Ultimately, she decided that her vision of her relationship with God required her to take such statements on in the future: a fairly gutsy decision in iconoclastic Silicon Valley. "Now when I hear someone say that, I say, 'Hey, that's my Lord,' and get them to stop."

"My spiritual life is huge," Molly says. "It's my air. And God is fire. Consuming fire."

GERALD

Gerald considers himself a Christian, but is not affiliated with any church and doesn't think he needs to be. "I go to church occasionally for the sermon," he says, "but I really don't like the 'stand-up, sit-down, fight-fight-fight' stuff."

Gerald is chief financial officer for a laser equipment company. He is turned off by the structure and the politics he usually sees associated with churches. Not being active in a spiritual community makes him aware of the need to weave his spiritual beliefs into other aspects of his life. "I relate to God through the principles I've been taught," he explained.

"I tie my morals and ethics very closely to my spirituality, and everything is a test. What do you do if you see someone drop a buck? Are you honest with customers? With vendors? Do you compete fairly in sports? Do you omit or commit things because it's temporarily expedient, even if it's wrong? Do you disclose fully to investors and analysts? How do you treat people who make mistakes? How should you respond when competitors lie, cheat and steal? How do you report company earnings? Do you cheat Uncle Sam when you can? Do you conceal things from auditors? How do you treat your wife? If someone cuts you off on the road, do you flip him off? Are you the kind of person who can be trusted to do things on a handshake? How do you react when things are not going well, at work and at home?

"None of these are black and white. But they're examples of the kinds of tests we face every day. And how we respond to the tests is between us and God. We have to live it, not preach it."

His vision of God is that of a mentor: providing guidance, direction, hope, and "... a path you can rely on when the chips are

---

One of my favorite stories is about a boy busily drawing on a large sheet of paper. His mother asks him, "What are you drawing?" He answers, "I'm drawing God." His mother says, "But no one's ever seen God. No one knows what He looks like." The boy says, "When I finish my drawing, they will."

Esther, a Valley homemaker

down. My God is loving and forgiving. But some established religions are neither. I can't accept the teaching that whole continents are damned just because they don't have the right religion. On the other hand, I believe missionary types are often very sinful in *pushing* religion rather than *teaching* it. I think that's a crime.

"Because of the way they live, some people who go to church and believe in Him may still not get anywhere near heaven."

MELINDA

"When I was 17, I actually thought of joining a religious order," Melinda recalls, "but then I realized I liked boys and dating too much."

Of such stuff are life decisions made.

Melinda works out several times a week at the Decathlon Club, and that's where we met for our discussion. The Decathlon is *the* upscale fitness facility in Silicon Valley. It's also a fine networking spot, both socially and for business. Conversations are heavily skewed toward sports, startups and cybersurfing.

At 2:00 in the afternoon only one other table besides ours was occupied in the Club's lounge area. When I sat down Melinda said, "You asked how I hear the voice of God. Sometimes it's just in the most improbable things. While you were gone I could hear some of those guys' discussion at the other table. They're talking about spirituality and God and the Bible. Two tables, two spiritual discussions. Got to be a first for the Decathlon Club."

Melinda is a licensed therapist. That profession represents a major midlife career change. Previously she was an administrator at a large Valley biotechnology company. Before that she worked as a sales rep for a telecommunications equipment manufacturer. Eventually, the tech world and the corporate environment became dimensionless: places where she earned a paycheck, period. She needed more. She wanted work that had meaning, work that would allow her spirit to speak and participate. She did her training, got her MFCC license, and started a new adventure.

Melinda was born into a Presbyterian family. Although she didn't join a religious order at 17, she did convert to Roman Catholicism. A tempestuous relationship was thereby launched.

After a few years of church participation, she felt its tug on her declining. She stopped going in her mid-20s, except for a brief period following the divorce from her first husband.

In her 30s, she felt she was back on a search path, but one leading in a completely different direction: philosophical rather than theological; psychological rather than spiritual. She neither needed nor wanted religious institutions during this phase.

About six years ago, in her early 40s, Melinda noticed thoughts about the Church sliding gently into her consciousness again. After a while they dropped the subtle approach, began knocking on the door of her psyche, and demanded admission.

She decided she'd open the door enough to talk, but keep the chain on until she knew the intruder wasn't dangerous. She went to a function for ex-Roman Catholics called the "Give Us Another Chance" retreat. It worked. She's giving it another chance. She expects the relationship to stick this time.

"There are still things I don't like about the Roman Catholic Church," she says. "For example, its position on women clergy. Somehow, though, I'm now at peace with the Church's shortcom-

---

The God of the Bible is a comfortable convenience. But those who have had problems with their fathers might have trouble with the masculine imagery.

Marie, a Valley homemaker and former marketing analyst

ings. I get a feeling of connection with God when I attend Mass, and the Church is the vehicle for that. But it's frustrating that the material world creeps back in so fast. The feeling of grace tends to fade 30 minutes after I leave the service.

"I don't like the God of the Bible that much. But the Bible is metaphor and allegory, not a literal work. I would like to think God is a loving God. It's hard to be sure. It's hard to make peace with the suffering of the innocent. But I understand that human justice is different from divine justice.

"God is cosmic, everywhere, not a robed person or a mountain. The vision of God I would most enjoy would be to see Him in every person I meet—even those I don't like."

CAL

They don't know each other, but Cal and Pete (whom you'll meet next) have something in common. Both of them initiated their first serious foray into religion to get dates with girls they had a crush on.

In Cal's case, the experience was not a keeper. Neither the religion nor the date stuck around for long. He found the religion "formulaic, dogmatic, and in denial." (He offered no further comments about the date. I didn't ask.) He looked into other denominations and found the same thing. He's still looking.

Cal is an accounting professor at a Valley community college. He classifies his parents as atheists. He classifies his own spiritual pursuits as "episodic" ("I look. I stop.") but he firmly believes in a Higher Power. He's just not sure how he should structure their relationship.

For a while, he went with a girlfriend to some meditation-based Eastern services. "Lots of drug addicts there," he says. He might still be going, but he broke up with the girlfriend, and she still goes there, and it would be uncomfortable.

"I'll probably end up practicing some form of Eastern religion. I feel I communicate with a Higher Spirit, but I don't see God as a personal God. My first choice would be to have a personal God. But I just can't buy it now. It's an 'I-know-You-exist-but-I'm-not-sure-in-what-form' thing.

"I do believe in the concept of collective consciousness. A biologist says all living things leave behind a 'spiritual residue' in some dimension, and I think I believe that. Maybe the collective, spiritual consciousness of every human who ever lived is my vision of God right now."

PETE

Unlike Cal's experience, when Pete jumped aboard his spiritual train to pursue romance, he stayed aboard.

Pete is in the thick of the Silicon Valley technology action. He manages an information services group for a large computer manufacturer. In an unusual scenario for the area, he's been there 15 years.

Pete's parents went to Sunday services, but he didn't sense any true spirituality in their lives. "It felt like they never really made the choice of having a life in God, as opposed to just going to church." He recalls being able to negotiate deals with his mother to avoid boring church attendance. Offers to vacuum the house or wash the car were among the more successful ploys.

Then the girl came along.

She wouldn't go out with him until he agreed to meet with her pastor. The pastor made a persuasive case. His mind told him committing to faith would be a rational decision. His hormones told him he *really* wanted to date this girl. He signed up. He's never regretted it.

His initial view was that Christian life was "a piece of cake." He remembers the incredulous responses he got to that perspective. It's an opinion he dropped a long time ago.

Several years ago, Pete made a decision which was good for his spirit but possibly deleterious to his career. There were a few other practicing Christians in his office building. They were interested in spiritual growth, and Pete was knowledgeable. He started a lunchtime Bible study and discussion group. Four or five of them met and talked over sandwiches and sodas, chairs cramped together in his small office, twice a week. If organizational advancement had been his number one priority, this was an error.

Pete is a sensitive, intelligent individual, firmly committed to high standards of professional performance and hard work. It was not the easiest thing in the world for him to hear that he was regarded as a "Jesus freak." It was not easy to deal with obvious disdain from colleagues, and averted gazes in hallways. No one asserted that his beliefs affected his work. But many found his practice to be jarring and inappropriate in that environment. To them, he became a dubiously regarded fringe member of the organization.

Occasionally, Pete would write Scriptural quotes on the whiteboard in his office. They were primarily to provide uplift and inspiration for himself. He hoped they might also be an upper for

During a guided meditation, I had a vision of bright, intense light and a sense of warmth and well-being that was absolutely overwhelming. My eyes were closed, but the vision was so intense that I could feel the heat. The feeling stayed with me for a long time, and the vision is burned into my mind.

Stuart, general counsel for a Valley instrumentation company

others, or at least an interesting mental refreshment from the day's travails. He found out later they were regarded by most co-workers who saw them as intrusive, or pretentious, or offensive, or all three. He discontinued the practice.

He also ended the lunchtime meetings and has changed departments. He's had reasonable career success. Was his success less than it might have been because of his spiritual activities in the workplace? Hard to say. Doesn't matter, anyway. He wouldn't have done it differently. At the time, he felt called to bear witness. It wasn't a call he would decline.

To Pete's delight, technology has permitted a workplace spiritual presence to flourish where the old-fashioned personal approach stumbled. Through the ease, ubiquity and comparative anonymity of modern electronic mail systems, believers at his company have a way to find each other and share matters of faith. The system has the capability for users to form "special interest groups," or SIGs, to exchange e-mail on topics of common interest. Some of the users wanted to have an electronic forum to do what Pete was doing at his office lunch meetings: talk about Scriptures. SCRIPT-SIG was born. Those who are interested can join in. Those who aren't can ignore it. No pressure. No offense. No mayonnaise on the carpet.

Pete's vision of God is one of grace and compassion, and very much the God of the Bible. He tries to consciously remember and honor his spiritual beliefs throughout his workday. This gets harder

The God of the Bible is the jumping-off point. The Bible gives you pinpoints of data, very tiny. We have to flesh out the full picture ourselves.

Loretta, a Valley homemaker and former corporate professional

when, for example, the system crashes or the network dies, just as critical information to high-ranking recipients is being generated.

But he tries. "God ought to say to me, 'Sorry, Pete, you've failed me too many times. I'm cutting you off.' But He doesn't, and that reminds me to try to treat others the same way."

SARAH

Sarah hails from upstate New York. She grew up in a conservative Jewish home that maintained kosher laws and Sabbath traditions. The family didn't get in the car on the Sabbath; they walked.

A major difference between Silicon Valley and her home town is neighborhood makeup. "I lived in a heavily Jewish neighborhood back East," she says. "Here, there's no concentration of particular religious groups in any area. We're liberal, we're accepting, and there's so much diversity."

Sarah feels that religious activity in the Valley is a much lower-profile part of the culture than it was back East. "A lot of my co-workers are atheists who don't believe in anything," she says.

She sees both goodness and badness in this. "On the one hand, intensity in religious life can have a dangerous side. That intensity can lead to fanaticism, intolerance, and antagonism between members of different faiths. On the other hand, I think a lot of the problems we have today can be traced to the shrinking of spiritual commitment. I see morals getting more questionable, and young people drifting without a course, and I wonder if a deeper and more structured spiritual life wouldn't make a big contribution toward dealing with these issues."

Sarah places herself among those whose religious life has diminished. Her attendance at synagogue has fallen off substantially over the years. She used to go every week; now she goes mostly on the major Jewish holidays.

She attributes this in part to the demands of her work as a pharmacist at a hospital—in part, but not in total. For whatever reason, perhaps many reasons, she hasn't found quite the same comfort level, hasn't been inspired to have the same involvement level, with the temple as she did back home.

Sarah thinks it's important for Jews, as a relatively small group, to pass on the religion to their children. At a personal level, she has found this to be difficult here—perhaps more so than it might have been in a more traditional setting. Her daughter married a Roman Catholic. Her son is still single, but told her he doesn't think he would marry a Jewish woman.

Although she regards herself as a feminist, God, to her, is very definitely a masculine presence. She is not completely comfortable with some of the changes which have been made in her synagogue's worship to eliminate differences between the roles of men and women in the services.

Sarah doesn't practice regular prayer times. She talks to God on an "as-needed" basis. "I don't really have a concrete picture of God," she says. "He's good and wonderful, and watches over us. I believe He does help those who make an attempt to help themselves, but I pray for help for anyone who needs it. When bad things occur I don't say 'How could God let that happen?' I just try to accept it. My parents died young, but I was never angry with God—I just took comfort in my spirituality and my connection with Him."

> *I see God when I see people acting together as a community to accomplish good things.*
>
> Frank, a Valley bank executive

DOREEN

Most of us can cope reasonably well with trauma on the job front if our personal lives are supportive and fulfilling. We can generally make it through upsets and disappointments in the personal sphere if our professional pursuits are hitting on all cylinders. When the personal and the professional both head south at the same time, we're likely to feel emotional quicksand closing over our ears.

Doreen remembers that feeling. She had been having a dicey affair with a man who was separated, but not divorced, from an acquaintance. The relationship was falling apart. At the time, she was working for a small sporting goods company which was being run into the ground by an inept and alcoholic CEO. "I was losing my job at the same time my love life was failing," she recalls. "And I was alone. When you're having the kind of affair I was, you don't tell a lot of people."

With the help of a friend who had a strong spiritual life, she was able to keep a grip. Things took a big-time turn for the better when she got a job at a well-known Valley optical instrumentation company. It proved to be a bastion of sanity and stability compared to the sporting goods fiasco. It also contributed mightily to her personal life: one of the executives there was the man destined to become her husband.

Doreen's path started in the South, with a father who was "jealous and overbearing." He was also a minister. "Mom just loved him, and gave and gave," Doreen recalled. "I would have hit him on the head with a frying pan." She came to California at age 19

> *God lives in people. He is cheerful, loving, fun-loving, adorable and accepting.*
>
> Rochelle, CEO of a Valley counseling group

to work on a youth services project, and stayed. The crisis point of simultaneous bad job and bad love has long passed, and life is good, but Doreen has continued her efforts to define and direct her spirituality. She has always felt the active tug of her spirit. She just hasn't settled on the precise practice and format which will fit it best. She regularly attends a mainline Protestant church, but has not joined. She does foster parenting, and serves on an urban ministry board.

"I need to know God is God," she says. "I wrestle with this fundamental issue. I want to know He's real and who He says He is. I need to have Him be a part of my daily life. I need to have that knowledge as firmly implanted in me as the faith of a Gandhi or Mother Teresa. I need it to be so grounded I'll never question it at the fundamental, down-deep level. I'm positive of my husband's love. I just don't have the same confidence regarding God's love.

"I think there's a difference between people's view of God here and back home. People are more honest here about what they do and don't believe. In the South, more people go to church; it's more of a lifestyle. There, the focus is on the traditional. Here, it's on the new. People are more self-reliant here, and it leads them to believe they don't need God. There's something about admitting you strongly believe in God that's unpopular in this area.

"I don't always get what I want from my spiritual life, and I don't always feel God's presence. But if I devote the time, I get what I need. When I pray I get communication back: thoughts,

No one will run away from a life in God if introduced to it properly. It's like getting honey from the hive—you might get stung, but it's worth it.

Hamza, a Valley Sufi Muslim leader

not specific words or an audible voice. I have felt turning points where God was speaking to me."

THERESA

"I'm currently a Catholic Church shopper. I want a church that has an intellectual approach to Roman Catholicism, not a simplistic one. I don't want a bureaucracy, and I don't want a monarchy. I want the focus to be on what Christ made, not what man made."

Theresa is the human resources department manager for the Silicon Valley operation of a very large, foreign-owned technology company. Her road to the Valley started in a Polish Catholic Chicago neighborhood. Her road to finding the right church will be made a little more complex by two facts: she's divorced (although she was granted an annulment after 10 years of marriage); and her current husband is not Roman Catholic. They were not wed in a Roman Catholic ceremony. She is confident that these issues will not be a problem in the right setting.

Theresa remembers that her mother went to church more than her father, yet somehow she felt that her father had the deeper spiritual beliefs. She is definitely not into form over substance. "It makes a lot more sense to fix a wrong than say five Hail Marys about it," she believes.

She remembers her initial vision of God. "When you're a kid, you pray to God and you know if you play by the rules, good things will happen, or at least nothing bad. But eventually you learn praying is not enough; you have to get involved in shaping your life."

Theresa observes that most religions have similar tenets. Most promote ethical behavior. She thinks she could be happy within any of their frameworks, but she'll probably stick with her roots.

During the day she has an ongoing dialogue with God. She likes to use the *Aha!* approach to these interchanges. As thoughts and ideas take form and percolate through, she believes she's hearing God's voice when an *Aha!* kicks in.

An example she gives relates to the Catholic Church's prohibition on birth control. She didn't agree with it. She didn't understand it. She initiated extensive dialogue about it.

An *Aha!* eventually struck. There needs to be an entity on earth that holds life sacred. The Roman Catholic Church is that entity. Birth control represents a form of denial of life. It's part of a package: if life is truly sacred, the steward responsible for upholding that view would be in violation of its charge if it permitted the intentional stoppage of life formation.

She adds a subtle but important clarification. She still doesn't necessarily agree. But she understands why the Church takes the position it does, and she feels she has no further quarrel with it on this issue. "Now I'll deal directly with God on this," she says.

Theresa's adult vision of God is one of energy. "Energy can't be created or destroyed, and that's God, or like God. That energy is a force that attracts goodness. It pushes people to do good things."

"IS GOD DEAD?"

For the past 30-plus years, a recurring question, usually asked by sociologists and mass-market magazine covers, has been, "Is God dead?" There is an ironically-humorous-verging-on-bizarre aspect

---

I know the experience of perceiving a vision of God, but I can't put it into a specific box. The Unnamable One, the Light, the Luminous Consciousness, a powerful universal presence, spacious, the totality of all life and all there is.

Victor, a Silicon Valley teacher

to the way the question is phrased. The issue is usually whether people have entered a stage of widespread disbelief, casting off the traditional faith of their youth. If there is a God, the idea that our disbelief would cause His death is a marvelous example of our egos subconsciously wriggling, coiling and sidewinding us into a position of logical absurdity. (Of course, it could also be no deeper a matter than unimaginative, slogan-oriented, lazy headline writing.) And if there isn't a God, there never was, and the question is infinitely moot.

In *The Disappearance of God*, Richard Elliott Friedman looks at one aspect of this question from the perspective of the professional spiritual leader:

> *But why be a* theologian *if God is dead? If people stopped wearing shoes, a shoe store owner would have the sense to switch to another line. The same applies for any other product that became unavailable. Only a theologian would stay in business in the absence of the product.*

Aha! There's another possibility.

Much of the traditional vision of a Higher Power, particularly as promulgated by mainstream religions, may be fading. Or perhaps there have always been faded sections, and now they're coming under close scrutiny. This scrutiny does not necessarily imply rampant iconoclasm or naysaying. It may be the reflection of healthy

---

My God is a God of judgment and grace. When I listen, I hear His voice guiding me, reassuring me, setting me in the new direction I need to follow. But more often than not, I'll pray, and then not wait to hear the answer.

Ray, a Valley software company CEO

questioning of assumptions, willingness to adopt new perspectives, slates wiped clean enough to accept fresh insights, a rejuvenated search for workable wisdom.

In the introduction to her book, *A History of God*, Karen Armstrong says:

> *Despite its otherworldliness, religion is highly pragmatic. ... it is far more important for a particular idea of God to* work *than for it to be logically or scientifically sound. As soon as it ceases to be effective it will be changed—sometimes for something radically different.*

This is very different from gratuitous rejection of the traditional just because it's the traditional. There is some of that. But I don't think it's the real story. The real story is that people feel motivated and free to find what *works* for them.

It takes energy, emotional focus and mental horsepower to formulate visions of Higher Powers. Occasionally, while discussing this topic, the television warning that says something like, "Don't try this at home, you might get hurt. Proper supervision required" popped into mind.

The fact is, I detected only trace elements of this view. Developing visions in settings which may be unsupervised, trying them on in the privacy of the home, and being willing to exchange them if they don't fit, seem to be common in the Valley.

I have a theory about the recent resurgent interest in angels: they offer a cultural icon of instant, safe spirituality. Angels provide awe-inspiring imagery and do beneficial things for people without the demands and rules of a God.

Loretta, a Valley homemaker and former corporate professional

Sam Keen says:

*Authentic spiritual language about God does not
confuse the map with the territory, the symbol with the
thing. Literalism concentrates on the letter and misses
the spirit; it gets the words but never the music, creates
a spiritual tone-deafness. You can starve to death
trying to eat a cookbook.*

A cookbook containing a robust collection of recipes has been created here, from which some tasty dishes have been produced. It's a potluck from which all are free to partake, or not. Some people are advanced spiritual chefs. Some have just opened a can or two. Some like to look at what's on the plates, but aren't inclined to do any cooking themselves at present. Others find it enjoyable and useful to ask for a taste of what's on someone else's plate. Most people know someone who's living on junk food, whom they hope will turn to better nourishment. Few, if any, seem inclined to fruitlessly munch on the pages of the book.

I'm fumbling toward communication with God. I need to get my own words out of the way so I can hear His voice.
Loretta, a Valley homemaker and former corporate professional

Valley clergy had these observations on how people here form their visions of Higher Powers:

People born into a religion start with the Biblical God. Later in life, the vision tends to be much more personal. Then there's a search to find some commonality between the personal vision and the God of the Bible. In California, we're more willing to go with our own feelings and use our own imagery, and share it. We're not as tied to Scriptural references and descriptions.

Most people don't explore visions of God beyond what we teach third graders. The God they encounter is the God of the Bible, the God they hear preached, or more accurately, the God of Sunday school.

One person in our congregation sees God as the Good Mother she never had.

The traditional view of God as patriarchal, bearded, sitting on a throne, has largely been rejected, particularly by women.

The biggest issue people have in their vision of God is dealing with misconceptions. Most people feel God is aloof or angry. We have to convince people there's mercy and grace in the real, living God. We have to peel back the layers of 2,000 years of misconceptions.

We live in a high-tech environment, and we expect change. Because He doesn't change, many people see God as archaic. In their vision, He's covered with cobwebs.

More so here than elsewhere, people want a blessing. They're not necessarily looking for God at all. If they could be one with the Star Wars "Force," that might work. They want energy and power. They want to enhance themselves. But people who are just looking for energy and power miss God, who offers only Himself.

The Biblical, anthropomorphic view of God—the elderly man with the white, flowing beard—is fading or gone. God as spirit, God as energy, is in. The Star Wars trilogy "Force" may represent more people's view of God than theologians ever dreamed.

Some people use standard prayers, some make up their own. But I don't know if there's much reflection or listening to God. I think there's lots of one-way communication. People in Silicon Valley are so busy and moving so fast. They think they're in a rat race. I think it's more of an ant race. But it's so important that they find the time to listen.

CHAPTER FIVE

❧

Homes for the Spirit

"Meditation was invented as a way for the soul to venture inward, there ultimately to find a supreme identity with Godhead ... Whatever else it does, and it does many beneficial things, meditation is first and foremost a search for the God within."

Consciousness theoretician Ken Wilber, quoted in
What Really Matters—Searching for Wisdom in America,
by Tony Schwartz

Ornish has come to believe that the single most important factor in "opening" the heart— physiologically and otherwise—is the degree to which people are able to find a greater sense of meaning, contentment and connectedness in their lives.

Tony Schwartz discussing internist and mind/body theoretician Dean Ornish in *What Really Matters— Searching for Wisdom in America*

101

"Do you think we should check the prototype?" he
asked.

*"Let's not risk it. Kevin warned me that it could
die at any time. Let's just leave it in the hands of
God."*

*"I'm glad to see you're coping with all this strain
by turning to religion."*

Jerry Kaplan, *Startup—A Silicon Valley Adventure*

Those of us who use well-known personal com-
puter programs for applications such as word processing and spread-
sheets are familiar with a function called "cut and paste." This
function allows you to pick pieces from one file and plunk them
down into another. You can repetitively pick and plunk, selecting
and combining the contents of as many files as you wish, keeping
only the portions you want, leaving behind or ruthlessly overwrit-
ing the dross until the final creation is precisely to your liking.

Great concept. Just doesn't go far enough.

What we need is a function called "Real Life Cut and Paste,"
designed to address the fact that everything in life is a package.
Anything big enough to really matter is going to be a combination
of good and bad: houses, jobs, lovers, friends, cars, religions, communities, racquetball partners—the list could go on indefinitely.
Following are some examples of how "Real Life Cut and Paste"
modules might work on these complex packages.

Let's suppose you're in the market for a new home. You like
the exterior of one house, but prefer the interior of another. "House
Cut and Paste" would allow grafting of, say, the better floor plan of
house A onto the landscaping of house B.

In the realm of romance, "Lover Cut and Paste" would allow us to combine the body of person C with the personality of person D, saving us from a frequently vexatious selection dilemma.

To manage the complexities of friendship, we introduce "Friend Cut and Paste." This handy reengineering tool permits the overlay of energy and creativity from friend E onto the humor and supportiveness of friend F, thereby crafting the all-purpose, no-compromise friend.

For professional pursuits we have "Job Cut and Paste" ... but I am sure the concept is now clear.

Many Silicon Valley residents have crafted an approach to their spiritual lives which might be called "Spiritual Life Cut and Paste." They have made the personal decision that none of the prefab packages of spirituality fit them well enough to be acceptable. Therefore, they have reached into their inner tool kit, pulled out metaphorical blueprints, hammers and nails, and either constructed custom-designed homes for their spirits, or at least applied for the building permits.

SALLY

"Christianity never did it for me," Sally said. "I just can't accept virgin birth stories. I wanted to know more about what happened to Mary. I finally decided Christianity didn't have much for women."

Sally is a former technical writer. She currently teaches in one of the Valley's most prestigious school systems. She has been a Presbyterian and a Congregationalist. Now she regards herself as a spiritual searcher and leader. She expects to require no institution, no previously defined religion.

"My husband is a fallen-away Mormon, and he's rabidly anti-religious," she says. "My mother is being recruited by the Jehovah's

Witnesses, and I really don't like the Jehovah concept. My best friend is a man who was raised as a Quaker, and now shares my husband's negative view of religion. I've tried to convert them or open up their spirituality, but nothin' doin'. So it's just me and the women now."

She currently leads a small group of seekers. They meet every two weeks. They are trying to create a spiritual practice which includes pieces from many sources they feel have valuable ideas to offer. Their focus is on developing a feminine religious practice, because they sense a predominantly masculine orientation in traditional religions.

The practice Sally and her group are fashioning includes the Goddess religion of eight cycles, and Jungian psychology. Sally has written up rituals and formal celebrations of the eight ancient holidays of the Goddess. Through their practice they honor the environment, the seasons, Mother Earth.

Ultimately, Sally would like to see partnership and balance between feminine and masculine energy in all spiritual pursuits. Her group would be delighted to have men join in their celebration.

She does not believe in one God, whether the Judeo-Christian or any other anthropomorphic vision. She believes there *is* a greater spirit or essence, and that perhaps the American Indian Great Spirit or the Hindu concept of multiple God-spirits might be closer to the truth. The limited minds of humans are not designed to comprehend it, but altered states might allow us to channel into this truth. Sometimes jogging peacefully through the pristine beauty of an old redwood grove can put her into that altered state.

"I believe in something divine, but the term 'God' annoys me. I like Carlos Castaneda's 'web' idea. He says someone will happen into your life who appears human but isn't, and that being will direct you down the right path if you don't miss her or him. I think maybe I missed mine. If I get another chance, I don't want to miss again."

Sally has difficulty finding the right approach to communication with her deity. She was not raised to pray. An early, Michelangelo-inspired image of God as decidedly masculine made her feel uncomfortable in prayer. She tried chanting and Buddhism, but had a problem with what she saw as patriarchal Buddhist priests. She also discovered she was just too nervous and hyper to meditate successfully. It was the Goddess who called her to her rightful path of spiritual growth.

What she tries to do every day ("badly—I fail") is connect from the heart to everyone she meets, and to live in the present. Exercises to strengthen and enhance the ability to connect are a part of her group's spiritual practice. She believes people may manifest spirituality in many ways—some of them strange—and participation in an organized religion has nothing to do with true spirituality.

Sally's decision to redirect her career from a corporate technical writing job to part-time teaching involved substantial financial sacrifice. Occasionally, while engaged in somber consideration of her checkbook balance, she wonders if she did the right thing. But not for long. She is positive that returning to the corporate environment would kill her spirit.

"In the corporate world, I felt surrounded by people who were visually and spiritually blind. They had a lot to learn about how to treat women. There was no place there for my talents and creativity. I was inside. It was dark. I was missing the seasons.

"One day I left to pick up my kids and the trees were blossoming. The season had changed and I hadn't had time to notice it! It threw me into a spiritual crisis. I decided I had to quit the job.

I chose freedom and spirituality. I also knew I might be choosing poverty. But I was going to die if I stayed."

Sally subsequently met the man who was to become her current husband. ("After we had dated for a while, I offered to keep a coffee mug of his own at my apartment. When he accepted, we both knew we were committed.") Although he has elected not to participate in her spiritual life (or any), they're a two-income household and poverty has been avoided.

"Change is coming to Silicon Valley," she says. "The male/linear/math/science orientation must allow sharing with the feminine. The more of us who get involved in spiritual life and bring it into companies, the more the companies will change for the better.

"Women are being bombarded by little snowflakes of change—and so are men, whether they know it or not. It's in the air. Magically, mysteriously, good people are being moved by the spirit, and all of us are being exposed to a new way of doing things.

"We're reaching for the global village. Spiritual life means trying to get past polarities and finding out about people, even if you can't stand them. A spiritual heart will reach out past the forms, past the rules, and connect with the spirit living in the hearts of others."

Can one be spiritual even if one does not believe in God or practice a religion? If spirituality means just recognizing something beyond the body and the physical, yes. But I think I'd answer the question no. What is it if it's not God? The purpose of our being here is to bring light into the darkness of the world. That's done by bringing God to people, and to me, any practice that doesn't include God would not be called spiritual.

Aaron, a Silicon Valley rabbi

MATT

In 1995, the large company which had acquired the small company for which Matt worked threw in the towel on the acquisition.

Matt joined the company in the early '80s. He worked hard and well, and enjoyed a gratifyingly consistent upward organizational path. He attained the chief financial officer title. He even enjoyed it for a while. Then the company's numbers turned bad, and his stomach lining followed suit.

Reductions in force were inevitable. The revenue wasn't there, so some employees had to not be there also. Matt was obliged to terminate people he had known for a long time. He developed a rash which made his skin look like his stomach lining felt.

Ultimately, the day of reckoning arrived. Matt had spent a ghastly year living the lie that the company should be tracking to an impossible financial plan. The parent decreed they would now receive the fate they deserved as a wayward, miscreant child: a new foster home would be found, as quickly as possible, with anyone who would take them. However, the process was to be kept highly confidential. Matt had the additional pressure of not being able to share with most of his employees and co-workers the fact that something was in the works that could have a significant impact on them.

During this period Matt's personal life took a turn that added further drama to his situation.

He had married his high school sweetheart shortly after they graduated. They had two lovely daughters. His wife worked when she wanted, stayed home when she wanted. Matt's career was always successful enough to make a second household income optional. In his view, they had an idyllic existence.

Matt's wife, Lydia, saw it differently. Matt sensed she was drifting away from him and the marriage. He had no idea what to do. They tried counseling; it didn't help. About the only things they still seemed to be sharing were their kids and the sport of racquetball.

They had both taken up racquetball. They got serious, and they got good. Matt was playing three times a week, Lydia as many as eight times a week. Sometimes, even while they were playing doubles together, Matt sensed hostility from his wife/partner. "It seemed like she was hitting me with her racquet a lot," he recalls.

"That's bound to happen occasionally with four players on the court," I responded comfortingly.

"Yeah," he said, "but the last time it happened I was standing by the water fountain."

On Valentine's Day, Matt planned a romantic dinner *à deux* at an intimate restaurant. They were seated at their table. Then Lydia cleared her throat and said she needed to discuss a couple things.

OK, Matt said.

First, she informed him, she had been thinking about the upcoming mixed doubles tournament, and the strategy which would be required to prevail over the competition. The bottom line was, she thought she'd have a better chance of winning if she played with one of the other guys at the club instead of partnering with Matt. She had already made the arrangements with the other player.

Matt was stunned. OK, he said. He didn't know what else to say.

The second thing she needed to discuss, Lydia continued, was that it wasn't just the racquetball partnership that wasn't working for her. It was the whole life partnership. She wanted a divorce. She wanted to start planning the separation immediately. Her mind was made up: no chance of change.

Happy Valentine's Day, Matt.

Eventually, both divorce settlements were agreed on: Matt from his wife, the company from its parent. A buyer was found for the company. Its new CEO proposed restructuring, further lay-offs, and extraordinarily long work hours for those who remained.

For the first few weeks after the sale was complete, Matt worked long and hard to integrate the company's financial operations with those of its new owner. Then one morning he got up and pondered the days stretching into the foreseeable future that awaited him at the office. He considered the twinges in his gut, and the stress rash that made him look like he'd had an overdose of tropical sun. To paraphrase an old folk/rock song, some kind of message shot through.

He tried to make an appointment with his superior, the new CEO. All he needed was five minutes to resign with dignity. He couldn't get it. On a Sunday afternoon, after a week of trying to meet with his boss, Matt's phone rang at home. It was the CEO, calling from his car phone. He only had a minute. What did Matt want to talk about? Through the cellular static, Matt told him.

Within a few days the stress signals from his innards had subsided. The rash was gone. He knew his decision would create new, perhaps unpredictable challenges, but that was fine. He had opened up his life.

After the usual number of dubious dating adventures in the singles world, he met Tanya. Things clicked. They dated, they moved

---

There's lots of spirituality without religion. During a recent TV channel-surf, Deepak Chopra was on one channel, and another had a woman whose spiritual philosophy was "fake it 'til you make it."

Stella, public relations manager for
a Valley networking company

in together, they got married, and they're happily blending together a family with his two daughters and Tanya's son.

On the career front, Matt has decided to become an entrepreneur. He has gone through training, and has hung out his shingle as a financial planner affiliated with a national financial services company.

I was particularly interested in hearing what effect the "opening up" of his life might have on his spiritual views. We met at his comfortable East Bay home, and sat in the breakfast nook of his newly remodeled kitchen. He offered me a choice of several coffee blends, made in any of the five types of coffee makers he owns. Our caffeine levels properly elevated, he talked about his path.

Christians sometimes speak glowingly of new developments that are causing a major new synthesis of science and theology, so that these two disciplines that previously have been quite diverse, now are merging into one new discipline of the future, a new paradigm, a new synthesis of science and faith. Science will bring validation to religion, and religion will bring transcendence to science—a New Age.

It is important to appreciate the great temptation that such New Age thinking poses for modern people immersed in a scientific world but looking for a means of religious expression. We must be prepared to distinguish between appropriate interactions between authentic science and authentic theology and the general tendency to move toward pseudoscience and pseudotheology as the ideal thought patterns.

Unpublished lecture notes from *Putting It All Together: Seven Patterns for Relating Science and Christian Faith,* a 1996 seminar series led by Richard H. Bube, Professor Emeritus of Materials Science and Electrical Engineering, Stanford University

❧ Religion and Spirits ❧

"I'm very spiritual, and my spirituality has increased now that I'm not in the corporate world. I try to do transcendental meditation twice a day. I talk to spirits all the time. From my perspective, they're all over, including the larger variety, which some might call God. Some spirits are dead relatives. I talk to the ones with whom I have interests in common.

"Before Tanya and I met, she befriended a lonely, elderly man whose wife had passed away. He was in poor health. She took care of him, and he told her that when he died he wanted half his ashes scattered in the Bay Area and half in Hamburg, Germany. The first half is done, and the second half is sitting in a jar upstairs. One day we'll go to Hamburg and honor the rest of his request. In the meantime, while the jar with his ashes is upstairs, I talk to his spirit. He doesn't have a body, but he's still a person. Some people have 'hardware' and 'software,' some are just *on the Net*.

"My ex and I didn't connect on spiritual beliefs. She went to church regularly, but she was never a spiritual partner. When she moved out, the spirits in the house had to rebalance themselves. Tanya has been a Mormon and a Roman Catholic, but now she's very much in tune with my spiritual life.

"My parents sent us to Sunday school when we were kids," he remembered, "but it didn't take long to figure out why. They just wanted to have some time to themselves. That seemed a little hypocritical, and gave me a negative attitude toward religion. In fact, it set me on a crusade to never participate in one.

"Then I got to studying history and I learned about all the misuses of religious power to inflict pain, cruelty and genocide, and act out obsessions, and it just reaffirmed my decision."

❧ Lives and Death ❧

"I look to my spiritual path to help me better enjoy life, and to prepare me for death. Someone once said 'death is the biggest kick of all, and that's why they save it for last.' In the long run, most things in life aren't important, particularly in the context of death.

"Death is just the necessary step in the cycle of continuing lives, ongoing learning, and attainment of higher states of consciousness and enlightenment. There's no heaven, unless that's it. It's not a question of *believing in* reincarnation. It's *there to be seen*, a matter of personal experience. If you haven't figured this out yet, you haven't been paying attention.

"It's very sad when people spend a lifetime and never get in touch with their own spirit. They die, but they haven't prepared for it, and their next assignment might be to come back as a snail. This wouldn't represent a very positive evolutionary process.

"Everyone has a soul or a spirit, even if they never experience its awakening. Just because a rock doesn't know it's a rock doesn't mean it's not a rock, although I hope most rocks do.

"The two biggest obstacles which keep people from embarking on spiritual paths are organized religion and television. Organized religion is always placing things like 30-centuries-old dogmatic documents, or a spiritual bureaucrat, in the middle of the path to block it up. And television just empties people's heads out until there's nothing left.

"Since our spirits recycle and are always here, they always have been here. Fifteen billion years ago, everything was in a state of complete harmony of material, energy and spirit. There was perfection. Then we all made a decision to have some fun, and the universe was created. We were all there, and we all made the decision. If you're not having fun, you're not paying attention.

"There's a spectrum of consciousness in all living things. Redwoods must think we're just awful. We're not that important in the scheme of the universe. But when I see some of the things we do, I think if I were an alien looking at earth, I might be tempted to flood the planet with an antitoxin to protect the universe.

"Recently I was feeling a little insecure, and went into a meditative session looking for a spiritual contact. I received a strong thought or direction which said, 'Seek me through my other children.' I was looking for a hug; instead I got a homework assignment."

❧ Doing What's Right ❧

"There may be some connection between people's spiritual beliefs and their moral and ethical codes, but the connection is far from universal. Spiritually and intellectually enlightened people may develop very similar codes of morals and ethics. But some who profess religion don't seem to have the codes I would expect, and some intellectual people don't seem to have a very good understanding of the difference between right and wrong.

"My personal ethics aren't based on laws or government edicts. I will do what I think is right before I obey the government. I would have been willing to smuggle Jews out of Nazi Germany even if it was against German law. I go over 65 miles per hour

Religious practice and spirituality can each exist without the other. In the Christian tradition, spirituality says there's a divine essence. To reach it, you have to touch a sacred dimension beyond yourself. The spirituality is the grace part, and the practice is the human part meeting the grace.

Ron, a Silicon Valley pastor

when I know it's safe. My primary concern is what's healthy for myself and for others.

"One of the toughest parts of living in the Valley is time demands. The challenge for me is to better integrate my spiritual life with life in the material world. My new career direction should make that possible. I want to see helping other people become a priority. I'll keep working on my program, continue finding myself, and stay engaged in daily spiritual life.

"Silicon Valley has always been a breeding ground for new ideas. It's a creative zone for the planet. I hope the tolerance and acceptance we have here will permeate everywhere, maybe even to troubled places like the Mideast and Northern Ireland. Technology like the World Wide Web will allow us to accept and enjoy our differences instead of hurting each other."

MARTA

"When one opens one's self to the life force, when it's got breathing space and is welcome, one can't help but become aware of the sacred," Marta says.

Marta is a tech writer for one of Silicon Valley's icon organizations. She was born in Germany, and moved to Minnesota as a child with her mother. Her mother had her baptized as a Lutheran because she felt that Minnesotans valued membership in institutional religions. Marta has been in Silicon Valley for 28 years, and that's been more than enough time to explore spiritual alternatives.

Several years ago, Marta embarked on a process to expand her inner frontiers. Her childhood religion was uninspiring. Her ex-husband was "a capital-A atheist." She had been in a spiritual stall. It was time to open up. She had previously taken a number of personal growth seminars and programs, and felt she was ready for new enlightenment.

When she opened herself, she expected the Christian spirit to enter her and come to life, but that is not what happened. Christian traditions were high on her exploration list, but she found nothing she could put her arms around. A substantial theological roadblock for her was the doctrine of original sin. She doesn't buy it. She doesn't believe we're "bad and black deep down," and she feels focusing on sin is "getting off the mark" of a true spiritual pursuit. She felt no connection with churches or church communities. "I remember thinking maybe you had to be a nun or a monk to get Christianity," she says.

A friend introduced her to some of the concepts of Zen Buddhism. She found them interesting. She bought a book on the subject and read it carefully. As she went through it, she methodically checked off things with which she resonated. It ended up being a substantial list, and she decided to explore Zen retreats.

The quiet, tranquil ambience of the retreats was a dramatic contrast to the inner maelstrom they brought her. Meditation opened paths to issues and conflicts with which she had never dealt. She found a prayer which she felt was allowing the Creator to flow through her. She cried extensively while meditating. She felt she was being broken open, made vulnerable, being given a road to "inward time" as a medicine for the frantic pace of life.

During one retreat, between meditations, an older woman said something to her which triggered "an emotional storm of terror and catharsis." It didn't have much to do with what was said. It had everything to do with the presence of someone Marta felt was accepting and nonjudgmental, the nature of the retreat, and the process she was going through.

("This woman told me she once spent a whole year crying," she recalls. I asked Marta if she knew why. "I guess it was just her year to cry," she said.)

Marta regards herself as "closest to Buddhist" in terms of applying a label to her spiritual path. "The practice is hanging out with whatever comes up, going through your mind and feelings, letting it go, witnessing, and coming back to your breath. It's the place of quiet." An image she likes is that of the upright toy with the weighted base: life throws punches, and may knock her to the side, but her spirituality helps bring her upright again.

The vision of God which speaks to Marta is closely akin to the Buddhist view of "a web of life with causality." God is the unmanifested potential, the pervasive substance. All creatures are God made manifest. She doesn't see a separation, with "God over there and creation over here." Everything's integrated. What we put out affects the world, and comes back and affects us, too. When we die, we go from the manifested back into the pool of the unmanifested.

A meaningful metaphor for Marta is God as ocean and humans as waves. Waves are differentiated, manifested, temporary. They have birth, fruition, death. They're made from, and always part of, the ocean. "Meditation is about coming to that still, calm place that says 'ocean.'"

An emerging part of Marta's practice is to combine prayer, meditation and exercise during brisk walks. As she passes other

---

Ethical or moral behavior is not so much an arbitrary decree from above as the natural outgrowth of careful attention to the consequences of one's thoughts and emotions.

Tony Schwartz, discussing Buddhism, in *What Really Matters—Searching for Wisdom in America*

people, she has a prayer for them: "May you have peace; may you have no suffering; may you be connected to God." Prayer may not change the color of a wall, she believes, but it can cause the wall to glow with a different light.

Twenty-five years ago, Marta's prayer channel opened up for two-way communication. The message she received was "Risk! Learn to let go of yourself. Learn to love in a larger way." She is trying to follow this direction. She feels confident that God talks to all of us, through our intuition, if we're open and available to it. She doesn't think the obstacle is that God is shy. The obstacle is that this is Silicon Valley, and our incoming lines are busy.

Marta thinks interest in Buddhism in this area is growing. She regards it as a fine foundation for building a custom home for one's spirit—particularly for those who are disenchanted with mainstream Western religions.

"Western civilization thinks man is a special case and doesn't have to obey natural laws," she says. "Not true. We are not exempt from nature. If we're going to survive, we have to find our connection with nature and each other. Our outer manifestation has to spring from inner values. Maybe it takes a spiritual renaissance."

HELENE

Helene, a Silicon Valley minister, was born and raised a Baptist. She has come to believe there are many paths to workable spirituality and connection with deeper meaning.

The diversity of viewpoints and philosophies the area sports and supports led her to establish an organization focusing on interfaith sharing. Its goal is to facilitate communication and understanding among those of disparate beliefs, and encourage pooling of wisdom to assist in the search for truth. She says, "Spirituality is not so much a list of beliefs as a relationship which can't necessarily be defined." She thinks this perspective, combined with the area's frequently negative view of the traditional, will make New Age approaches much more attractive than mainline churches to spiritual newcomers in the Valley.

BRAD

After exchanging a series of messages via each other's answering machines, Brad and I finally connected for an online, real-time, bisynchronous telephone conversation. He's a Roman Catholic priest. I had been told he was doing interesting things and might have some valuable insights on spiritual dynamics in the Valley. We agreed to meet at the Los Altos Peet's for coffee. He said he'd be wearing teal.

A priest wearing teal ... sounded interesting already.

Turns out he's not currently working in his clerical role. His spiritual vision has become tightly woven with a passion for education, and a desire to help teachers teach. He and two colleagues have established a nonprofit foundation to develop courses, training tools, and seminars to make educators more effective. They are particularly interested in working with the area's high-tech companies to "break down the walls between religion/spirituality and science/technology."

The foundation will also develop and offer support programs for educators, with emphasis on showing them how to incorporate the teaching of ethics and wellness into their subjects. Seminars to help people deal with long-term illness are also in the works.

Contributing to the effectiveness of Silicon Valley's educational infrastructure has become a core part of Brad's view of his spiritual journey. There is no legacy he would rather leave than to see people who are better educated, and more spiritually and ethically aware, coming out of the Valley's schools and corporations through his efforts. It's a logical continuation of his life.

Brad was born in upstate New York, and received most of his education in Roman Catholic schools. As he grew up, he developed respect for clergy who took the lead in social issues. Daniel Berrigan was an early hero. Brad entered seminary because he wanted to follow those footsteps, help change society for the better, learn to use religion to pursue the common good. He saw that the Church could be a "critical conscience" in our culture.

After ordination he worked as a parish priest for two years, but discovered what he really enjoyed was working on educational projects. If he'd been a member of an educational order, he believes he might have cheerfully embarked on a career of academic administration. But he wasn't. So he looked for other routes to involve himself with teaching.

One day he woke up and asked himself, "Self, do you really want to spend the rest of your life in Buffalo?" Self responded resoundingly in the negative. He ended up in Silicon Valley, a place he finds intriguing for its leading-edge economy, openness to change, multicultural diversity and strong educational institutions.

Wozniak and Jobs started Apple in a garage. Brad's following the mold, renting rooms and working out of an empty convent while getting his foundation rolling. As we sipped French roast, he shared his observations on the Valley's spiritual scene.

"Everything here is so competitive, so product- and process-driven, that the care of the soul has taken a back seat. Affluence grabs hold and takes over. New product introductions give people such a rush that they've practically become the drug of choice.

"But the work can be draining and exhausting. People some-times start wondering if 'that's all there is,' and that may open the inner door a little. I've talked to many VPs who have been downsized. These were people who had virtually enslaved them-selves to their jobs and their companies, then got flattened. They felt they had done all the right things. Then they went from six-figure jobs to no-figure jobs.

"But those with some spiritual component in their lives dealt with the whole thing so much better. They seemed to be able to transcend the devastating circumstances. They realized they were still good husbands or wives, still good parents, still valued mem-bers of a community. They kept their dignity. I believe it's people who bring dignity to work, not work that brings dignity to people.

"Sometimes I start retreats by asking people to think about a scene from the movie *Philadelphia*: the one where Tom Hanks lets an operatic aria just *transport* him to another place while he's in conference with his lawyer. Then I ask them, 'What's the music in your life?' In Silicon Valley, I'm not sure people know what that music is, or are ready to hear it and be touched by it.

"People back East ask me what it's like living in Silicon Valley. I tell them it's like having all 30 NFL teams located between San Francisco, San Jose and Oakland, all competing for the same fans. Competition and survival are the focal points.

"People here have such tremendous aspirations. What hap-pens if they don't achieve them? Bust times may come again. The soul is the one thing we should invest more in. We'll need it if the Valley turns back into prune orchards. I don't know if people are ready to take care of their souls yet. They know they should, and they'll flock to Kepler's or Printer's Ink or East-West Books to buy literature, but they may not be ready to find the music and devote the energy.

"People here know they're making history, and the business is addictive. Andy Grove wrote a book called *Only The Paranoid Survive*. OK. How long do we want to be paranoid? Is that a way to live? Sooner or later everyone takes a kick in a sensitive portion of their anatomy. We have to be able to keep it in perspective. For many, it might take something as big as failed health or failed families to snap the money and the success back into perspective.

"In *Habits of the Heart*, Robert Bellah made the case that we have become a nation of individuals, not a community. That applies even more to Silicon Valley. But when individuals don't have a community to share their spirituality with, the spirituality tends to fade. The most true spiritual expression I've seen in the Valley has been at Alcoholics Anonymous meetings.

"I think the image of God many people in this area have is the one they're most comfortable with for their authority figures: he's the CEO. One thing I still like about the Catholic Church is that they teach a God of compassion, not of wrath. But there are some people in the Valley who are hungry to find simpler, black-and-white things in this incredibly complex environment we live in. There are some fundamentalist churches starting to thrive as some of these people join, and they're hearing about a wrathful CEO.

"People don't have to practice a religion to be spiritual, or even believe in the usual concept of a deity. The inner spirit, the

---

The problem with spirituality without an organization is that it emphasizes an individuality which leads to isolation, renunciation, and self-righteousness. Churches require sharing. "I can be spiritual alone" is a great way to escape responsibility, and promotes a false experience. If I'm a person of faith, I'm also a person reaching out to others.

Pat, a Valley pastor

thing that brings purpose, joy, exultation, may be experiencing God even if the mind isn't at the moment. I believe there are five ways people experience God that involve no formal worship:

❖ first, just having self-worth and self-respect;

❖ second, having the capacity to give unlimited love;

❖ third, dealing with our own mortality;

❖ fourth, having hope;

❖ and last, raising children, the willingness of every generation to sacrifice for the next.

"The human spirit *soars* during these five situations. It doesn't have to be mystical or magical. The moments of spirituality are in the ordinariness of daily living.

"The people who are the most spiritually grounded are people who like themselves and don't want to be someone else. Spiritual people won't be *users* of others. They see people as creations like themselves, to be reverenced and respected, not as subjects. They don't always have to be playing the trump card and controlling others.

"A key ethical conflict everyone has to work out before taking a job is, 'If I go to work for you, how much of my soul am I gonna have to give you?' Another one is, 'Can this workplace be a place of meaningful conversation, or does it have to be what the boss wants to hear?' A good environment must ensure mutual success, and not end up with a posse of burned-up, burned-out souls.

"I think it's a part of American culture to respect team spirit, and I don't think the Valley is an exception to that. And team spirit is a form of spirituality. Most folks like to see others who show great team spirit succeed. When people demonstrate spirituality in their business relations, no one begrudges them their money or their success.

"In terms of my personal spiritual path, I'm going to keep doin' what I'm doin'. My passion is for education, and for teaching people how to take care of their souls, making it possible for them to teach others the same thing. If I never presided at another Eucharist it wouldn't matter. I didn't get ordained just to wear robes. It was about moving forward with a social vision and making it happen. Heroes are fine, but what we really need are role models.

"I don't know how the Valley will end up blending technology with spirituality—I just know it needs to happen. You can't stay paranoid forever."

STREET SCENE INTERLUDE

As I waited for Victor in a downtown Palo Alto coffee shop, a compelling figure shuffled repeatedly into the shop, then back out. He looked 42 going on 106. His clothes were an unrelated collage of old, tired cotton. His full beard was mostly black, streaked with gray. So was his mane of wildly disheveled hair.

I found some of the same adjectives popping into mind as I looked at his eyes: Black. Streaked with gray. Disheveled. Wild.

The eyes stayed fixed dead ahead as he moved. He left his shopping cart—brim-full of ancient garments, two canteens, and unidentifiable objects wrapped in untraceable pieces of plastic— by the bench in front of the shop. I sipped blueberry Italian soda and watched him come ... through ... the ... door ... at ... a ... painstakingly ... slow ... pace, ... careful ... step ... by ... careful ... step. My inner metronome, used to the manic Silicon Valley clock speed of life, was going nuts.

Eyes straight ahead, he moved glacially past the service counter to the rear of the shop where large burlap bags full of coffee were stacked. His mission was a mystery. From behind the counter, the coffee server/cashier watched, radiating discomfort and indecision. The stranger wasn't hassling anyone. But he also wasn't buying anything, and his bizarre looks and behavior might scare the customers away. What to do?

Outside, a woman crossed the street and sat down on the bench, a few feet from his cart. She was plump and blonde, wearing blue jeans which looked worn and faded enough to have been handmade by Levi Strauss himself. What was left of her boots indicated similar vintage. She looked 34 going on 106. She gazed through the door into the shop for a few moments, then grimaced or smiled (no way to tell which). Her teeth didn't look too good. She closed her eyes in the late afternoon sun.

The bearded man retraced his steps and eventually made it back out the door: his fourth round trip. He looked at his cart, the bench, the woman. He stood statue-still for about 45 seconds. Then, with the same torturously slow tread, he moved toward the woman. If she heard the shuffle of his approaching feet, she gave no sign. Her eyes stayed closed. Her hands were folded in her lap. He finally arrived at her location. He paused. He leaned over. With utmost gentleness, he kissed her. She did not move or open her eyes. He stood up, turned around, headed back toward the shop door with the same timeless rhythm, entered, and began his well-defined return journey to the burlap bags. The woman opened her eyes and stared straight ahead, face completely expressionless. No clues were in evidence to tell whether she knew the man, or that she had been kissed.

I felt an almost overpowering urge to get up, introduce myself to both of them, and request an interview. What would be their thoughts about spirituality in Silicon Valley?

Victor pulled up outside the shop, dismounted from his bicycle, secured it and joined me at my table by the window. The bearded man exited, and this time did not return. I scored a blueberry Italian soda for Victor, and we began our conversation.

VICTOR

Victor was born in Illinois, but has lived in Silicon Valley for over 20 years. His father was Jewish. His mother belonged to a mainline Protestant denomination. He was baptized, but his parents let him make his own call about his spiritual direction. At 13, he decided not to go through with confirmation into his mother's church. "My path will be neither Jewish nor Christian," he says. "It will encompass both, and other things. An image I sometimes use for my spiritual life is a butterfly. The wings are Judaism and Christianity, and the body is the center I'm trying to get to."

While in college, Victor spent summers in Japan, and he lived there for two years after graduating. "Life in Japan made me realize I'm not Japanese," he recalled, "but it gave me some shelter from the spiritual confusion I felt at the time. What I had to realize was that my journey was not geographical, it was *inward*. Once I got to that point, I decided that the Bay Area was the place for me to be. This is an excellent environment for exploration, for quests, for me to find out who I am."

Fluent in Japanese, Victor is now a language instructor. Finding his spiritual destiny is at the top of his priority stack. He includes Quaker meetings, Buddhist meditation and labyrinth walking in his current practice. "I find the Quaker style nurturing in the sense that the silence offers space and balance. Teachings come from within. People speak if they are 'moved to speak.' "

"Connectedness" and "centeredness" are terms Victor used frequently during our discussion. They represent core concepts of his path. "The connectedness has to be with what's authentic in me, not what's superficial," he says. "Mindfulness meditation is a bedrock to my pathway. I'm using it to achieve a sense of wholeness, of completeness, of authenticity. To get to a place where I can say '*Aha!* I am *this*, and I am *this*.' And sometimes, when I'm meditating, or praying for direction, things will become known, and I'll say '*Aha!* It's been made clear! Thank you!' "

Although he values the Valley's freedom to explore and experiment, Victor also has a healthy concern for the area's snares for the unwary. "The overstimulus provides a tremendous challenge to remaining centered and authentic," he says. "We're like fish swimming upstream. We have to constantly keep our eyes out for hooks. One of them is the increasing sense that technology determines your value, and that the faster modem, the better Internet connection, the more advanced program will lead to fulfillment. It's almost as if the servant has become the master.

"One of my biggest spiritual challenges is trying to keep a balanced sense of compassion and understanding when I'm feeling attacked by my boss. It's been a struggle. My boss is a jerk. But maybe his parents were jerks, and maybe all he knows is how to be a jerk. So the challenge is not to grab onto his 'jerkness,' but to see past it, see him as a person, stay centered, but still make my point.

"I'm looking to my spiritual life to lead me to peace within myself, and to allow me to fully express my gifts. I need greater balance between involvement in the outside world and focus on

Nature lovers could be closer to God than people realize. Maybe closer than those practicing in churches.

Rhonda, a network equipment company program manager

the inner world. I may be doing longer periods of silent meditation—perhaps even a 10-day silent retreat. We need to counter the speed of the Valley, and return to a natural human rhythm. We need the spaciousness of quiet."

TRAIL FOR TWO

An issue discussed at greater length in Chapter Nine is what happens when one partner in a marriage or relationship has a spiritual life but the other does not. There's another version of the question: what happens when both spirits are alive and well, but each partner wants to build a different spiritual home?

Additional subtext may arise when the home one or both of them have in mind is very much a build-to-suit project rather than a prefab. Making up the rules as we go along can be liberating, but also confusing. The fact is, it's hard enough to blaze a new trail just for oneself. Making it wide enough for two to stride side by side adds much to the task. And for some, walking the path without a partner is just not their first choice. Things might end up that way, but not by preference.

For many years, Paula and Gavin have been members of an established, mainstream Protestant church in an affluent Valley community. They have come to feel that the relationship with this institution is no longer working well for them, not doing what it's supposed to do. However, this is not a joint decision. It's two individual decisions, for two different sets of reasons.

GAVIN

Gavin is a biology professor at a local community college. He's a tenor in the church choir, and takes great pleasure in making music in that setting. He belongs to the church men's club, and enjoys the social experience. Music and mixing are happening for him there, but not much spirituality.

Part of the drawback to his spiritual experience at the church relates to the idea that familiarity can breed, if not contempt, then at least irreverence. Gavin has come to know the long-time minister almost too well. He knows his foibles, sees his human failings, enjoys the camaraderie. But his acceptance of the man as his spiritual leader has faded. Not by design. It just happened.

In a way, Gavin feels that his religious involvement peaked in his teens. He had a great time in the church youth group, and he went to Mass with a Roman Catholic girl he was dating to show her he cared. After high school, life took over, and he wasn't interested in getting back onto a spiritual path until children came along. Then he and his wife put a great deal of energy into shopping for a church, but he felt it was more for the kids' benefit than his.

A few years ago, Gavin felt his spiritual life had leveled out. Then a guest speaker at the men's club gave a presentation on meditation. He tried it. He liked it. So did some of the other men. They have formed a group which meets every two weeks for meditation. Gavin now meditates three times a week for 30 minutes—or tries to. He says it has made a big difference in his life, made him calmer. He gave an example:

"I was walking through the Price Club parking lot with a shopping cart full of stuff, and two cars honked at me. In the past that would have made me very angry. I was going fast enough. Let them wait! But meditation has mellowed me out, so I didn't get angry. Then I saw they were honking at me because a package of 5,000 napkins had fallen off the bottom of my cart."

At this point Gavin doesn't know exactly what his spiritual life is, or what he wants to get from it. He wants to be more in touch with himself, more in control of himself. "I want to be more the driver than the car," he says.

Mostly what he'd like is to be able to recreate the spiritual feelings he had as a child. He didn't know as much then. Now, his scientific orientation is putting up a real barricade to internalizing some tenets of Christian belief.

"I have a hard time accepting things on faith anymore," he explained. "I want an explanation of the miracles. 'The Red Sea gets shallow at certain times'; 'locust mating patterns support the plague schedule'; that kind of thing. And as a biologist, I just can't handle virgin birth. Mary and Joseph have to have been fooling around.

"But in my men's group, I would have a hard time expressing my doubts. I would get, 'What, you don't believe?!' I wonder how many people in church on Sunday have primal doubts about doctrine and God and life after death. I suspect a lot of prayers are the adult version of 'God, please increase my allowance.'"

Gavin's vision of God is right in sync with the observations of clergypersons Roland and Pat in the prior chapter: something like the "Force" in *Star Wars*. He observes that sometimes things do seem to happen when people pray together, and thinks maybe God functions like a cosmic network server to which everyone connects.

> *Without the leavening of a creative intellectual focus, the quasi-therapeutic blandness that has afflicted much of mainline Protestant religion at the parish level for over a century cannot effectively withstand the competition of the more vigorous forms of radical religious individualism, with their claims of dramatic self-realization, or the resurgent religious conservatism that spells out clear, if simple, answers in an increasingly bewildering world.*
>
> Robert N. Bellah et al., *Habits of the Heart—Individualism and Commitment in American Life*

But he also observes that there are too many people praying to too many Gods for conflicting things, and he's troubled by the inherent contradictions. How can He take sides? How can He not? Why does He let so many bad things happen? If He has the conscious control of His creation which people ascribe to Him, how can you not blame Him for the world's problems?

He doesn't have the answers to his questions and doubts, and he hasn't settled on a well-defined strategy for getting them. He thinks he may focus more on exploring Eastern religions via retreats, mantras and continuing meditation. But he likes the people in his church, and likes the music there, and he's not going to walk away. The current pastor is approaching the end of his reign. Gavin thinks having a new leader will be healthy for the congregation, and might help him refocus his journey.

PAULA

Like her husband, Paula has come to the conclusion that their church no longer meets her needs. She was born into an affluent, mainstream Protestant family in Colorado, and she's fairly certain that her family and old friends would look harshly on the direction her path is taking. She has not yet disengaged: she feels ties to the church community and some aspects of traditional belief. But she is energetically engaged in the pursuit of the right alternative.

"The church is hierarchical, and structured on centuries of patriarchy and male domination," she says. "There's a wound to heal, and issues to deal with. There are a lot of very controlling male ministers, and when you look at what traditional churches have foisted off, it's appalling. It's a power play, backed up by hellfire and damnation.

"The Christian boat is sinking. But if you jump, where do you jump and who do you jump with? I think I'm looking for the Goddess, for the pre-Christian harmony of humankind and earth. 'Christian feminist' may be an oxymoron; some might call me a pagan."

Strong feelings that traditional religion just didn't add up entered Paula's consciousness in her late 30s. She concluded that organizational structure was a big part of religion's problems. She thought she could be a part of the solution by becoming an organizer and activist within her spiritual community. She did research. She prayed for direction.

She made little progress. She remembers sitting in a church committee meeting and being struck by the lack of diversity of thought and perspective in the group. She couldn't restrain herself. "We're inbred and incestuous," she said. Everything stopped. There was silence. Then the discussion continued as if she hadn't spoken. For the first time, the thought came to her that it might be time to leave, time to find something new—or start it.

Then she saw a play that changed her life. It was written and performed by one woman, built around a series of scenes reflecting women's relationship with spirituality over the ages. She took several women to see it. They were all moved. They decided to form a group to discuss its concepts.

Paula put a blurb in her church newsletter to announce the formation of the discussion group. She felt it was a relatively modest undertaking, not requiring the minister's approval. He saw it

The more I accept that I can't accept some of the theological details of my Christian faith as truth, the more the Holy Spirit deepens within me.

Celeste, a Silicon Valley attorney

differently. He called her on the carpet for not going through channels. He told her the whole thing sounded like she was trying to form a new sect.

She told the minister that henceforth she would seek the appropriate clearance. Furthermore, she would commemorate this resolution by having T-shirts printed up saying, "We have safe sects with our minister."

"It'll be a long time before a woman is the senior minister here," she says. "Teaching and healing, yes. Leading and decision making, no.

"I want a numinous connection to the higher spirit. I want to feel connected to the God/dess within. I can understand why people become mystics or hermits—it's a powerful experience, and may be the best way for many to find that connection. But I need to find it with a community, although stepping out of the mainstream makes it harder to find that community. Starhawk [a well-known Bay Area Wiccan practitioner] has written a wonderful 'Tree of Life' meditation, and the image is connection of all through the roots, and strength through the trunk.

One can probably be spiritual without religion or belief in a God, but it might be somewhat superficial: like ordering a cheeseburger, hold the meat and hold the cheese. One can be humanistic, but the question of what's the difference between the humanistic and the spiritual is a tough one, and the answers are full of gray. The commonality seems to revolve around the sense of peace. The humanist is at peace because he has accepted *the human condition. The spiritualist is at peace because he has* transcended *the human condition.*

Richard, a Silicon Valley software company executive

"I've been an energy vampire for much of my life, and now I want to stop taking and give. I'll do my part, if I can just figure out what it is. Or if 'someone' will tell me.

"Silicon Valley has a very open culture, and it's easier to explore new directions here than it might be back home. I think I'd have to be cautious, more careful, if I tried to talk about my 'alternative' beliefs there. And if I were accused of witchcraft there, I'm really not sure who would stand by me and who would join in stoning me.

"What I'm looking for is unity between God and Goddess, but since traditionally we get taught more about God, maybe we have to focus harder to find the Goddess. There was a point in my life where I came to feel that, as a woman, I had been dealt a hand with no face cards and no trumps, despite having brains, education and money.

"Men have to focus on being humble. Women have to focus on being equal. Men have to get in touch with their nurturing side, women with their power side. Women are usually the keeper of the spiritual flame, the home, the religion. Western society gives women more permission to be contemplative and spiritual than it gives men. It seems like men have to wait until they retire to get that chance.

"I had a deeply emotional experience while I was walking the labyrinth at Grace Cathedral. I was trying to figure out where my spiritual path should go and what I should do about my relationship with the church. I started to cry. Then I realized I didn't have any tissues. I didn't want to weep. I didn't want to leave all the good parts of Christianity behind. I said to Jesus, 'I don't know where I'm going. Will you walk with me?'

"Yes," He said.

"Then I said, 'Will you carry me?'

"No," He said.

"Then I said, 'Will you hold my hand?'

"Yes," He said.

"My friend was behind me on the labyrinth. Suddenly, she reached out and held my hand. I started to cry again. She started to cry. Her hand touching mine at that moment was the Holy Spirit in her touching the Holy Spirit in me. It felt like lights could have come on and a host of angels lifted us up. Our souls had connected.

"I'm not sure how my search for the Goddess and my Christianity will play together. I believe that if Jesus came back today he would put his head in his hands and weep—and then the male-dominated institutional power structure of religion would crucify him all over again.

"To some extent, the relationship of women to the church is like a wife to an abusive husband. I will not leave Jesus. He personified all that was good. But I will leave the church. And that makes me feel very sad and very tired. It takes a lot of energy to build a new structure."

You can achieve a limited degree of spirituality on your own. But to realize your potential, I think you need some sort of guide. I cannot imagine an Olympic athlete without a coach.

The fact that one ostensibly follows a guide, however, is certainly no guarantee of spiritual enlightenment. I can't remember the exact circumstances or words, but Gandhi was once asked why, since he believed in the teachings of Christ so much, he never became a Christian. He replied that he never found a Christian denomination that followed the teachings of Christ.

Neil, a former Silicon Valley programmer

CHAPTER SIX

℘

Soul Tracks

Many trainers and consultants maintain that the soul belongs at home or in church. But with little understanding of the essential link between the soul life and the creative gifts of their employees, hardheaded businesses listening so carefully to their hardheaded consultants may go the way of the incredibly hardheaded dinosaurs.

David Whyte, *The Heart Aroused—Poetry and the Preservation of the Soul in Corporate America*

"Our nervous system isn't just a fiction; it's a part of our physical body, and our soul exists in space and is inside us, like the teeth in our mouth. It can't be forever violated with impunity."

Boris Pasternak, quoted in *What Really Matters— Searching for Wisdom in America,* by Tony Schwartz

135

For every man and woman, midlife is a pivotal time of internal rebirth. No matter what we have accomplished or what we command, midlife calls on us to experience it in a new way, to birth ourselves into a new kind of usefulness. Returning from years of work … we know now the sacredness and soulfulness of belonging once again.

David Whyte, *The Heart Aroused—Poetry and the Preservation of the Soul in Corporate America*

Spiritual matters are inherently nebulous and elusive, a characteristic which provides built-in tension between them and well-defined technical knowledge. That elusiveness doesn't deter some people from expressing their spiritual views with striking certainty. However, of all the topics discussed in this book, none caused as much hesitation, reflection and uncertainty during interviews as the issue of "soul." Even interviewees who sailed through most of the questions with breezy conviction often sputtered a touch here.

THE GREAT DIVIDE

Consideration of soul might be divided into two perspectives: its nature and significance during life, and its nature and significance after life. Almost everyone, even those with no spiritual life at all, felt there is something within humans, somehow different from mind or body, that might be called *soul*. And when asked, "Do you believe a soul is inherent in all people, even if they never experience any spiritual awakening of any kind?," the answer was, almost unanimously, "Yes." Many people added provisos, however: strongly held beliefs that qualitative differences would exist between souls which inhabited people with spiritual lives, and souls which didn't.

The question of the soul's significance after life (if any) is the more abstract and metaphysical issue. Yet, in a way, it's easier to consider than the question of significance during life (if any). Discussion of human afterlife has been around for a long time, and most doctrines about life after death (if any) invoke some form of soul. This is a well-debugged application of the concept.

It's also an application which causes a curious sort of comfort: most people have accepted the fact that they may have *beliefs* about soul's role in an afterlife, but they know they're not going to be able to prove or demonstrate the accuracy of their beliefs until they get there. Therefore, there's no specific action item required at present.

However, if soul plays a role while a life is in progress, then it is during that life that one must figure out what the role is, and how it should be connected with life: a somewhat less theoretical, more immediate issue, requiring somewhat sharper attention. Of the two "significance" perspectives (after life/during life), it's also the one we might conclude we have been given less time to noodle through.

There is increasing recognition, both in literature and, I believe, in the general consciousness, that there is a special part of us which the grindstone of life agitates, abrades, hones and molds. That special part is not related to skills and abilities, likes and dislikes, personality traits or accomplishments. I would characterize it more as *convictions*, as the piece which says, "Here is what I stand

---

A friend once said, "It didn't hurt me to not exist before I was born, and it won't hurt me to not exist after I die."

Cal, a Valley college instructor

for, here is what I believe is valuable and right, about me and about the world. Here is what I would fight for, and make great sacrifice for, although no one would tell me to do that, and no one has the power to force me to do that."

It takes time for this special part to declare itself and take lasting shape. Perhaps its emergence is a core portion of the midlife experience. When it does emerge, the Pasternak quote at the beginning of this chapter carries a message of importance for all of us: ignore that part at great risk.

A picture which emerged from interviews with clergy is that soul may be a concept which is less defined than other aspects of their theology. Substantially different visions were offered, even from clergy in the same religion or denomination. This is not surprising. The attempt to visualize and describe the soul is that leap into an unknown which has tantalized us for as long as there have been humans to ask deep philosophical questions: what are we *really*?

It's easy to understand the connection between traumatic developments in personal life and the sudden onset of spiritual interest. But a slower, subtler process may take root and grow: an awareness of being *part of*. Part of a group. Part of a community. Part of the universe, a being whose body is made, literally, of stardust. (The very early universe contained only the elements hydrogen and helium. All the heavier elements, of which human bodies are made, were manufactured by the nuclear processes of

> *The soul is the light of the universe coming through our physical manifestation. It's our purpose, our path, our work, our intention, the reason we're here. It's not often seen because it's hidden by many masks. It's like a flame. Some flames have burned low, some are shining like a Roman candle.*
>
> Victor, a Silicon Valley teacher

stars. Then the particles were distributed by stellar explosion for subsequent usage. Crosby, Stills, Nash and Young were exactly right when they sang "We are stardust" in Joni Mitchell's song *Woodstock*, although it is unlikely they were aware of this, or that they would have been particularly interested in the technical correctness they were displaying.)

And finally, perhaps, an awareness grows of being part of a family of human souls. Depending on one's vision, it might be a very large family.

JERRY

Jerry started his career as a lawyer, which proved to be excellent preparation for his current calling: rabbi of a large Silicon Valley synagogue.

As a lawyer, Jerry felt a profound disconnect between the work he was doing and the life he wanted. He was looking for meaning and involvement. He wanted to feel his time was being invested, not wasted.

Jerry sees the interplay of many factors in the spiritual awakening of people in the Valley and in his congregation. Joys and sorrows; existential anxiety; success and failure; pressure to succeed; doubts about the right definition of success; children; the dehumanizing effects of modern existence; pursuit of goals which prove to be vacant and illusory; progressive materialism; workaholism; narcissism; the approach of midlife.

"One thing we learn from Eastern religions," he says, "is that spirituality is not an event, but a product of sustained, disciplined engagement which can open us up and allow us to grow. There's some similarity to the dynamics of joining a health club or going on a diet. The reality of the discipline often means people don't stick with it. Tough commitment is required. Faith is meaningless without faithfulness.

"We live in an agnostic time and place, and people don't know what to believe. Religion has become so tied up with pop culture that spirituality is almost disposable. People want to mix it with water, get instant spirituality, and pour what they don't drink down the drain. They'll get more out of their spiritual pursuits if they see themselves as *partners in creating* a spiritual community, rather than just being *consumers* of community. A journey of faith without a community seems to me like reading sheet music and never hearing it played.

"When some people tell me they're not religious and don't believe in God, I say 'Tell me about the God you don't believe in.' When they do, my response is often, 'Well, I don't believe in that God either.' Then, maybe, we can talk about a God we *do* believe in.

"Soul is that aspect which survives us, the aspect which contains the divine within us. Christianity often differentiates body and soul, with the body being the source of our lusts and our appetites. Jews tend to see body and soul as a united whole, and the body as a source of potential holiness.

"Back East, I was president of the local clergy association, and hosted the annual holiday dinner. We had a scrumptious black forest cake for dessert. A minister came back for seconds and said, 'This is what we Christians call sin.' My wife smiled at him and said, 'This is what we Jews call pleasure.' I don't see the body as

---

Soul is the essence, the flame, the drive that gets us up in the morning. When you're doing the things you were created to do, the soul is like a balloon that keeps expanding until you feel it's going to burst because you feel so good.

Kate, a Valley church office administrator

distinct from soul, and I don't see the body as inherently bad. It's possible for talk about soul to miss the mark on its relationship with the body and the rest of the person."

MELANIE

"I try to approach questions of soul and afterlife scientifically," Melanie says. "Unfortunately, it's hard to get good data."

Melanie is a computer scientist and engineer who spent most of her career at one of the Valley's flagship research installations. Her vision of soul is a mix of ingredients from life observations, multicultural theology and analytical scrutiny.

Melanie's father was Roman Catholic, her mother Protestant, and she ended up with no real interest in either. "All head, no spirit," she remembers. "Also, some people who go to church are very rigid and arrogant and self-righteous. Some of the worst arrogance is spiritual arrogance."

Her upbringing left her in a spiritual vacuum. Years later, as an adult, she felt her spirit beginning to wake for the first time during a trip to Egypt. "The leaders of the trip pointed out that Egyptian art reflected more living spirituality than all our organized religions." She was inclined to agree. "The same kind of thing is also true in India," she observes. "There's a living spirituality that everyone there seems to have. You don't see that when you're out and about here."

Eventually, Melanie joined a relatively small, nonmainstream religious group. Of her current spiritual life, she says, "If I do my part, I'll get what I need. I know that with inner certainty. It is not the certainty of faith or belief. It comes from 25 years of being a research scientist, from the scientific method, which says the data support my conclusions."

Melanie sees God "... primarily as the Divine Mother. Prayer is talking to God. Meditation is listening to God. I try to do both. Sometimes we get divine messages through signs. I ran a stop sign recently and got a ticket. I saw and felt it as a warning: 'You're not stopping. You never stop. Take your foot off the accelerator.'

"Soul is our consciousness, our thoughts, who we are. When I live life in a way that generates good karma, good things happen. If I live as if whatever I do to others will eventually be done to me, everything makes sense. When I'm rude to someone, next time I go into the grocery store the clerk is rude to me. I finally got the data on this! Maybe some of the starving people in Rwanda were Nazis in a former life.

"Believing that people create their own 'soul destiny' saves me the anguish of not being able to control or help what happens to them. It's also empowering, because I can control what happens to me by living a good life. It enables me to accept what is, and not

I believe that the soul becomes associated with the body at the time of conception and survives after death—not to come back into this world, but to progress through many other worlds of God, of which we are only dimly aware. It is the soul which experiences joy and illumination. As such, it is my belief that the soul is essential to consciousness.

Roger Penrose, a mathematician/cosmologist, has investigated the essence of consciousness in two of his books. He allows for the possibility of a spiritual aspect essential to consciousness, but as a scientist does not allow himself to believe it to be necessary. I find it difficult to explain certain discoveries in mathematics and science without a spiritual influence. I have myself 'discovered' things which I have absolutely known to be true, only later to be confirmed by rational thought. I think the soul is definitely involved in this process.

Neil, a former Silicon Valley programmer

hassle myself about what might be, which is a totally new way of thinking for me.

"For most of my career as a scientist, I was the only woman in my work groups. All-male groups, all male supervisors. At one point I was thinking about suing my employer for some rather blatant sex discrimination. I was trying to figure out what was the right thing and the spiritual thing to do. I talked to my spiritual counselor, and she said, 'We never sue for personal gain, but we do fight for principle.' There's strength in that! When you stand up for *principle*, you can't get pushed around. One woman who did end up suing became a basket case because she didn't have that spiritual anchor.

"It's really much easier to believe there is no afterlife. It's scary to realize there are spiritual consequences to our actions. A spiritual life is hard work. But Jung said, 'Unless you achieve a spiritual understanding, you don't make it to the later stages of life.' And that's been my observation.

"Again, I'm a scientist. I'm not looking for a belief system. I'm looking for something that works."

STAN

Until age 17, Stan thought there was a good chance he might become a minister. Then he discovered the world of technology. Engineers 1, clergy 0.

Stan is a highly educated engineer and technology consultant who reveres *intellect*. Intellectually, he's trying to understand the

> *The soul is a little mass of shining energy in our bodies, about the size of a grapefruit.*
>
> Olivia, a Silicon Valley homemaker

relationship between spirituality and the church. And intellectually, he struggles with the concept of a soul that can't be measured despite the fact that it has to be in there somewhere. He has an engineer's view of the reason there must be a form of eternal life: "Every person is a generator and emitter of energy. Those waves go on forever." When asked if those waves—and therefore, perhaps, a soul—are inherent in all people, even those who have had no spiritual awakening, Stan replies, "Absolutely. But the waves may have more desirable characteristics when one is spiritual."

RICHARD

Richard is vice president of strategic planning for an aggressive, acquisitive software company. He tries to balance a strong moral code and ethical values with business necessities when his company acquires another, and decisions must be made about the fates of the acquired company's employees. He works to keep candor and compassion in the forefront, particularly when the headsman's axe must fall.

In much the same way, he tries to strike a balance between the pragmatic reality he knows and the deeper issues he can never really know. In wrestling with the tough topic of soul, he is trying to

> *Science is not normally interested in nonmaterial, apparently mysterious things ... The soul is not an easy subject to deal with either scientifically or spiritually ... [But] the idea of the soul is perhaps the single, most significant, concept of our time: one that needs a current, scientifically relevant and heart-centered spiritual view.*
>
> Fred Alan Wolf, *The Spiritual Universe— How Quantum Physics Proves the Existence of the Soul*

craft the kind of elegant analysis and supportable thinking he might use for a business problem. He knows he can't get there, but he'll keep trying.

For Richard, soul or spirit is eternal partly through the impact we make on others. He senses communication with those who have died, through their impact on him; but he's pretty sure that afterlife doesn't involve going around saying hello to everyone you once knew. He finds this area a little anxiety-provoking, because he feels there are certain things he's supposed to believe, and he's not sure he does.

STUART

For many years, Stuart has been general counsel for a medium-sized Valley company which makes electronic instrumentation systems. Born into a mainstream Protestant family, he has continued to find comfort and satisfaction in the religion of his birth. That doesn't mean he hasn't had an occasional sag.

"Sometimes I've felt that my spiritual life was getting dry and needed some watering," he says, "but I've never felt it was arid. Doubt happens to everyone. Someone once said, 'If you haven't stopped believing in God at least once, you probably never did.' The idea is, if you've worked long enough and hard enough on your path, you're going to have those moments."

> *Since this is Silicon Valley, I'll use a personal computer analogy for my view of soul. Our bodies are the keyboard, monitor, hard drive, etc. Soul is the electric current which allows them to run, and the "principles of life" program that tells them what to do. Soul is God's way of turning on our switch and booting us up.*
>
> Michael, a Silicon Valley priest

Stuart's view of soul is "the essence of a person's being, the person's core, wrapped up in all the person's beliefs. What some might call 'heart.' It's what's left when you've stripped away the clothes and the body, what prevails when the person is in the highest emotional state. It's what animates us, and what goes on to eternal life.

"We get messages from our soul through dreams and the subconscious. We have to learn how to separate what's coming from our active consciousness from what's coming from deeper within.

"When you die, you continue your spiritual journey in a realm beyond space and time. Given *enough* time, even Hitler's soul could come to God's presence. You continue to have the opportunity to approach God after death, even if you were the most confirmed atheist imaginable during life. There's never permanent estrangement; there's always the chance for reconciliation."

ERIC

Eric is a technical publications editor who has had a whirlwind tour through the technology tangle over the past few years. He spent three years at a high-profile startup, worked like a maniac along with everyone else, then saw the effort crumble into oblivion due to fatal flaws in the company's product and market vision. Bummer.

Then he joined a software megacompany and became one of 18,000 employees, working in a corporate headquarters campus big enough to qualify for nation-state status in selected historical

> *The opportunity [of midlife] is to get on with the real work of your Second Adulthood—the feeding and crafting of the soul.*
>
> Gail Sheehy, *New Passages*

periods. Good pay, interesting enough work. But after sampling the involvement and excitement of the newly born enterprise, it's hard, very hard, to be a blurry face in an army-sized crowd.

He floated his résumé and the right call came. He's back with a startup, and this one looks like it's going to make it. He's a happy camper.

Although Eric and his family have always been active in a church, he senses that his spiritual path is becoming an increasingly important part of his life. "I nurture my soul through worship, reflection and singing," he says. "I don't consciously listen to my soul—it's me, not separate, and I have a hard time prying the two apart.

"I'm a Christian, but I believe in the combined concepts of responsibility and karma. The soul's destiny depends on the quality of actions during life. A person's life, deeds and work produce a legacy that makes up one part of the soul. The other part is God transcendent.

"What you leave behind, based on what you did during your stay, is a form of afterlife. I'm intrigued by the idea that somehow, in some form, we can visit earth after death. The 'web you weave' determines what happens to you in the next life. Maybe we shouldn't risk a bad life!"

DISCOVERY BAY

On a day punctuated by rain squalls interleaved with luminous cloud formations and sudden, unexpected rays of pale sun, I drove 45 miles north and east of Silicon Valley to Discovery Bay: a top-choice residential community for boating buffs. Eastern Contra

When someone feels hurt, it is the soul which is hurt.
Dana, a former Silicon Valley training manager

Costa County, just south of the Sacramento Delta complex of waterways, islands and levees, is a hopscotch blend of the old and the new. Once, it was almost all agricultural. Much of it still is, featuring well-tended orchards, a variety of produce farms, and rotund cows enjoying their brown and green Northern California salad bars.

Increasingly, however, much of it isn't. The sky-high cost of housing in the Valley communities has provided builders with incentive to construct outlying housing developments. It has also provided buyers with incentive to put up with excruciating commutes in exchange for owning a bigger, newer house for $200,000 less than they'd pay for a smaller, older one in the heart of the Valley. There are a lot of those houses, smack in the middle of what was farmland not long ago. More—many more—are on the way.

Sharing the landscape with the new, large housing tracts are old, small towns such as Brentwood and Byron. Driving through them, one feels in touch with years such as 1941, or perhaps 1955. Virtually no building in the older section of Byron, residential or commercial, seems without its very old, very rusty car part or piece of equipment or unidentifiable artifact accenting its lot. Fifteen minutes down the highway, 200 brand new houses snap the observer back to the '90s.

> *"I had spent my entire life studying science ... only to be met with the wretched realization that science was, not wrong, but brutally limited and narrow in scope. If human beings are composed of matter, body, mind, soul and spirit, then science deals handsomely with matter and body, but poorly with mind and not at all with soul and spirit ..."*
>
> Consciousness theoretician Ken Wilber, quoted in *What Really Matters—Searching for Wisdom in America,* by Tony Schwartz

Railroad tracks crisscross the turf, many of them unused for years. The planned community of Discovery Bay is built around waterways, and it's on the water, not the tracks, where the action is now. This is a stellar location for boating enthusiasts. Many of the houses have fingers of the bay gently sloshing right outside their back doors, with private mooring spots allowing residents to step from their boats to their patios. The port of San Francisco is a few leisurely cruising hours away, the exact interval depending on how much horsepower one is cruising with. On this day, multitudes of mallards and gaggles of gulls floated and soared on and above the water made silvery by gray clouds and unpredictable shafts of sunlight. Their quick flash of wings and adventurous plummets from midair to underwater added to the ambiance, and kept the fish honest.

RUTH

Ruth and Mel have lived in Discovery Bay for three years, and like it. Mel is a successful Silicon Valley entrepreneur who has dabbled in an impressive variety of economic endeavors. His early career was as a manufacturing manager and executive, eventually with one of the Valley's seminal technology leaders. Those were heady days. Mel thrived.

But a large pool of restless energy is part of Mel's makeup, and eventually the corporate world seemed too tame and well

Soul is the human spirit, the "essence" of the person, but the soul is not eternal. The Hebrews could not conceive of a disembodied soul. The whole person dies, body and soul. Then resurrection is given as a gift of God, and there is a new body of some kind, and a new soul.

Walter, a Valley minister

known. He quit and went into business for himself. He left the world of high-tech materials manufacturing for the world of—sandwiches. He bought a catering company. After a time, he sold that and bought a vocational school. Now he's a financial consultant, tax planner, accountant-for-hire, and real estate investor. For added excitement, he serves as a county sheriff reserve commander.

Ruth's professional track could not have been more different from Mel's. She balanced out his exploits by bringing an element of predictable stability to their life. She taught elementary school for 35 years in one of the Valley's larger school systems.

Ruth and Mel became interested in boating several years ago. They bought a boat, and grew to love life on the water. Ruth's retirement was coming up. There was no reason they couldn't build their life around the boating activity they enjoyed so much, and the friends with whom they shared it. They sold their house in the Valley, and bought the house in Discovery Bay. A year later, Ruth was diagnosed with cancer.

We are constantly being asked to turn our faces away from our own internal images of what is right, true, and most of all alive for us. The very simplicity of these images may seem to speak against them. They may be images of harmonious relationship, a vital company producing useful things, a new product, a life in the country, a loving family, or clear, simple images of flames, swords, feathers, iridescent birds, or enticing forest paths. We give them away thinking they cannot be reflected by the complex experience of the world in which we have learned to live. But giving them away, we find ourselves strangely empty. Finally, we understand that though the world will never be simple, a life that honors the soul seems to have a kind of radical simplicity at the center of it.

David Whyte, *The Heart Aroused—Poetry and the Preservation of the Soul in Corporate America*

Ruth has always felt there was a spiritual component to her being, but its form and magnitude have varied greatly over time. She is currently putting much energy into deciphering her path and beliefs. She is thinking extensively about soul.

Ruth comes from a Seventh Day Adventist family ("the Puritan version," she says). She didn't like it much. "No dancing, no fun, no meat," she recalls. "Mother wanted us to look like good Christian ladies, but really, we looked weird. And if she'd had to choose between the church and my father, she'd have chosen the church." This made for a household Ruth found critical, unloving and oppressive.

Eventually, Ruth was able to start down her own path. She grew comfortable with the idea that God would not zap her with lightning if she drank a beer or had some ham. She vowed that her childhood environment would never be inflicted on her family, and particularly not her husband, when she married.

It hasn't been. Put off by the early exposure, she has pursued her spiritual life without formal religious association. At the beginning of the interview, when I asked if she belonged to any religion, her answer was, "Absolutely not. Dead set against it."

Ruth's cancer treatment has required surgery, and she is currently undergoing both radiation treatment and chemotherapy. "When the cancer came, that was life saying 'get moving and start growing again.' I don't like the concept of people turning to God just as they start to fear dying; it's kind of like whining. As a matter of fact, this isn't the worst thing I've gone through. My divorce from my first husband was worse than this, but it was also another

---

We tried to set up a spiritual retreat for executives. The topic was 'care of the soul for businesspeople.' Not one soul came.

Brad, a Silicon Valley priest

example of a message: 'get rolling, be independent, take care of yourself.'

"I feel so grateful for all the good things. I owe the world a lot, and I need to give much back. I couldn't dream of saying to God 'Why me?' regarding this cancer. When I think about it, I actually think, 'Well, why *not* me?' I was born an American, given two daughters, an education, so much good life. I wonder if I've done enough with what I've received. Perhaps what I'm supposed to do, what I'm here for, what I can give back, is to walk with this and show it can be done in grace and spirit. When I'm having my chemotherapy, I say, 'Thank you, God, for teaching people how to do chemo.'

"The soul is your spirit, the part that remains. Soul is what comes back. It's what chooses what to learn, and what to teach others. Some souls decide to devote their entire life to helping others. The body gets recycled. The soul gets reincarnated.

"My two daughters are so different that I think the only way to explain it is to think in terms of soul difference. One is a physician, successful and comfortable in just about every aspect of life. There's an old soul there. The other has a very young soul, maybe a special soul. At 17 she married a guy who can't seem to do much in life. They have always lived just one step above poverty, but they've stuck together for 24 years. Their son is autistic. He's 18 years old, 6' 6" tall, good looking, and can't say his own name.

"Some souls come here just to teach us lessons. I think this applies to the handicapped son. He's teaching us patience and humility. But I don't know what *he's* getting out of it. What kind of

---

Soul is spiritual DNA.

Brett, a Valley engineer

wonderful soul would be willing to give up a whole lifetime to teach us?

"I had a session with a 70-year-old woman who channels for an Indian shaman spirit. She went into a trance, and I spent an hour talking to the spirit. I told him I wanted to feel that my soul had done well in this life, that I had done what I was supposed to do, and had given back enough. In a guttural voice, he said, 'You Americans always think you have to be *doing* something. Just be. Our souls chose our parents, and our mission here is to be.'

"I think it's more than that. We're here to learn and grow. All of us, and our souls, keep learning. There's more magic, more miracles, waiting to happen and be discovered.

"Nothing ever disappears or goes away. Form may change, but our atoms are always here. During radiation treatment, I visualize the cancerous cells being broken up, and the molecules freed by the radiation, freed to go out in the atmosphere and become a rainbow, not trapped in cancer cells anymore. And then the molecules go from the rainbow to the clouds and become healing rain and fall on the desert and provide healing and nurture to the lizards and plants and sand—and sometimes the treatment is over before the visualization and the dream ends."

Rest, as we all know, brings perspective, vitality and good humor. But it also brings a relaxation into inner silences and images that are sometimes too difficult to face. We might wonder if this has anything to do with our addiction to being busy. Concerning ourselves with the music of the busy outer world, we might not have to face the inner music that was composed as a score for our future destiny.

David Whyte, *The Heart Aroused—Poetry and the Preservation of the Soul in Corporate America*

HAMZA

Shortly after sending a letter to a relatively new Muslim mosque, I received a response via electronic mail. I had written to describe the research I was doing for this book, and to request an interview. The e-mail message came from a member of the group which founded the mosque. He is an engineer with a large software tools company, and he graciously volunteered to arrange an interview with Hamza, the Sufi Muslim group's spiritual leader.

An evening interview was set up at Hamza's residence. When I arrived, a group of followers offered tea and refreshments. Hamza appeared, invited several of the other people present to join us for the discussion, and led us upstairs to his study.

Hamza has been in Silicon Valley for four years. He believes that every human heart is a mosque, but that spirituality in this area is drowned by the focus on business and material pursuits. "Everyone is a carnivore. We eat each other. We want what each other has."

He observes that many churches are heavily focused on ceremony and social activities, perhaps to the detriment of true spiritual seeking. These are barriers to the success of the churches and the fulfillment of their members. He thinks that Native Americans may have the deepest spirituality among Western belief systems.

Hamza sees Americans eventually migrating away from the dogma of their religions to truer and more direct spiritual paths.

Soul/body dualism is not a helpful way to look at things. What is helpful is to see ourselves as integrated beings, capable of both joy and stupidity. I'm not sure what we'll look like in the afterlife, but it will be the best of us.

Sam, a Silicon Valley pastor

He believes there will be increasing interest in Sufi, Buddhist and Hindu teachings. "Sufism is from the heart."

Asked for his vision of the human soul, he says, "According to Islam, soul is the spirit known only to God. It is the unseen. It cannot be defined. It is out of our knowledge. But we have many signs that soul exists. For example, if we say a person is generous, the statement gives no description of the person's physical makeup. It's a reflection of the nature of his soul.

"Soul is like an inner, frictionless moving object. It keeps people moving. Soul is God-made electricity—the divine version of the electric energy which keeps your heart pumping. Maybe we should focus our technological efforts on developing a 'spirituality chip' for humans, so the electricity would power that also."

DEAN

Just before the outbreak of World War II, Dean's parents moved back to their native Japan, and that's where he was born. His parents had no way of foreseeing the war, nor had they any way of knowing that if they had stayed here they would have ended up, with other Japanese-Americans, in a relocation camp. After the war, when they could, they moved back to the U.S. with Dean.

Dean's parents practiced the traditional Japanese beliefs of Shinto and Buddhism. As a small child in Japan, Dean remembers asking his mother "Who is God?" and getting an answer that made him believe there was a God. At age 12, in California, he recalls

> *Soul is what Jung calls "Self with a capital S." It's that piece of God which we are given and called to reflect into the world.*
>
> Erica, a Valley pastor

going into a Christian church for the first time. Into his 12-year-old mind came the words, *"Aha*, God is here."

It took him eight years to accept the sign he had been given, and, as he put it, "… to figure out who Jesus Christ was. Also, my pride got in the way. I kept wanting to say, 'I don't need these beliefs, I'm capable of living my life without them, thank you.' "

Dean attended a major university in Southern California, earning a master's degree in electrical engineering and computer science. After graduation, he worked for several years as an engineer at two large computer companies. Then, something unexpected happened. He began to feel God calling his name, tugging on his sleeve, insistently, unmistakably, to suggest a career change.

He accepted the suggestion. The computer engineer became a pastor. He currently serves at a church whose congregation comes primarily from the Japanese-American community in the Valley.

"I was the youngest of five children," he recalls. "In my parents' eyes, becoming a Christian minister made me (to use a double metaphor) both the black sheep and the prodigal son of my family.

"I had many concerns about leaving the engineering profession and entering full-time ministry. I did it very gradually. I've seen many ministers suffer and sacrifice for their calling. I've seen too many former pastors selling insurance. But it's worked for me, and I wouldn't want to be cooped up back in the computer world.

"Our church encourages non-Christians to consider the good news of Jesus Christ. Ninety-eight percent of Japanese-Americans are non-Christians. Buddhism is the predominant Japanese-

---

I strongly believe in a woman's right to choose. *I also* strongly *believe unborn babies have souls. This makes abortion a tough issue for me, and it leaves me frustrated and conflicted.*

Kate, a Valley church office administrator

American faith. In fact, I've never seen a Japanese Christian funeral. We're a minority of minorities, and we know it.

"I think people have a lot of inner conflict about what they want from religion. San Jose sponsors a festival of lights to celebrate Christmas, but there was pressure on them to remove the manger scenes from the festival. How can you have a celebration of Christmas and censor out the image of Christ?

"I've been to secular events where they ask me to lead a prayer as part of the proceedings, but someone will tell me, 'Do the prayer, but don't pray in the name of Jesus.' After one event, a guy actually came up to me and said he had been offended because I mentioned Jesus in the opening prayer. In general, if you invite a Christian minister to lead a prayer, you're likely to hear Christ's name.

"My view of soul is that we're all made in God's image, but in the way we think, feel, express ourselves, we show that each of our souls is unique. Soul is the totality of who you are.

"Each person has a vacuum in their heart that they try to fill with something. Most try to fill it with material possessions, but it can really be satisfied only with eternal values.

"Many people are hurt, and their souls need healing. They want to be 'all that they can be' in God's army, even if they don't think about it that way, but they need comforting first. My job as pastor is to comfort the souls who are hurt, and discipline the ones

> ... *we eventually come to the realization that it is injurious to the soul to remove portions of our life from exploration, as if, at work, certain parts of experience suddenly lie out of bounds. We simply spend too much time and have too much psychic and emotional energy invested in the workplace for us to declare it a spiritual desert bereft of life-giving water.*
>
> David Whyte, *The Heart Aroused—*
> *Poetry and the Preservation of the Soul in Corporate America*

who are complacent. Some will avoid discipline, but some are wise enough to know they need it. People can sharpen each other, and improve each other."

LORETTA

Loretta was born in Memphis, but her family moved to California before she was old enough to develop any Southern drawl to hint at her roots.

She sees her spiritual development in distinct phases. Her family belonged to a mainstream Protestant denomination, but until age 15, Loretta felt no spirit moving in her. At 16, she decided she would be a nun. This inclination lasted until she was 20. Then she realized that marriage and family were calling her more strongly than the cloth.

While attending Stanford she engaged in a certain amount of religious exploration. ("Lots of undergraduate epiphanies," she says.) She's done time in the corporate world, and her husband is in the thick of the high-tech race as a marketing manager for a leading-edge hardware company. For the last few years her focus has been on her home and three children, and on pursuing the right spiritual life for herself and her family.

She has discovered that exercise has a spiritual dimension. While jogging, she's conscious of the discipline it builds, of the way it makes her pay attention to herself. She's aware of taking care of the body she's been given to house her soul. She notices the beauty of the flowers she passes, and rejoices in the way the air smells and feels as she runs through it: moist, opaque, mysterious in midwinter; warm, fragrant, beckoning in early summer. She makes it a point to actively notice, actively be thankful.

Loretta writes when she can. Some of her writing is pure recreation, such as the unfinished murder mystery featuring a properly aged, thoroughly poisoned Napa Valley cabernet sauvignon. Some is pure soul expression, such as her essay on a chapel window she fell in love with while in the choir.

"Soul is the part of your being that touches eternity," Loretta says. "But the body and soul are tightly coupled. We will have bodies after our resurrection. Something will go on, and maybe death is the seed from which it grows.

"There's a soul in everyone, even if they never experience any spiritual awakening. You can keep God at arm's length throughout your life, but you will get one opportunity, one second, at the end of life to choose God.

"I want my spiritual path to play more and more of a role in shaping my daily life. I want to pray, write and exercise every day. I would like to be transformed; to get rid of all the internal grunge; to feel that I've scraped all the barnacles off my soul."

While similar, spirit and soul are different. For now take it that spirit is unmanifested vacuum vibration, while soul is the same thing but reflected back on itself so a pattern within it can be seen. The soul is able to manifest intent *through this reflection, while the spirit is not. The spirit desires but knows not what it does nor even what it desires when it spews out matter and energy. The soul desires and knows what it is about and what it craves. The spirit is potentially conscious and potentially unconscious, while the soul is conscious.*

Fred Alan Wolf, *The Spiritual Universe—
How Quantum Physics Proves the Existence of the Soul*

PERRY

Perry and I had scheduled our meeting downtown, but only the most oblivious would have failed to realize we had been given a perfect park day. We decided to migrate in Perry's van to a nearby park, a move which required shifting a large number of books from the passenger seat. One of them was enormous: they could use it for bench presses at 24-Hour Nautilus. Moving it made my biceps feel buffed.

Perry's a scientist. Most of his career was spent at one of the Valley's premiere research institutions. He assured me the technical importance of the book's contents justified its preposterous size.

Recent heavy rains had given the park's foliage the color of the Emerald City. The grass felt 8" thick. We pulled up at a stone table half in the shadow of a California redwood. The interview was closely supervised by a fearless, inquisitive squirrel. Between trips up the tree to shuttle acorns and other goodies to his cache, he perched on his hind legs a few feet away, and scrutinized us closely. He radiated a no-nonsense attitude: stay sharp, or incur his scorn.

Perry has been in Silicon Valley for 34 years. He's been a member of the same mainline Protestant religion all his life, but it is not that membership per se that is central to his spiritual life. "I could be anything," he says, "as long as there's belief in a deity. Specific format of worship is not important. My current church is

---

One certainly has a soul; but how it came to allow itself to be enclosed in a body is more than I can imagine. I only know if once mine gets out, I'll have a bit of a tussle before I let it get in again ...

Lord Byron, in a letter to the poet Thomas Moore

fine, and I might miss the forms if I left, but I could find God through other paths.

"God is just 'there.' I don't waste my time trying to think about God in terms of a physical form that I could never recognize anyway. God is a real and central part of my life, part of everything. I don't sit down and figure out words to pray. I don't meditate. I'm dyslexic; it's not easy or enjoyable for me to read, so I don't do much spiritual reading. My spirituality is oriented toward action and feeling: trying not to hurt others, trying to see God in everyone I talk to, even avoiding accidents when I'm driving. I *live* my spiritual life and my prayer.

"My vision of soul is similar to my vision of God: transcends everything, no physical form, no relationship to the body. Lots of relationship to attitude toward other people. Our souls were probably here millions of years ago, and will probably be here millions of years from now. Configuration-wise, soul is a miniature of God, a part of the deity. God is an accumulation of an infinite number of people's souls, sort of an Omega Point.

"The way I am today is all God's fault," he smiled. "Through my soul, I am part of Him."

TERITA

Terita arrived in Silicon Valley 17 years ago from her native Iran. Her father was an Iranian Muslim, her mother a French Catholic, and Terita was raised Catholic. It didn't stick. "Roman Catholicism seemed very static," she says. "You stay in the box."

She remained a practicing Catholic until she became 21, but found the religion increasingly unfulfilling and hard to accept. She had no inclination toward another belief system as she left her Roman Catholic upbringing behind. If Roman Catholicism was not of interest, she expected no more appeal from any other religion.

Terita met her husband soon after she became a Silicon Valley resident. He was a Baha'i, a faith with which Terita had not been familiar. She liked much of what she saw in the Baha'i belief system, and decided to learn more. Among the things she learned was that Baha'i is considered an illegal religion, Islamic heresy, in her native country. Members of the faith are frequently imprisoned and killed, and are certainly not granted passports to leave.

Terita became a Baha'i. She appreciates having found her new faith in a location where she enjoys complete legal and social freedom to pursue it.

Among the many things which attracted Terita to Baha'i was the concept of "progressive revelation." Everything is evolving, including mankind's spirit. Baha'is believe all the great prophets of the past—Buddha, Moses, Jesus, Mohammed, among others—were valid and right for their time. The prophet for our time is Baha'u'llah, the founder of the Baha'i religion. In a thousand years, another prophet will emerge for that time. "God sends teachers to guide us, and at different stages in our development we have needed different teachers," Terita says, "just as we have different teachers while we progress through school. Many teachers, many religions, one path, one God."

Terita agrees strongly with other Baha'i tenets: acceptance of all cultures, world unity, equality between men and women, and universal, continuing education and search for truth. The latter is a

---

Soul is a difficult concept. It's intellect, heart, feelings, innermost thoughts and being. It's hard to articulate in a way that doesn't sound like you're trying to write a Hallmark card.

Trent, president of a Valley telecommunications company

striving she applies with particular vigor to her own spiritual path. "Baha'i has made me see that truth can be looked at from many angles, and is never completely known. You must always struggle to learn truth, although the search is endless."

Most religions depend on clergy to provide spiritual teaching and leadership. There is no Baha'i clergy, no formal place of worship. "In the past, clergy were needed because people weren't educated," she points out. "Now, education is available to everyone."

To help each other achieve enlightenment, groups of Baha'is gather in members' homes every 19 days for sharing, discussion and reading. Terita likes the idea that she can't depend on formally vested authority to chart her path, that the ultimate responsibility for success or failure in finding truth rests firmly in her own hands.

"But we do need the prophets," she says. "God is an unknown essence which we will never fathom. We have different 'kingdoms' on earth: mineral, vegetable, animal. Each is not necessarily aware of the one 'above' it. God is the one above us, and we can't grasp or be fully aware of Him/Her. The only way we can glimpse Him/Her is through the Messengers He/She sends.

"The soul is the person's true identity, the part that continues. Our fundamental nature, or reality, is that we are spiritual beings. Our physical bodies are simply clothes we're given to wear during our stay in this plane. Our purpose in this plane is to develop our spirits.

"When a baby is in the womb, he's developing parts even though he has no idea what the parts are going to be used for. In this world, it's our spiritual qualities that have to be developed. We're going to need them when we're 'born' into the next world, even though we don't know what they'll be used for. Without them, just like a baby who's born without some of his parts, we'll be crippled.

"Baha'u'llah says death is a messenger of joy, taking us to a much better plane than this one. If people knew what was coming next, they'd probably commit suicide to get there faster. People who have had near-death experiences don't want to come back.

"It seems to be the law of this plane that we grow through suffering. Maybe we're like plants, and we have to be pruned and trimmed to become better. Ultimately, this world is like a school. But it's a vocational school, not a playground. You put in the effort, then you take a test to see what you've learned. If you pass, you move up.

"When you're born, you have gems in you, and the job in life is to bring them out and polish them and make them beautiful. Many people don't know this and miss the whole thing. There is choice and free will, and every person has a different capacity. Some have been given a cup. Some have been given a thimble. The goal is to fill whatever you've been given."

A soul is but the last bubble of a long fermentation in the world.
George Santayana, *The Life of Reason*

CHAPTER SEVEN

❧

Righteous Lives in the Material World

Michael Lerner argues that liberals have "framed their intellectual commitments around a belief that the only things that really move people are economic entitlements and political rights"; they miss the fact that "human beings have a deep need to have their lives make sense, to transcend the dynamics of individualism and selfishness that predominate in a competitive market society and to find a way to place their lives in a context of meaning and purpose."

Stephen L. Carter, *The Culture of Disbelief: How American Law and Politics Trivialize Religious Devotion*

We are hungry to recover the sense of the sacred that is currently painfully missing from our love affairs, families, jobs and politics. No week passes when some

friend or stranger does not speak to me about the
yearning.

Sam Keen, *Hymns To An Unknown God*

If one hankers to start a fiery debate, a good topic might be whether the office is any place to bring "deeper meaning": issues relating to philosophy, morality and spirituality. One view is that intangible "spirit care" centers should do for the soul what child care centers do for the child: keep them safely out of the way until they're picked up at the end of the day. Most would probably say that's the right way, and certainly the safest. Some disagree. Their number may be increasing.

The concept of "righteousness" in American business culture—how personal and social values coexist with economic realities—has been a ponderous sine wave, moving with changing times back and forth between tight definition and laissez faire. There have always been conflicts between individual and business needs, between societal and corporate values. Silicon Valley's maverick culture and plethora of individualists seem to have developed their own version of these dynamics. And, as one would expect, they're changing at a brisk pace.

Do those who have spiritual lives necessarily derive different moral or ethical belief systems from those who don't? It's important not to let a subtle bias creep in here: ethical and moral codes are possessed by all. It is by no means a given that spirituality automatically leads to higher standards of behavior. In fact, many who have strong spiritual convictions are convinced they do *not necessarily* lead to better ethics or morals.

The belief-based conflicts and dilemmas which confront people in the Valley don't generally stem from the ambient sea of affluence. Nothing during the interviews indicated any widespread sense of guilt, or even burgeoning diffidence, regarding material success. For one thing, people work very hard. They naturally assume that anything they have they earned, and earned well. For another, most of those who have made their careers here are conscious of having been part, directly or indirectly, of a technological revolution which changed the world.

No one questions that the change is for the better. It's a given. A well-known, associated fact of life is that high-impact players reap high-impact rewards.

CASE IN POINT

A few years ago I went through a shopping experience that seemed to faithfully reflect a certain part of the Valley scene. I had decided to give myself a gift (which I felt I had earned, and earned well): a large screen television. No more 19-inch stuff. It was November. The season's big football games were coming up. I proposed to watch them on a screen appropriate to their importance. I narrowed my choices down to two: a 40-inch rear projection model, and a 35-inch direct view model. Both were newly introduced sets; both sold for over $3,000.

It was a bit of an eye-opener to find out that all the stores which carried these sets were having a hard time keeping them in stock. They came in; they *flew* out—so I was told. The first time I heard this, I attributed it to retail hyperbole and cheap sales psychology. I was wrong. They were, in fact, flying out. Most stores I went to had even sold their floor models, and could not confirm any specific date when they might have more in stock.

When I finally bought one, the store's sales manager checked his computerized inventory system and told me two units were in stock and he'd deliver one the next day. Well, he didn't. Instead he called and said that both the units had been sold the prior evening from one of their other stores. Since both those sales tickets were time-stamped earlier than mine, those customers got TVs and I got an empty promise about getting a unit from the next shipment.

I ended up buying a set from another store, which I happened to catch at the right time with exactly one unit left. Due to demand level, the first store had been unable to get another set to sell me.

The striking point was that these were $3,000 *television sets* which were selling faster than they could be trucked in. Three thousand dollars is not a small sum. A large-screen television is not a life necessity. This minor marketing phenomenon seemed to capture both the Valley's affluence level and its love of trendy technological toys.

Debra is the minister at a medium-sized church in the heart of the Valley, and she sees a full laundry list of issues which bring conflict to residents. "People in Silicon Valley know we have enough food to distribute to everyone, but we don't do it," she says. Certainly, the juxtaposition of inadequate food supplies with insatiable demand for multimegabuck TVs contains the ingredients for a

---

In Silicon Valley we hit the ground running in our 20s and spend the next 15 years trying to get what it looks like everyone else has: the house, the Beemer, the toys. We never climb up the mountain and take a careful look around at the terrain.

I'm recovering from a serious case of business ennui, and I'm trying to redefine myself with a purpose that doesn't include "stuff."

Alden, a Valley insurance broker

possible moral struggle. But I don't believe Debra's statement realistically captures the primary nature of this particular tension.

It's a fact of life that often-brutal time and energy demands conspire with high levels of expectation and uncertainty to siphon off large quantities of inner resources. In a more benign setting, those resources might be available to, and targeted for, traditional social and community concerns. As it is, moral and ethical considerations tend to swirl around a much more prosaic locus: what's right for *here*? There is widespread recognition of the uniqueness of Silicon Valley culture. No one worries how things would play in Peoria. There's a Valley way, and it doesn't have to pass muster elsewhere.

This does *not* mean that individuals in this area are less generous, less concerned, or less principled than denizens of other regions. Quite the contrary. As discussed in Chapter Ten, there is reason to believe the Valley may ultimately play a leading-edge role in social redefinition and betterment on a global scale. Issues are being pondered. Directions are being found. And the Valley is never shy about sharing its discoveries.

STACY

The evening was clear, lots of stars visible considering the right-in-the-middle-of-the-lights-of-civilization setting. A pre-Christmas cold snap was in the air: a great night for sipping Irish coffee; Hennessey cognac; or syrupy, unctuous Northern California merlot or zinfandel. I had the zinfandel, and Stacy had the merlot.

We sat in the attractive bar area of a Silicon Valley restaurant well known for power lunches and business dinners. Having beaten the crowd by a few minutes, we were able to homestead a table adjacent to the fireplace and the Christmas tree. Despite the substantial noise level from the jolly and well-lubricated holiday crowd, it was a fine setting for our conversation.

Stacy has been in Silicon Valley an action-packed four years. She came here from New Jersey to join a medium-sized network equipment company as marketing communications director. As sometimes happens, the shifting sands of corporate politics ended up depositing her in an untenable situation. She left after less than two years, and joined a startup company which had developed some leading-edge wireless networking technology.

At her new company, the monsoons of corporate temperament eventually blew her into conflict with an influential member of the senior management group. She left. She now works as field marketing director for a software utilities powerhouse. So far, so good in her new job, but she has learned to be wary of the speed and power with which things move and change in her new locale.

Stacy's mother belonged to the Church of England. Her father was Jewish. They told her she could take her pick. She feels the influence of having been exposed to Jewish culture, but ended up becoming a Presbyterian.

Stacy is acutely conscious of the tendency of work to fill all life's nooks and crannies. She's a motivated professional, but she doesn't want that to happen to her. The breakup of her 10-year marriage a few years ago threw her life into a state of imbalance. She wants to rebalance, and she wants the balancing act to include some form—the right form—of spiritual connection.

She recalls seeing one of her company's group vice presidents three times in a two-week period. Each time, the woman was wearing the same suit; the last time was on a "casual Friday."

"That's not casual," Stacy pointed out good-naturedly.

"You forget—I have no life," the VP responded. "I don't have jeans. I have pajamas, and I have suits."

Stacy does not want to live a jeans-free life.

As a matter of fact, one of her most memorable spiritual experiences involved not church and Sunday-go-to-meeting outfits, but jeans and hard labor. Some friends invited her to join them doing missionary work in Alaska. They were going to renovate a dilapidated Eskimo school building. She went, and spent days doing things like sanding overhead door frames. "My arms ached for a week," she says, "but I was proud of what we did. It was incredibly wonderful. We laughed, because we were doing things, like scraping mildew off walls, that back home we pay others to do."

During her marriage, Stacy and her husband drifted away from any spiritual involvement. On a Sunday shortly after their emotionally devastating divorce, she was driving past a church and noticed a sign that said the sermon for the day was, "God heals a broken heart." She hit the brakes and went in.

She now attends services frequently, although she's not sure what role church will play in her eventual spiritual path. She has explored New Age spirituality, but it hasn't done much for her. "You can't solve your problems by holding up a rock or a crystal," she says.

Stacy finds that her communication level with God goes up mostly when she's in trouble, although she does say "Thank you" when things turn out well. "I've had a couple of medical things that have made me get down on my knees and say, 'Please, God, let the biopsy come back negative, and I'll be a good person from now on.'"

The bumper sticker that says, "He who dies with the most toys wins" is a sad commentary.

David, a Silicon Valley minister

❧ Balancing Act ❧

Stacy's relationship with her brother has caused her to do some serious thinking about the tension between spirituality and life in the material world. His fundamentalist brand of faith is one to which Stacy most assuredly does not subscribe. He believes that buying insurance reflects lack of faith, so he doesn't buy any. Debt is counter to his beliefs (a principle of faith which, spread widely enough, could bring the modern world economy crashing down). His faith that God will provide makes him comfortable with his family's perilously marginal financial status. Stacy does not share his comfort level, and has taken him to task on this point.

"The problem is that when they're in a real bind and looking for 'God to provide,' it usually comes in the form of a check from our mother or from me. Then they feel their prayers have been answered. They're thankful to God, but not to me. I guess I'm just the vehicle. My brother knew the money would come somehow. In some respects it must be a nice way to go through life, but I couldn't abandon myself to that."

The president of the first company Stacy worked for when she finished graduate school was a mentor. Perhaps, just as parents imprint their children during formative personal growth periods, early bosses imprint subordinates during formative professional growth periods. Stacy observed this person making tough decisions that she felt were highly ethical and "right." That's how she

> *I was told it was not a good idea to discuss my Christianity at the office. Part of the reason the relationship didn't work was they weren't sure that as a practicing Christian, I could be aggressive enough for a Silicon Valley startup.*
>
> Colin, marketing manager,
> recalling his brief tenure with an employer

wants to do it herself, and that's how she'd like to see businesses run.

"It's a dilemma when you see someone succeeding at work who's downright bad, downright not a good person," she says. "If the world was right, this wouldn't happen. I don't have the kind of faith that gives me an answer to this, but I don't push myself too hard on it anymore. You just have to figure that what goes around will come around.

"I believe in God, but I try not to investigate or question it too closely. I want to accept it on faith, and not have the conversation with myself about where He is, how the universe was created, or other things that might hook my scientific side.

"But I believe in right and wrong and punishment, and that it's important how you live your life. A phrase I picked up here in the Valley is the 'karma bank.' You make deposits and your balance goes up. You make withdrawals and your balance goes down. And Someone is keeping score.

"I work with a vice president who's responsible for $4 billion in annual business. He's been married to the same woman for 27 years, and I asked him how he's managed to be so successful while maintaining a balanced life and a good marriage. He said, 'You don't *get* these things, you just *keep working* on them.' In the same way, I don't think one day you can say you've *gotten* your spiritual life. You keep working on it, and that's what I'll do."

RAY

Ray describes himself as *very* competitive.

It's probably a prerequisite for his job as CEO of a small educational software company, and it contributes to his frequent success on the tennis court. But he focuses on keeping it in check when it's not needed.

It is not unusual for Ray to find his competitive side teaming up with business pragmatism to pull him one way, while his ethical beliefs are tugging back in the other direction. "You always have opportunities to treat people in an unfair fashion," he says. "It's a struggle—and it's revealing.

"Occasionally our salesmen find themselves in a position where they could charge the customer more than they should. When I don't approve it, they sometimes think that my ethics, which are closely tied to my spiritual beliefs, are a detriment to the company."

Ray's father was Roman Catholic; his mother was Protestant. He was raised Catholic, but by the time he hit college he was growing away from it. For over 10 years he had no spiritual practice. When he and his girlfriend decided to get married, they chose a Protestant church because they liked the minister and his acceptance of the fact that they were already living together.

Despite his long absence from any religious practice, Ray had always thought that life in the material world, by and for itself, was rather empty. He and his wife became actively involved in an alternative group which practiced and taught a unique blend of homegrown philosophy and spirituality. Eventually, they turned off to the group and left.

The arrival of their first child had great spiritual impact on Ray and his wife. During this receptive period, a neighbor introduced them to a church they grew to like. They have stayed there and become active members.

❧ Man Talk ❧

Ray was instrumental in starting a small men's group which meets regularly to share events and feelings relating to their spiritual lives. All the members are in the technology business. Ray's group provides a forum for members to discuss the challenges they face living out their spiritual beliefs in the material world. It also serves an important function as what Ray calls an "accountability group": they feel responsible for, and accountable to, each other for the ethical and moral content of their decisions and actions.

His description of this group struck an interesting chord, largely because of a theme that repeatedly popped up during the research for this book: men often have a much harder time than women talking about their spiritual lives. Many men are acutely uncomfortable doing it at all. Some will go to great lengths to tune out any such conversation which might unexpectedly spring up around them. If it's the only distraction available, I have observed guys in such circumstances desperately and intently focusing on television commercials for household cleaning products as a means of opting *way* out of the ambush of a discussion about some personally sensitive topic.

Five years ago, a local church published an announcement of the formation of a new support group. Twelve women showed up and started a group which still continues and has bonded many friendships. The same church subsequently announced the formation of two new groups for men: one for spiritual and general life sharing; the other to provide (euphemistically) "job transition support" for those who had been fired, laid off, or experienced other

---

"You are what you buy," is the message we get, and it's hard to remember that's not the truth.

Victor, a Silicon Valley teacher

potholes in their career path. The church had, unfortunately, a substantial number of men in this situation.

There were no signups whatever for either men's group.

❧ Court Case ❧

A challenge to Ray's ethical standards which has stayed with him long and vividly—perhaps because he believes he failed the challenge—came on the tennis court. He frequently plays in tournaments. Recognizing the strength with which his competitive juices flow, he prays before starting a match that he will compete fairly.

In a tournament playoff, at a critical point, his opponent hit a short ball that landed just over the net on Ray's side of the court. He streaked in, got there in time, and hit a winner to put the point away. However, his racket hit the net during the swing, which means his shot should have been disqualified.

Ray looked up, and realized his opponent did not know Ray's racket had hit the net. No one but Ray did. He could take the critical point and keep on playing. Or he could blow the whistle on himself and tell his opponent the point was his.

Ray kept the point. "I still feel bad that I didn't insist on the other guy taking the point," he says. "When I came to a critical spot, my competitiveness beat out my ethics. It was a real lesson for me.

" ... people ... are working in banks, in corporations, or at the university where they find it is very difficult to live out the Christian life and they're very lonely and they mustn't be."

Father Morrison, Episcopalian Rector, quoted in
*Habits of the Heart—Individualism and Commitment in
American Life* by Robert N. Bellah et al.

"Someone who is spiritual has a sense of something bigger than themselves. Most people would probably think of that as a relationship with some kind with God. But in sports, there's the concept of 'team spirit,' and that's also a way of connecting with something bigger than oneself. I've felt it when I was involved with athletic teams, and I've felt it sometimes by being part of a company."

Ray believes that religious or spiritual beliefs provide a basis for setting moral and ethical standards. "I'm concerned that some of those standards are going away," he says. "In American culture, tolerance is almost a religion. But tolerance taken too far is a problem, because some things should not be tolerated."

ANITA

As Anita opened her front door, my peripheral vision registered something exploding past me at ankle height, heading for the street. It appeared to be furry, and approximately the color of a Granny Goose cheese puff. It braked, executed a screeching Immelmann turn, and gazed expectantly at the front door, eyes glowing in the light from the large entryway windows, radiating self-satisfaction at its accomplishments.

"Comet, get back in here," Anita said.

Comet failed to respond with adequate dispatch. Anita strode forcefully down the path and scooped up the wayward cat. In the semi-darkness, it looked big enough to eat schnauzers.

Once back inside, Anita introduced me to her other two cats. Titus, panther-black and panther-sleek, was about Comet's size. Artemis, the only female of the group, was introduced in absentia, and did not join us. Anita explained that Titus had turned Artemis into a "Lady Macbeth of neurosis" by constantly stalking her and trying to play with her. To give her a break, Anita brought Comet into the household to be Titus' pet. As the evening progressed, Titus tried repeatedly to nibble my pen. Finding it lacking in both flavor and texture, he eventually settled for giving it a periodic nuzzle to keep it on its toes.

Anita has been in the right place at the right time twice. During the early '80s, she was with one of the Valley's legendary garage-to-multibillion-dollar technology companies. Later in the decade, she was a member of the management team at a company that correctly read the emerging market for networked desktop computing, and also joined the multibillion dollar sales club in record time. "The first company bought my home," she says. "The second one bought my theological education."

In between, she and two colleagues resigned their jobs to form a startup company. Anita's Valley experience has included two Goliaths and one David.

Anita executed a midlife career change, took the fruits of her labors at the second company, and put herself through seminary. She's now a minister. In fact, the evening we met followed her first day of work in a new pastoral job. Her life differs greatly from her days of duking it out in corporate conference rooms.

She reflected on her early work experience.

"When I came to Silicon Valley it seemed like they just started throwing money at me. I ended up with a six-figure compensation package. It was intoxicating.

Baha'is use a consensus-building style of conflict resolution, and sometimes I actually welcome conflict. It gives my spirituality a workout, and increases my spiritual muscle tone.

Terita, a Silicon Valley homemaker

"I was 29. I was visible and I was credible. We were on the cutting edge. We had great toys. We were royalty. At that time, do you think I would have considered giving that up to 'wash people's feet'? Come *ON*!

"In the late '70s the Valley culture was young, crazy and intense. People were looking for community and affirmation—that they were OK, connected. The '80s were like the T-shirt one of the company founders made up for us: '80 hours a week and loving it.' The expectation was that everyone would give their life over to the corporation."

Although most things change quickly in the Valley, this expectation has demonstrated great staying power. While enjoying her status, her money, and her new car, Anita began to sense tendrils of discontent, of something missing, snaking themselves around her inner being.

❧ Calling ❧

Her family had attended a church through most of her childhood, but after getting married she lost interest in the church and spiritual pursuits. Then she and her husband divorced. "He got our social crowd," she recalls. She felt she had been left without a community, and that church might be a quick way to find one. The World Wide Web hadn't been invented yet, so she used a tried and true, low-tech search method: the *Yellow Pages*.

The church she went to clicked. She found more than community; she found people who seemed to her to be truly committed to their spiritual path. That influence teamed up with her growing sense of needing more from life than a continuous string of technological triumphs. She felt things stirring and waking. About a year and a half later, the stirring and waking evolved into an imperative inner call to change direction, to devote herself to a life of the spirit.

She was not pleased. "I went to my minister," she says, "and asked him to talk me out of this."

He didn't. Anita embarked on the simultaneous challenges of corporate management and seminary study. This was too big a load to sustain indefinitely. Eventually, a watershed moment arose.

"We had a *major* project starting. It was part of the company's initiative to migrate to a completely new product architecture. I was given the opportunity to manage one of the groups for this project. It required a three-year commitment. It would be totally consuming for that period: everything else would have to be subordinated. It demanded *passion*.

"So I had to go home and ask myself what I was passionate about. And the answer came back that it was definitely not Reduced Instruction Set Computing. I couldn't sign up for three years of life dedicated to that. So I quit.

"I was 36 when I left, and I was already starting to feel middle-aged in that environment. I know some very young 'techies' who are still there, and I kind of enjoy their attitude about my being a minister. They're interested. They accept it. Some of them actually think it's cool. They're not impressed, but they're not unimpressed, either. Beats hostility!

"I think people here are still looking for some kind of affirmation. They want someone with some kind of authority to say, 'It's

> *God's priorities are God-community-spouse-children-vocation. In Silicon Valley we turn it exactly around: our priorities are vocation-children-spouse-community-God. Every day I try to reverse people's priorities. Can you imagine how hard that is?*
>
> Roland, a Silicon valley pastor

OK being who you are,' and there's so little of that in the Valley. Even engineers can figure out that what they get rewarded for are not the cardinal virtues.

"Part of my reason for leaving the corporate environment was the degree of spiritual bankruptcy I saw in upper management. It wasn't so much that they didn't care about the right thing; *they genuinely didn't know what the right thing was*. They're cultural role models, maybe, but not spiritual ones. They just don't show an ethic.

"At my second company, I had to lay my job on the line every 10 days. I had to go in and say, 'Look, it's ethically and morally wrong to treat people like this,' or 'We can't ship our customers bad product.' There was always the element of cluelessness."

❧ "Goofy Insanities" ❧

"I think it's very revealing that a favorite slogan in the Valley is, 'Be careful what you pray for—you just might get it.' People think God is out to get them, like a Cosmic Trickster. It's God as adversary, God as lawyer, God waiting to trip you up in the wording of your wish.

"People here don't rest in God, don't feel safe with God, don't think God wants them to be joyful. People see Jesus as a great guy, a good teacher, a snappy dresser, a moral exemplar, but not an incarnation of the Creator of the universe.

"Even in the churches, I sometimes think they're all neo-Gnostics in the pews. All that 'Flesh bad, spirit good' stuff, as if the part of us that's going to live after death will be like Casper. I'm not a Casperite. Whatever causes me to breathe in and out is what God has given us, and He's given it to us all. It's too wonderful!

"I was talking with the Bishop a few years ago, and he asked, 'What's the coin of the realm down there in the Valley?' I told him that up to a point it's money, but after that it's competition: 'What makes me better than you?' The Gospel stands completely at odds to that world, and calls us to do impossible things. I just adore that!

"Christianity invites us to necessary but goofy insanities. 'Love your neighbor' is ludicrous. 'Love your enemy' is even worse. These are nutty and counter-intuitive, and only the grace of spiritual life can get us there.

"The Valley has an almost Sesame Street mentality in terms of needing constant stimulus to keep us engaged. But the rhythm of spirituality is the rhythm of the sea: slow and eternal. It's hard to be patient and wait for the rhythm of the spirit. We want everything fast and action-packed. No sermon can run over 12 minutes—people tune out.

"Everyone wants instant communication from God, but no matter how much we want it, God doesn't e-mail us. A prayer He may hear often from this area probably says something like, 'It's almost the 21st century, Lord—please get an Internet domain!'

"We've had so much economic success in this area that we have the disease of believing everything we think is important; that we don't have to listen to anyone else; that we know best. But this makes us isolate ourselves, and spiritual life needs community.

"A type of comment I hear a lot that comes from that isolation is, 'I don't need a church, I can worship God just fine in the redwoods, alone.' I don't think it's enough. The redwoods may be the lecture, but the church is the lab, and most people need both.

"A lot of the engineers I worked with were scornful of religion, particularly Christianity. One was a friend I used to really enjoy philosophical jousting with. He was a secular humanist. He had very spiritual principles for living his life, but aggressively disavowed any God. I once asked him why he thought golden-rule concepts were valid, since in his mind they didn't come from any real voice of authority. That stumped him at first. Then he got back to me later, and said he had an answer: 'It's important to be kind, because what goes around, comes around.'

"On the other hand, many members of my current congregation have a scientific background. They want meaning. They want to make a difference. They're not satisfied with easy answers.

"In seminary they always ask, 'Why do you want to be a minister?' I used to tell them, 'I don't. God wants me to be one.' Then I wanted to say to God, 'Don't make me do this.' But I've made the change, and now I'm at the opposite end of the spectrum: spiritually rewarding work, and practically no money.

"I worked with some engineers on a book over the past year, and dipping back into the Silicon Valley culture reminded me how invigorating it can be. At first it was a problem mentally keeping up with them: my bandwidth had gone back to 'normal.' But now it's back up, and I feel like I'm running at 9600 baud while the church operates at 2400 baud. In church I feel *serene* and *content*, but not *sharp*. The spiritual life is not as stimulating in some ways as the technical life, and maybe that's what derails some people from the spiritual life.

"In the last 25 years, I think the Valley has moved from hostility to laissez faire to intellectual curiosity regarding spirituality.

I have observed that middle-aged adults who have done the demanding work of figuring out their own spiritual beliefs are more able than others to make moral decisions and stand by them, even if the decision causes them some pain. In short, these people make the best leaders.

Kathryn D. Cramer, *Roads Home—*
Seven Pathways to Midlife Wisdom

Religion in this area has been a sort of forbidden fruit: 'Don't tell me about your underwear, and don't tell me about your religion.' The new people coming into the Valley seem less rejecting. Very diverse spiritual paths are available, and it's easier to try different approaches now than it used to be. I think that's a good trend, and I'm optimistic about the prospects for spiritual growth here."

RHONDA

After the latest in a string of reorganizations, Rhonda is part of a corporate subculture she knows will take some getting used to. She works for a company that makes computer communications equipment. Her entire career has been in sales organizations, most recently as director of sales operations. She is about to say hello to a new job in an engineering group. She hopes she survives the experience.

If time devoted to the job is the key variable, she will have no problem. She's a battle-proven veteran of nonstop, 60- to 70-hour work weeks. During the rare periods when this level of commitment has not been required, she has almost felt guilty about wimping out at 50 hours.

No. Willingness and ability to work long and hard on a sustained basis are not the issues. But as Rhonda contemplates her new responsibilities, she is also giving thought to the structure of her life. The way we spend our time defines our priorities. Are hers in order? Is she making room for the right things? Is she, by any chance, using a jam-packed work schedule as a way of avoiding the contemplation of other priorities?

"It *plagues* me that I don't have a regular meditation schedule," she laments. "I just don't get my lazy butt out of bed early enough to do it. I feel guilty about it, along with many other things, probably thanks to the great guilt training I got from my parents' church. I know what I would like my daily routine to be. I just haven't disciplined myself or my workplace to accommodate it yet. But I know I could."

Rhonda was born in Wisconsin, and grew up in the Midwest. She reflected on her initial impressions of spiritual life.

"My mother belonged to the altar guild at our church, and I went with her while she did altar guild stuff. My memory is of a cold building, a cold and bleak church, illuminated by weak, wan winter light. Even now, when I go home to visit my folks and we go to church, it seems cold. There's no abundance. Everyone's pale. No one wears makeup. The organ music is thin and screechy. It doesn't feel life-giving or life-supportive."

She gave it a shot. In her teens, she read psalms and prayed for guidance before going to bed. "I never got any answers," she recalls. "I finally came to feel, 'this does not serve me; I'm not getting anything out of this.' It was pretty much like I was out there alone, and being told to go figure it out. I was kind of a rebellious kid anyway. The lack of response from God made me think that instead of staying in the Girl Scouts and becoming a fine young woman, maybe I should run off to the coffee shop and hang with the 'other' crowd and smoke cigarettes."

Her rejection of the religion of her youthful years was complete enough to let her start over, as an adult, with a blank piece of paper. Now, figuring out what to fill it with is her challenge and her opportunity.

Too many ministers fail to talk about the practical applications of spirituality. Some people turn to spiritual lives to find solace for the unethical decisions they've had to make in their professional lives.

Rochelle, CEO of a Valley counseling group

Several years ago, Rhonda took yoga and meditation classes. She realized meditation and prayer were closely related, and meditation has become her "preferred form of communion." Through calming and quieting the mind, she feels more open to receiving answers from the "All-Knowing." However, she's had to struggle with the time commitment a regular meditation practice requires.

She went through a period where she was meditating twice daily, with one 20- to 25-minute session after work. But the relaxation it brought, coupled with the energy drain of her action-packed work days, usually caused her to fall asleep for a couple of hours. When she woke up, realizing that a large chunk of time had passed while she snoozed, she became cranky and irritable. This was, of course, in self-defeating conflict with the objective of meditating.

That meditation schedule was consigned to the trash bin. She now tries for at least once every other day, with no trailing naps permitted.

❧ Loner ❧

Rhonda has tried a couple of retreats, but she characterizes her present spiritual pursuits as *very solitary*. That's not her first choice. She wishes she could find a church or group with which to participate. Although she admits she hasn't done a heavy search, she has never found it. "Whenever I go to groups or churches, everything seems so contrived," she says. "I find both overreticence and overemphasis unattractive when people talk about their spirituality. My spiritual life is more experiential than intellectual.

"Eventually—and this would be quite daring—I would like to go public, come out of the closet, and join a group or church. I don't know why. But somehow I think it would add oomph or power to my spiritual life to share it with a group. When you're fumbling around in the dark, someone might know where a light switch is.

"It could force quite a change in my marriage, though, so there's some risk. I don't know if my husband would join in that sharing. He has a rich spiritual life through meditation, but he's very much a loner. He grew up in a Unitarian Fellowship church. His mother's an atheist. UF takes 'em all."

Rhonda hopes to reap several benefits from her spiritual life. Peace of mind. Increased tolerance of her fellow humans, of situations she can't control, and of herself. Confidence that her actions, thoughts and decisions are appropriately in harmony with a Higher Power. Assurance that outcomes will be fine. Connectedness. A sense that she has a role in the grand scheme of things.

She likes to read inspiring, spirit-affirming literature, and finds that associating with successful people can be uplifting. "You can learn from them how to work through life, and be balanced and moderate," she believes. "I enjoy moderation. I don't enjoy extreme rigidity or extreme indulgence."

Rhonda attributes her moral and ethical codes chiefly to her upbringing. She doesn't see much connection between moral code strength and spiritual commitment. "Some people are very religious, but believe in the death penalty," she observes. "But some who are atheists don't believe in killing. Some people who deny a God still have an extremely ethical code of personal conduct which distinguishes them as folks of the highest caliber. Yet they may not care a whit for spiritual practices.

Because they live in a fast-moving, high-tech world, many people in Silicon Valley want to see the same thing in their worship. Others want just the opposite: to balance the fast pace and constant change in other parts of their lives with worship that is slow and unchanging. The two views don't meet.

Audrey, a Valley minister

"Material prosperity and abundance may be a deterrent to people feeling a call to a spiritual path. But sometimes it can work the other way: once material needs are met, people may begin to wonder if there isn't more to life than all their *stuff.* Sooner or later everyone has to face some of those personal negatives and challenges. Prosperity and abundance can't buffer us from that.

"I have a soul I'm renting from the Higher Power, and it's through my soul that I'm connected to and influenced by that Power. Part of what was going on in my childhood was I didn't know how to work this body and this soul. I've learned how to run myself now, and I hope I get good at it before I leave."

AARON

Aaron loves Silicon Valley. There's nowhere he'd rather be. And he's got plenty to compare it to.

That's not to imply he doesn't see the area's problems. As rabbi of a small, marginally funded synagogue, he gets great insight into the challenges faced by his flock, and faces a few himself. "But this is exactly the kind of place I want to be," he exults. "I enjoy the challenges, I enjoy the technology. Finding ways to use the technology to serve God is perfect for me. I love the pace. In Silicon Valley you can't tell anyone what to do. But I never wanted to direct, I always wanted to guide. This is perfect!"

After being ushered into Aaron's modest office by his assistant, I waited a few minutes while he briskly stroked the keys on his computer. "I'm putting together a newsletter, and a friend just sent me some clip art over the Internet. Let me finish my download, then we'll talk," he said.

Download successfully completed, he described his background. Born in London. Progressed through school at what might be termed an accelerated pace, starting junior high at age 9. From England, went to Israel for rabbinical studies. Lived for a while in France, then moved to New York, where he met his wife. In the Valley for 16 years.

A key word, a central, unifying concept of Aaron's view of what spiritual leadership in the Valley must embrace, is "outreach." This term is often used to describe charitable contributions made by religious organizations, but Aaron has a much broader definition. He believes spiritual leaders must be proactive, innovative, and entrepreneurial in reaching out to the community. Not just to get money in or out, but to craft a delivery system that distributes the important messages of life everywhere they need to be.

"Religious practice here is more freeform than structured," he says. "Translating the traditional into practice doesn't happen much. People don't necessarily equate traditional views of God with spirituality. They have all kinds of visions. The motto I've developed for our congregation is, 'Communicating tradition in a modern world.'

"I want to see emphasis on spiritual outreach, on getting people involved. Ninety-five percent of the people I deal with are not religious. And we're so insular. Lack of community is a real problem. I've been trying to create an environment which gets away from that.

The organization controlling the material equipment of our everyday life is such that what in itself would enable us to construct it, richly plunges us instead into a poverty of abundance, making alienation all the more intolerable as each convenience promises liberation and turns out to be only one more burden. We are condemned to slavery to the means of liberation.

Raoul Vaneigem, *Basic Banalities II*

"The need to excel in the career here often overshadows religion. That might also be true on Wall Street, but it's so consuming here. We have a competitive, dog-eat-dog mentality, and heavy emphasis on materialism. Everything's so expensive, and people have to work so long and hard just to survive. It makes introspection difficult.

"It's not so much that people here reject religion. Actually, I sense a collective backlash against the negativity toward religion. It's more that they're caught up in the excitement and demands of the technology, and they're just too busy. Sometimes we need to stop. In Silicon Valley, no one stops. But some people find their toys starting to feel a little empty, and that sometimes leads to the start of a spiritual path.

"Because everything is new here, spiritual life tends to be shallow and sparse. You don't see grandfather's plaques on many walls. It can take generations to form a solid religious organization. But the flip side is that there's an excitement to religious life here that's not available anywhere else. That's because it's based on *choice*. No one *has to* do it.

"And we have such a wonderful physical environment around us. Sometimes I look at the beauty of nature in our area and wonder if this is what the Creator's eyes saw.

"If you are religious and believe that God created you and put you here for a purpose, when faced with a dilemma you will consider it in the context of why you're here. Without religion, you might just ask, 'Will I get caught?' or 'Aren't I here to do well

---

Pure spirit, one hundred proof—that's a drink that only the most hardened contemplation-guzzlers indulge in. Bodhisattvas dilute their Nirvana with equal parts of love and work.

Aldous Huxley, *Island*

materially?' Religion gives a deep sense of responsibility and the tools to withstand temptation.

"I got a call recently from someone who had been offered big money to pirate out some software his company owned. He was very tempted, and he asked me what he should do. I told him not to do it. He didn't. The following Monday, he received a bonus check from his company, one he wasn't expecting. The check was exactly equal to what the pirate offer would have given him—*net*, after taxes."

I will conclude this chapter with the stories of two Silicon Valley couples. Both were high-achieving, two-career households. Both made the decision to trade their professional and financial success for a different model of success.

DANA AND NEIL

Dana was born into a Christian family in Illinois, but the religion wasn't a take. She regards herself as having been an agnostic until she discovered the Baha'i faith. "When I began my spiritual search," she recalls, "my plan was to start with the latest religion, Baha'i, and work my way backward. Since Baha'u'llah (the Baha'i prophet) discusses the major previous religions and explains the progression and purpose of each, it seemed the work was done for me. In their essence, without man-made rituals and dogma, they all come from God and they are all one."

> *Gossip at work is contrary to Buddhist teachings. When I notice I'm in a gossip session, I don't like it.*
>
> Marta, a Silicon Valley tech writer

For many years, Dana worked for a Valley telecommunications company renowned for its growth, its progressive policies, and the length of its employees' work weeks. She started in sales, and over time made her way into management. Although she was rigorous and active in practicing her faith, she wanted more from that part of her life.

Reflecting on the challenge of balance, Dana says, "I find myself engaged in a daily struggle to maintain a proper perspective on life and its spiritual meaning. While working in Silicon Valley, this struggle was even harder because my tendency was to awaken and start thinking about work, or whether I should cut short the prayers to squeeze in a little exercise, or whether I had time to do a few house chores before work. I always seemed to be rushing. I'm convinced it's because I hadn't given my spiritual needs the right priority.

"It took a long time to realize that when I prayed and meditated first, when I tended to my spiritual needs first, it determined the quality of my contribution during the rest of the day. I still have to stop and remind myself of this important reality."

Dana's view of her spiritual mission includes work for social transformation and human unity. Her husband, Neil, is of a like mind. This goal was destined to lead them to a bold decision.

Neil was also the product of a Midwest Christian family, and also did some early exploration of alternatives. "I attended various churches while I was growing up," he recalls. "In college, a group

---

All businesses have temptations. Silicon Valley is not a 40- or 50-hour per week kind of place. The danger is that the fast-moving, exciting, engrossing technology can shut one down from all other pursuits. It's a big price to pay.

Ted, a Silicon Valley rabbi

of friends would get together every week or so to party. This usually included philosophical discussion. I started reading Western
philosophy, even though I hated it as a university course. In retro-
spect, I wish I had also investigated Eastern philosophy, but Iowa
didn't have many eclectic bookstores."

Neil's spiritual path eventually led him to Baha'i. His romantic path led him to Dana, whom he met at a Baha'i meeting. His
professional path led him to become a systems programmer for
one of the Valley's legendary computer manufacturers. Their combined success led them to a comfortable life in a beautiful house in
a very upscale Valley neighborhood. Financially and professionally,
they had it made.

Then they decided to give it up.

It wasn't that they hadn't been living faithful or contributory
lives. It was that they had come to a point where felt they could,
and should, do more. It was time to *devote* themselves. "I remember coming to a realization that I was at a life crossroad," Dana
says. "I could continue living as I had for the past 20 years—or I
could move on."

They resigned their high-paying technology industry jobs.
They sold the house. And they accepted an assignment to live,
work, teach, help and offer spiritual resources in a South American
country which is one of the poorest in the world. For three years,
their existence was an exercise in the most extreme contrast imaginable to their Valley lives. While there, Dana wrote, "Upon reflection, I was quite poor in a rich country, but am becoming rich in a
poor country."

Their spiritual commitment, their conviction that they were
doing something important and right, didn't eliminate the impact
of the traumatic change in their daily lives. They missed friends
and family. They missed telephones and personal computers. They

missed electrical power that worked more than two hours a day. They missed a moderate climate; convenient, comprehensive health care; not having to check the house for insects the size of fax machines; and lots more. But they stuck, prevailed, stayed faithful to the mission for which they had signed up.

"It is common for Baha'is to think of themselves as world citizens," Dana says. "Sometimes that means you leave your own country to serve others."

❧ Richer and Poorer ❧

"Living in a third-world country should be universally required," Neil believes. "Life without running water, reliable electricity, or garbage pickup, but with rampant disease, sounds unendurable. But I discovered generous, spiritual and openly friendly people throughout this environment. Also, there was a peacefulness and beauty there that I rarely find here.

"I remember one individual there who invariably described people in terms of how their soul appeared.

"Spiritual life in Silicon Valley is virtually nonexistent compared to what we found on the coast of South America. There, nearly everyone discussed spiritual concepts as part of their daily life. I think this was at least partly due to the fact that people there have almost no physical possessions.

"Unfortunately, television sets are becoming more available, and the most watched show is *The Young and the Restless*. To me, this is not instilling positive values in the minds of the watchers. Professional wrestling was also very popular, and 99 percent of those watching could not distinguish between acting and reality."

Dana observes that "... spiritual life seems easier in a less complex society where there aren't a lot of material distractions. Complexity and materialism make us struggle to stay focused on spiritual matters. I believe one can have a meaningful spiritual life wherever one lives. Some places just make it easier than others.

"Recently a television program showed Madonna singing her hit song containing the lines, 'We are living in a material world, And I am a material girl.' Here's what I'd like to have said: 'We live in a material world and many beautiful things have been put here for our enjoyment. But we are *spiritual* beings, and we must not allow material things to become obstacles to our spiritual growth.'

"The moral and ethical codes flowing from the first statement would probably be quite different from those coming from the latter.

"It may appear we gave up a lot to go to South America, but in reality it was nothing compared to the worlds and opportunities for growth which opened up to us. There was more emphasis on relationships. People spoke freely about spiritual things like breathing the air. I felt more in tune with the natural rhythm of life, waking up at dawn and going to bed about two hours after sunset. I served others more and gave more of myself.

More and more, I feel comfortable letting people know when I think what they're asking for is unethical. I try to find out what the objectives are, and then see if there's a way to meet them in an aboveboard way. For example, we've had some harassment cases. Simple acknowledgment that one person hurt another can go such a long way toward healing that breach. The healing makes sense for the company, and it's a spiritual value for me.

People might say, 'You're a lawyer, Stuart. We're not asking you for spiritual *advice.' Well, they can always get rid of me if my act is wearing thin.*

Stuart, general counsel for an
electronic instrumentation company

"I'm not sure what they learned from me, but I know I learned much from them. We are all related, and all connected."

I asked Dana and Neil if their Silicon Valley work experiences had caused them any spiritual conflicts. The answer was, not really.

"In the office it was generally known that I would not use or listen to obscene language, gossip or backbiting," Dana remembered. "I think I've been lucky to work for and with people of tremendous integrity, people I've respected."

"I haven't had inner spiritual conflicts," Neil says, "but there have been times when my beliefs have clashed with my manager's. We had one incident where he was yelling at and belittling a computer operator in front of several people in the computer center. I felt this was wrong, and completely unjust, and told him so later in his office. I also told him he should apologize. He did, in the presence of others. I think we both felt better.

"Our management approaches differed markedly. I tended to use a participatory, consensus-building style. He was motivated by power, and had an autocratic style. When we met several years later, he asked, 'Have you learned how to manage yet?' I just laughed and said, 'I guess not, from your point of view.' "

Commenting about future spiritual directions, both for himself and Silicon Valley, Neil says, "I see myself continuing to learn about all sorts of things, a pursuit I associate with spiritual life. Perhaps I'll leave the U.S. again, to try to assist others in learning and applying technology, while simultaneously trying to convince them that acquiring 'stuff' is not the ultimate goal of life.

Where there is the necessary technical skill to move mountains, there is no need for the faith that moves mountains.

Eric Hoffer, *The Passionate State of Mind*

"I am not very sanguine about the future of spiritual life in the Valley. Too many people, by the very nature of their jobs, do not allow themselves time to reflect on the reality of life. There are too many workaholics and too many people trying to buy the latest technological toys. There's nothing wrong with enjoying material things, but they do seem to get in the way and impair spiritual progress."

Dana is a little more upbeat. "Some observers of the sociological scene are already suggesting that as baby boomers age, they are becoming more interested in spiritual matters. We may see this trend in the Valley.

"As for me, each day presents new challenges. The quest for greater spiritual depth is never-ending. There is a beautiful quote from 'Abdu'l -Baha [Baha'u'llah's son] which sums up what I would like my future direction to be:

> *It is possible to so adjust one's self to the practice of nobility that the atmosphere surrounds and colors all our acts. ... At such a degree of evolution one scarcely needs to be good any longer—all our deeds are the distinctive expression of nobility."*

BRETT AND ROBERTA

"I went into physics because I wanted to find out what the universe was about," Brett recalled. "Also, some nut of a physics professor said physicists made more money than anyone else."

Even in universities—bastions of the search for truth—bad information is available.

Brett is from Missouri, and was an early-life adopter of the "show me" perspective: an atheist from the get-go. He was soon to discover the art of compromise.

With many of his peers, he did a tour of duty in Vietnam. He had started dating Roberta before he left. They corresponded. When he got back home, he was ready: he proposed to her two weeks later.

"She said, 'I can't marry you because you don't go to church,'" he remembered. "My hormones kicked in. I said I'd go, but I wouldn't necessarily believe. I guess that was good enough. She said she'd marry me if we could move to California."

Move to California they did, arriving in a Silicon Valley economy ready to explode. Brett's technical degree landed him a job with a major defense electronics manufacturer. "They were hiring 19 people a day," he recalls.

He kept his commitment to give church a try. Some issues harking back to his upbringing had to be dealt with. "My parents left the Roman Catholic Church because they felt that churches were just interested in the money. My grandmother went to Rome and *bought* an indulgence so my mother could go to heaven. My parents wanted to raise moral children. But they saw God as a crutch."

Brett was baptized at age 27. He remembers the minister telling him, "You know, Brett, these things don't usually work out, coming to Christianity this late." This aroused his Missouri stubbornness. His scientific training sent him on a reconnaissance

---

Sometimes I leave a meeting where we've discussed some "political correctness"-type issues and I ask myself, "Did I just sell out?" But I can't impose my Biblical values on the corporation.

Trent, president of a Valley telecommunications company

mission for facts. He asked lots of questions. He tried to understand why people came to church. He struggled with a feeling that the Bible didn't ring true, that it could have been written by anyone. He agreed to teach Sunday school.

"But I was just teaching facts, not imparting faith," he says. "I couldn't—I still didn't have it myself. I needed help. I needed a sign."

Much of the defense work his employer did was classified, which meant there was a formal, rigorous document control system in place. A document under Brett's control disappeared. The document was classified "secret." Its absence had the potential to be a serious problem for Brett, and he was worried about it.

Shortly after the document vanished, Brett's phone rang. He picked it up. A voice he didn't recognize said, "Something lost has been found."

Mystery solved. The document had fallen behind a safe. But the unexpected words, from the unexpected voice, rang and reverberated. *Something lost has been found.* Driving home that night, he pulled his car over to the side of the road and thought about the words.

❧ Real Estate ❧

Roberta's professional route was real estate: she was a hard-charging broker working seven days a week—and seven nights. She was president of her local real estate board. She made big bucks. "I had time to do all that," she recalls, "but I didn't have time to think. My life wasn't producing fruit. Then I started to ask myself, when my life is over, what's going to be the final analysis? That I made a lot of money? That I helped people buy a house? That's all? That would be so sad."

The faith of her upbringing did not serve her well during this churning introspection. It had become a rote, intermittent practice, with neither intellectual nor emotional impact. The more she thought about the meaning of her life, the more depressed she got. She read a book which contained a chapter she felt captured her situation perfectly: *Dark Night of the Soul.*

"I got to a point where I couldn't think of anything I wanted," she says. "That's when you know you're depressed." One day she came home and threw herself on the floor, crying. "Help me, God," she sobbed.

The thought formed in her mind: "Don't worry—something good is going to happen to you."

"I knew it was God's voice," she remembers. "I was too depressed to have generated that thought myself. In a few weeks the depression was gone, and I have never doubted it was His spirit that brought me out of it.

"But I was still concerned about Brett's path. One day we were taking a walk and I told him, 'I can't stand to think of you getting to be 65 and retiring as an engineer, doing the same thing all those years.' We prayed that the strong hold that money, houses, and jobs had on us would somehow be broken. When we got back from the walk, we laughed that it was a scary kind of prayer, and the scariest part was that it might be answered.

"Not long after, Brett got a temporary transfer to the East Coast. I had to make 33 phone calls to disengage from everything I was doing. When we came back, he was told his job would be going away in a few months. I said, 'This is what we prayed for and it happened. We're free!' "

❧ Fruitfulness ❧

The new course for Brett and Roberta's lives was launched when they decided to have children—and couldn't. They tried for two years, and gave up when medical analysis found a problem. "Since we couldn't have children, we figured we'd just keep buying bigger houses and moving every six months," Brett recalls.

Then, after it was clear that it couldn't happen, Roberta got pregnant.

"It's a recurring theme," Brett says. "You try and try, and you can't get there on your own. There is no road there from here—unless it's what He wants. When you have wealth, or ability, or good looks, you rely on it, and it steers you in the wrong direction." Their child arrived. She was their "princess of the world."

"We should adopt another child," Roberta said one day, "so Melissa won't get spoiled."

"I'm not spoiling her," Brett replied. "I'm just being a good dad." But he admitted it wasn't a bad idea.

They found out that adopting a child when parents are over 40 can be tough. Someone suggested they volunteer for foster care, and they did. "Mandy, a cute little 14-month-old girl, walked into our lives and hearts," Brett recalls.

Mandy's mother had given birth at 16. She herself had been born to a 15-year-old alcoholic. ("Mandy's grandmother is younger than Roberta," Brett pointed out.) After seven months of foster care, Mandy's mother told Brett and Roberta, "You have the kind of family I always wanted. Will you raise my daughter?" They had found their second child.

Brett and Roberta had opened themselves up for new life priorities and directions. Independently and jointly, they were ready to devote themselves to work that *mattered*: a mission that would bring meaning and satisfy faith. Their introduction to the foster care system opened their eyes to its critically important role, its great potential, its many problems. Children were out there, needing help. They had found their mission.

Brett didn't look for another engineering job. Roberta no longer spends Sundays at open houses with "for sale" signs on the lawn. They refinanced their property, juggled the household budget, and started up a local affiliate of a nonprofit organization dedicated to the support of foster children and the foster care system. It's now their full-time pursuit. "This is what we were put here to do," Roberta says.

Brett is grateful for the opportunity to devote himself to community and spirit. He sees the possibility of tremendous social benefit from the formative-stage intervention foster care provides for at-risk children. He and Roberta will focus on getting foster parents trained and certified, developing support services (such as baby-sitting networks, to prolong foster parents' sanity by giving them an occasional night on the town), and getting charitable and spiritual organizations to do more.

"Ultimately," Roberta says, "fixing the problems that lead children into foster care doesn't depend on whether we spend more tax dollars or fewer tax dollars. The underlying issues are spiritual issues. Some people are rocket scientists, and some are babies of drug-addicted mothers. God has to find and be real to all of them."

One of the interview questions for this book was, "Do you think those who have spiritual beliefs are likely to hold different moral and ethical codes from those who don't?" Here are some of the responses from nonclergy.

We cannot judge that, cannot judge people. We don't know other people's places and situations.

Yes, but it's always important to guard against self-righteousness.

No, because the range of people's religion-based behavior is so wide. It probably parallels the scope of behavior of those who have no spirituality.

I go back and forth. There are good people in and out of churches, and there are hypocrites in and out of churches. Religion seems to promote both the best values and the worst. You can be very moral, very ethical, without religion. Secular humanism is spat on by religious conservatives, but it's a philosophy that can lead to as good values as any.

Yes. I don't see how you can have a moral code without spiritual beliefs. The existence of a moral code implies some spiritual sense.

Those who are founded in spirituality tend to be stronger and better able to stand the buffeting of the business arena.

Part of religion almost spells out spiritual and ethical codes. Some just make sense. If I don't have to worry about killing you or you killing me, I can keep both hands on the plow. "Don't have children with your sister" is just good biological sensibility.

Everyone has a spiritual paradigm, whether they articulate it or not. We are not humans struggling to be spiritual, we are spirits struggling to be human. There was a "stages-of-morality" study which seems to indicate no connection between active spiritual life and morality.

I know some religious people who are as crooked as the day is long.

Going to church doesn't make you better, and it doesn't make you worse.

Morals and ethics usually precede *religion.*

Might have the same code, but the underpinning will be different. Without spirituality, the motivation might be, "how can I look good?" or "what's in it for me?" God doesn't look at just the actions, He looks at the motivation, at the heart.

If you're just religious, *there's probably no difference. If you're truly* spiritual, *there probably is.*

You can arrive at almost any code via almost any path. Belief in God can still lead to Machiavellian morals, and atheism can still lead to good ethics.

It's not black and white, but knowing there's more to life than the material world drives a difference.

People who don't read the Bible might be less inclined to leave their money to the poor.

As people get closer to God, they get closer to good.

Not necessarily any difference, much as I would like to say there is.

Here are answers to the same question from some of the clergy:

I certainly hope so, although I'm not sure I can make such a statement. You might almost have to recap a list of what good people do. But religions have centuries of those definitions and applications behind them, and a community to support them. When people have a value system that is rooted in their beliefs, it's probably stronger.

Those with spiritual lives expect to hold themselves to higher moral and ethical codes.

It might almost be too easy for someone who does Sunday morning church, and tithes 10 percent of their income, to say "I can do whatever I want the rest of the time." So some spiritual people might have worse codes. If we feel we're only answerable to God for 10 percent of life, that sets us up as our own God for the other 90 percent.

Some nonspiritual people live wonderful lives and have exemplary moral codes. If people are brought up with good values, those values will stick around even if they never go to church.

Too many variables to say for sure.

The divorce rate in this state is 50 percent. I heard a statistic that if both husband and wife go to church, and know at least six people there by their first name, the rate is 2 percent.

Some people compartmentalize their faith journey from their work. I've seen nonspiritual people with good ethics, and spiritual people with no-good ethics.

People with spiritual lives have better views and understanding of the defects in society.

Those with spiritual beliefs tend to have a stronger sense of morality, but there's no guarantee they will live their morality.

Many people who feel unconnected with God may have moral and ethical codes which sprang from ancient spirituality, whether they know it or not.

The issue is conviction *versus* opinion. *Those whose spiritual lives give them* conviction *of what's right won't deviate. Those who only have* opinions *might change their minds.*

People on the spiritual journey seek integrity, honesty and wholeness, and are able to resist shortsighted, selfish behavior.

With a spiritual life you're likely to tune in to others more. The connection oozes out beyond you, into the world. You have less alienation, more humility, and the we/they mentality is not so acceptable. You realize you're not the center of the universe.

Without a spiritual life there's no external guarantor of ethical standards. That absence might justify anything.

CHAPTER EIGHT

❧

Techno-Souls in Cyberspace

*Cyberspace. Room for the human spirit to soar free.
Earth surrounded by a digitized halo of
information—a throbbing, ethereal matrix
coagulating into ever shifting patterns of revelation,
and giving birth to a rich stream of social, political,
and environmental initiatives. The individual
freedom once sought only within the cloister or in the
trenches is now to flow from keyboard, mouse and
glove, electrifying the initiated with raw and
unbounded potential for new being. An electronic New
Jerusalem, its streets paved with silicon and bridging
all cultural rifts, promises the healing of nations. Even
the hope of personal immortality flickers fitfully for the
first time through materialist brains contemplating
prospects for DNA downloading and brain decoding.*

And you, self-professed infonaut—from whose jargon I have fashioned this vision—you say you're not religious?

Stephen L. Talbott, *The Future Does Not Compute: Transcending the Machines in Our Midst*

"Speed is God and time is the devil."

Hitachi executive David Hancock, quoted in a *New York Times CyberTimes* article headlined "Quicker Pace Means No Peace In Silicon Valley"

How versatile the Internet! Shop for a car, research a paper, chat with others at a virtual cocktail party, get tax forms, read new product specs, check the latest sports statistics, ogle pictures of seminude starlets, exchange e-mail, troll for love, and—starting late but gaining momentum—pursue your spiritual path. Some may view this as technology in the highest possible service. Others may see the hand of the devil in these electrons. It's a happening thing.

Internet use is not unique to Silicon Valley. By definition, the Net is a fusion of people the world over. However, the soul, the heart and the guts of the thing were largely crafted here, and without question it throbs to the Valley beat. No discussion of the effect of technology on the spiritual and philosophical experience can ignore the impact of the Internet.

WWW.JUST.ABOUT.EVERYTHING

Many approaches extend their virtual hands to those seeking spiritual enlightenment online. Let's start with the collection of electronic documents and locations known as the World Wide Web.

The power of the Web's underlying technology has been thought out and harnessed well enough to make it relatively easy to use, even for those with limited computer expertise. This ease of use has fostered an exponential increase in the number of people logging on, creating irresistible market potential. An incredible array of organizations and individuals have created Web presences for themselves. Spiritual groups have dealt themselves in.

Websites usually consist of combinations of text, graphics, and links to other sites or pages. Organization is hierarchical, allowing browsers to "drill down" through subject areas, or peruse increasing levels of detail. The user interface is almost completely at the "point-and-click-with-your-computer-mouse" level, so Web surfers can easily navigate through storehouses of information. The biggest challenges are not technical. They are: a) figuring out what you want to see next, based on the limited descriptions, and b) patience.

The patience factor is required because use of the Web has outpaced its resources. The Internet frequently gets as choked on modem traffic as commute routes on auto traffic at 5:30 PM. Response time can be slow enough to make you want to check your modem's pulse rate to make sure it's still alive—then your own, to make sure *you're* still alive.

Everything's a package, though. Waiting for a busy website to finish downloading a document to your screen might be a fine time to catch up with your meditation.

A few months ago, a major Web indexing service listed over 5,000 links to websites in the "Religion" category. At this writing, the number of sites is around 9,000 and going up *daily*. The universe is both large and expanding. To give you an idea of the diversity of what's available, following is a partial list of what might be termed "mainstream" sites:

Category	Number of Sites Listed
Christianity	5,682
Judaism	724
Islam	257
Buddhism	175
New Age	137
Hinduism	109
Baha'i	60
Atheism	45
Taoism	12

Then, there is a multitude of what might be called "less widely practiced" offerings. Selected examples include:

Category	Number of Sites Listed
Paganism	113
Wicca and Witchcraft	82
Mysticism	71
Satanism	31
Cults	23
Shamanism	19
Druidism	17
Gnosis	11
Rastafarianism	7
Pantheism	4
Voodoo	3

And finally, some offerings in the range between "less well known" and "downright obscure":

Category	Number of Sites Listed
Asatru	17
Yaohushua	8
Santeria	4
Mithraism	4
Quan Yin	3
Cao Daiism	2
Ifa	2
International Raelian	2
Osho	1
Tenrikyo	1

A typical website access will yield words and pictures designed to give an overview of the subject, with options to select for further information or interaction. Some sites let you order books or materials, and provide event schedules. The more graphics content a website has to show you, the longer you can expect to wait and meditate while your screen fills up.

Most—not all, obviously—of the foregoing represent religious and spiritual doctrines which have existed for some time. The Net and the Web introduce a new way for them to meet up with followers, actual and potential. Perhaps a more thought-provoking dynamic is reflected by the introduction of spiritual pursuits explicitly designed for the Net. Please welcome Cyberculture Religions.

Some Cyberculture Religions are pure humor. Some are ill-disguised electronic ego trips ("**The Church of Overhead Projector. The true religion.** Currently has one member. Slowly expanding.") Some don't seem to be able to keep their Web server up long enough to matter. Some have used the new technology to attempt new blends of science and philosophy ("**Church of Virus**—A rational, atheistic religion mimetically engineered to fill an ecological niche in the idea-space of humanity created by recent advances in knowledge.") Maybe, just maybe, some will become impact players. Even if they don't, let's not underestimate the value of a good chuckle in a serious world.

Chuckle generators which somehow seem unlikely to make their mark include "**Dai-Uchu Jinja**—basecamp for the Space-Commanders. Approaching the secret of existence"; and "**Messiahs, Inc.**—How Jeremiah L. Hermastone starts a Church-In-Reverse, beats the IRS, patents God, and has more sex than Rush Limbaugh, but less than JFK."

Born-on-the-Net organizations more inviting of a closer look include such innovations as the "**First Internet Church of All**—A modern religion for modern times. A religion for environmentalists and those concerned with the state of mankind"; and "**Religion of the Humanities (ROTH)** is the first true CyberChurch. A new religion without a physical location. ROTH is completely 'of the net.'" There are others.

A quick review of the "Sermon of the Week" from the "**First Internet Church of All**" yielded a rather sensible if not groundbreaking treatise on water conservation and stewardship.

... if the excitement [about finding information on the Net] is not about actual encounters with expressions of the human spirit, what is it about? One gets the feeling that a lot of it has to do with a futuristic, almost religious vision of what the Net is becoming— and all these interim discoveries are more valued for the progress they indicate than for themselves. Signs for the faithful. Epiphanies.

Stephen L. Talbott, *The Future Does Not Compute: Transcending the Machines in Our Midst*

OK. A probe into the pastoral counseling facility of the White Oak Chapel Cyberchurch opened an e-mail window to the church. Might work for some.

A representative example of a cyberspace new spirituality shopping mall might be "**Spirit-WWW**: A Non-profit and independent Web-site," originating in Switzerland. It offers a wide array of books and links, billing itself as "A dedicated spiritual worldwide-website which comprehends spirituality in a modern context in review of ancient teachings and religious belief-systems. The site is independent of any kind of specific religious belief-system or movement, but tries to give an overview of manifold forms of spirituality."

David E. Gordon has written a graduate thesis discussing online spirituality, entitled "Religion and the Internet." Appropriately enough, he has posted it on the Internet. He makes several cogent points:

❖ The ease of access and the free flow of ideas on the Net will "... favor religions focusing on an independent relationship with the divine ..." If true, this would represent a dramatic departure from traditional religious perspectives.

❖ Physical location will become less and less important in defining one's spiritual community.

❖ Exposure to a wide variety of spiritual viewpoints will encourage the continuous, fluid formation of new philosophies and organizations. Seekers will find it easy to "cut and paste" ideas from diverse sources to compose their own approaches. Then they'll find it easy to propagate their ideas and encourage others to follow. If you post it, they will come. Those who sign up will find that their followers' supply kit needs little more than keyboard and modem.

But even the most intrepid, dedicated Web spiritualist could never explore all the options. New ones get added too fast.

NEWSGROUPS

Another category of online communication which has emerged as a robust application for spiritual pursuits is the phenomenon known as newsgroups, or the "Usenet." These are series of messages sent to "folders" which are organized by topic, and available for world-wide access via the Internet. Messages may be new thoughts or responses to previously posted messages. The chain of original message, responses and counterresponses ("thread") to a particularly incendiary, thought-provoking, or common-chord-striking message can go on for months.

Some newsgroups have assigned monitors to review items before they are posted to public folders, and verify that they're appropriate for the group. Most groups are not monitored.

Historically, there were seven newsgroup topic names and hierarchies:

news	news about newsgroups
rec	recreational topics
soc	messages about social issues
talk	for general opinion-swapping
comp	messages relating to computers and networks
sci	topics regarding the "hard" sciences
misc	everything else

Now there are scads more, sometimes referred to as the "alternative hierarchy." Some of these carry the designation **alt**, and the newsgroup **alt.religion** is where a significant amount of online spiritual newsgroup dialogue occurs. Within that category, as of this writing, there were 51 subgroups, most with either self-explanatory names such as **alt.religion.zoroastrianism**; or we-can-guess-at-the-intent names like **alt.religion.course-miracle**; or in-all-probability-no-one can-figure-out-what-the-topic-is-until-they-read-some-of-the-messages-in-the-folder names like **alt.religion.spangles**.

One finds the serious, the playful, and the difficult-to-categorize. A common acronym in the online world is FAQ, which stands for Frequently Asked Questions. Many Internet services and functions maintain a list of recurring questions and the answers to them for the convenience of cybervisitors. The newsgroup **alt.religion.monica** sported 20 pages of these questions and answers. I decided to find out a little bit about the religion called "Monica."

The first question in their FAQ list was precisely what I would have hoped for: "Who is Monica and what is the purpose of this newsgroup?" The answer:

> *Monica Mi-Yeon Chung is the Venus of soc.culture.korean. In less than a month, Monica has become more famous and has more followers than Jesus, Buddha, Marx and other net-gods combined. Even after her departure to convent, her thread and popularity has exponentially grown to the point where so-called "serious debates" have become virtually impossible ... alt.religion.monica is a radically retro-postmodernistic newsgroup devoted to discussing morality and subliminal messages of Monica Chung ...*

Newsgroups contain energetic discourse on the full panoply of topics relevant to most modern churches, spiritual groups, leaders and individuals. The postings number in the thousands. Missives assume any and all positions on salvation, creation, women's clerical roles, gay and lesbian issues, Mammon vs. Truth, first marriages, Second Comings, third mortgages, charitable donation percentages, spiritually dead churches, prayer requests, ministerial misconduct, sudden revelation and scriptural quotation—to thinly scratch the surface. Emotions run high. Manners run low. Imaginations run wild.

The following nugget is from the **alt.religion.all-worlds** newsgroup, authored by a person identified as "SwiftRain." SwiftRain was responding to a posting from a person using the online name "Collectively Unconscious":

> *Collectively Unconscious wrote, "Depending on your flavor of Zen Buddhist (mine is chocolate), meditation is just an expedient method for cutting back the noise in your head. There is nothing that needs to be transcended and no one needs to be transcending it."*
>
> *Actually, regardless of how off-topic we are, Zen Buddhism doesn't talk about "meditation" at all. "Meditation" is a (rather bad) translation of "zazen." Zazen just means sitting and being at peace.*
>
> *(And I prefer vanilla.)*

A writer using the name "SkyDotCom" offered the following thoughts in the same newsgroup:

> *I'd like to share an idea with those of you who may—as I do—reject the common notions of godstuff.*
>
> *Though the terms "atheist/atheism/atheistic" have served well enough to lump together groups of people who "don't believe in God," I find it ironic that we *choose* to be labeled by them.*

*Theism is "the belief in the existence of a god or gods."
Since I think (and you'd probably agree) that gods are
the creations of species man, it follows that the
natural state of humankind does not include any
god. A person who has no god isn't lacking anything.
Rather, the person with a belief in a god has chosen to
take on some "extra baggage."*

*Example: if a man has a tattoo on his forehead, then
he has a feature which is not part of the *natural
state* of humankind. You may choose to refer to him
as "the guy with the tattoo." But would you instead
choose to call everyone else "tattoo-less people"?*

*Then why choose to call yourself an "atheist"—a term
almost certainly coined by a "believer" (possibly to aid
in the persecution of early freethinkers)?*

*The dictionary calls an atheist "one who denies the
existence of God." I don't deny the existence of God!
There is no "God" whose existence I can deny!!!
Rather, I reject the very notion of a god. I am not an
atheist!*

Two writers identified as "Dartwin" and "Maith" engaged in
the following brief dialogue:

Maith: *"Atheists have almost as much (in some cases more) contempt for agnostics as they do for theists." Have we all got this straight?
The atheists hate the Christians, hold contempt for the agnostics, sidle
up with caution to anyone who is sexually, ah, ambiguous but *REALLY* love themselves.*

My! What hath their ever-flaunted absolute freedom wrought??

Dartwin's reply: *You're right. We're not worthy of your attention. You can leave now. Say a prayer before you cross over to the Christian bulletin boards.*

Also present are quasi-commercial messages (considered very bad "netiquette"), irrelevance, irrationality, obscenity, and incorrectly posted items. There is wheat, but there is also a lot of chaff. Usenet is a great place to check in on a very interesting subset of the world.

Despite the geographical and philosophical diversity of newsgroup contributors, the views can't be assumed to represent the population at large. Participation on Usenet is not difficult, but does require a computer and some rudimentary knowledge of how to navigate around a network. The opinions expressed are, therefore, those of a silicon-oriented community which is certainly growing, but is still a long way from including everyone.

FORUMS

With the advent of full-featured, commercial online services, the concept of the "Forum" has been deemed ready for prime time. Forums are a combination of communication channels dedicated to particular topics. Let's take a look at the "Religion and Beliefs" forums available on one of the major services.

When you select **Religion and Beliefs** from the **Life, Style and Interests** menu, you can choose from **Christianity, Judaism, World Beliefs, Spiritual Mosaic**, or **Ethics and Values**. If you click on **Christianity**, for example, the following options will appear:

❖   **Christianity Online**

❖   **Christianity on the Web** (A website Index)

❖ **The Catholic Community** (Message boards, features, websites of interest to Roman Catholics)

❖ **Focus On the Family** (Articles, functions and features sponsored by this well-known organization)

❖ **The Christian Forum**

Entering the **Christianity Online** area leads to a grouping which includes:

❖ **Message boards.** Similar to Newsgroups, with a suggested daily discussion topic. (The topic on this particular day was, "How should Christians respond to health issues facing today's society?")

❖ **Religion news update.** Click here to get late-breaking news stories regarding religion and spirituality.

❖ **Current News and Magazines.** This section provides access to electronic versions of current issues of selected newspapers and magazines.

❖ **Christianity on the Internet.** Offers an index to Internet and websites of interest. There is also a "church locator," to help people find churches in their locale and to their liking.

❖ Perhaps the most interesting resource is the gateway to **Chat and Live Events.** (Chat rooms will be discussed later in this chapter.) This is interactive communication. In chat rooms, people talk with one another, or with the "room." Live events usually involve a guest or host (often a celebrity or well-known name), who responds to questions or comments.

Mere Christianity—and More

The Christian Forum offers access to online libraries, websites, chat rooms, message boards, and a daily devotional. Approximately 500 message board topics in this forum include interfaith relationships, Christian teens, suicide, gay men marrying gay women, abortion, e-mail Bible courses, conservative churches, and "Gotta do more, gotta be more."

Curiosity piqued, I peeked into this last folder. It mostly contained exhortations to strive harder for righteousness in its various forms. Two postings, however, provided additional interest in different ways.

The first was a message which started out, "My mission in life is raising my identical twin grandsons. Custody wars, court systems and battles including welfare, military and gay issues were unknown in our past and were just as suddenly paramount. Our 32-year-old daughter ... was too busy living with her female lover to provide for God's Blessings. What a shock to us as we discovered she was Pregnant! Gay! And had no possible way to care for the newborns." This woman has written a book on these experiences, and hopes to "... reach the millions who are in our same boat."

> *The New Age, it appears, will be won with surprising ease. The wondrously adept principle of "emergence" accounts for everything. It will materialize delightful new organs of higher awareness, not cancerous tumors. As one Net contributor enthuses: "The nature of the organism resulting is the only question. ... Strangely, I think this organizing into a spiritual whole will occur without much effort. When human spirits gather in a common purpose, something happens."*
>
> Stephen L. Talbott, *The Future Does Not Compute: Transcending the Machines in Our Midst*

The second posting of interest contains a theme older than time itself. Its subject line is, "Cast your nets!! Are you ready?" The message reads, "Are you ready to make enough money so that money makes no decision for you? You can have all you want!!! I can show you how, it's easy! We are Christian and conduct our business in a Christian manner. We will work along side you to help ensure your success. For Free Info on how you can make BIG money, Email me …"

Selecting the **World Beliefs** option yields invitations to forums on Baha'i, Buddhism, Hinduism, Islamic/Muslim, and Interfaith. Each of these offers a banquet of boards and sites, resources and chat rooms, similar to **The Christian Forum** menu.

If you are getting the impression that there are *many* ways to explore, communicate and share spiritual journeys from your keyboard, you are right. Many are duplicative, but that allows seekers to find the forum most precisely tuned to their individual tastes. Several stores at the mall may sell jeans, but only one may have the pair you want—in stock, in your size—on a given day.

CHAT ROOMS

Many who pursue an online spiritual path are looking for real-time interaction, not electronic document treasure hunting. Rather than browse the Web or surf the Net, they'll log on to chat rooms. Where there's demand there's soon supply, and they can find rooms dedicated to spiritual discussion—at least nominally; there's no serious enforcement. While it's true that rooms with titles like **Christian Fellowship** are not as compelling to some as rooms like **Romance Connection** or **Flirt's Nook**, they get their piece of the chat action. People share spiritual experiences, ask questions about the meaning of life and the existence of God, inquire about good Zen temples in Wisconsin, call each other spawn of Satan, and put a lot of energy into the whole thing.

The concept of chat room participation is simple, but the logistics, format and tempo take some getting used to. A loose-fitting analogy might be attending a casual, open-house style, happy-hour party where you don't know anyone. The party is in a hotel, and there are many other such parties going on at the same time. I'll use the chat room structure of one of the major online service providers as an example.

When you log on to the service and select what they call **People Connection**, you are transported to a "reception lobby." You can actually converse with other people in the lobby, if you wish, while figuring out which "party" you want to attend.

To "talk," you simply type what you want to say on your keyboard. Everyone else who is currently logged into the lobby or chat room you're in will see your name at the left side of their screen, followed by your comment. When someone else "says" something, the screen scrolls upward and that person's "screen

---

... perhaps the most poignant symptom of the projection of a lost interiority lies in the new electronic mysticism. Images of a global, electronically mediated collective consciousness, of Teilhard de Chardin's [O]mega [P]oint, and of machines crossing over into a new and superior form of personhood are rife on the Net. Channelers channel onto the Net. Pagans conduct rituals in cyberspace. Most of this is unbearably silly, but as a widespread phenomenon it is difficult to dismiss.

Stephen L. Talbott, *The Future Does Not Compute: Transcending the Machines in Our Midst*

name," followed by their comment, appears at the bottom of the screen.

The software which controls and enables some chat rooms can accept only about 15 words at a time, so ability to communicate in one-sentence bites is helpful. The average sentence is probably five words. In an active room, the comments can fly at a very fast pace. Other rooms may have periods of "silence" when no comments are being sent. As with parties, each room has a character: shy, aggressive, anywhere between. You can participate, or just sit on the sofa and listen to the dialogue swirling around you.

Conversations take two forms: comments put out for the room in general, and comments directed to specific individuals. The live-party analogy might be the way you circulate around the room: sometimes you join a group, sometimes you're one-on-one.

One-on-one conversations usually require sharp eyes and good reflexes. If there are 20-odd people in the room and you're "conversing" with one, you need to pick the comments of that person out of the pack. Being able to think of replies quickly is helpful; so is having frisky fingers to type them.

As with real social gatherings, pests can horn in. You may be having a fine dialogue *à deux* with someone, but if it looks interesting to others in the room, they can try to get involved. If you and your cohort ignore them, there's not a lot they can do besides switch to all capital letters to protest, and say mean things about you. (Using all caps is the electronic equivalent of SHOUTING, and is considered bad netiquette.) However, if unsolicited outside comments make the two of you feel the neighborhood is going downhill, and you wish to repair to a more genteel, private locale, two options exist. You can set up a private room; or you can send "Instant Messages," which only the two of you can read, to each other.

Using the live-party analogy again, the "Instant Message" approach might be like the two of you stepping outside into the garden. The "private room" option might equate to the selected group hopping into a hot tub.

Most people don't hang around the lobby long. They head for a room with the chat topic of their choice. Major categories include:

❖   **Arts and entertainment**

❖   **Life**

❖   **News, Sports and Finance**

❖   **Places**

❖   **Romance**

❖   **Special Interests**

❖   "Country" rooms (**Germany, France, Canada**)

Chat rooms with potential interest for spiritual searchers are found in both the **Life** and the **Special Interests** categories, along with a host of other rooms. **Special Interests** rooms include astrology, ebony, art, gardens, born-again onliners, metaphysics, music, cars, computers and pets.

Life rooms offer a smorgasbord of conversation canapés for people in different stages and states:

❖   Age affinity rooms: **Teens, Twentysomething, Thirtysomething, Over 40, Senior Scene**

❖   Family role affinity rooms: **Parents, Careers and Family, Divorced**

❖   Gender affinity rooms: **Male Point of View, Women's Point of View, Gay and Lesbian**

❖ "Looking for love" affinity rooms: **Single Again, Single Parents, Widows and Widowers, In Limbo**

❖ "Searching for truth" affinity rooms: **Christian Fellowship, Philosophy**

People in chat rooms usually use "screen names," which are online aliases. Sometimes it's evident what a screen name refers to. Sometimes the choice is totally opaque, meaningful only to its owner. There's no way to find out the real names behind screen names like "Zephyr," "Silver Wraith," "Magik10," "Where'sMom1," "Angelbirdy," "Moonbats," "Bluuenikki," "HooknLaddr," "Lord Gizmo," and my personal fave, "PNutChelle," unless their owners choose to share the information. This they can do during conversation or by completing an optional member profile which is available for all to peruse. Some chat room participants do post profiles, but many choose to chat in mysterious anonymity. Such is their prerogative.

Entering the online chat world during midday in midweek revealed an interesting fact: many of the participants were midteens whom one would expect to be in school. Among their many other sociological roles, chat rooms may be emerging as a recreation of choice for the flu-ridden and/or the truant.

The words and thoughts in a chat room come and go, surge and merge, part, wane and die so that new words and thoughts may rise from their ashes. Statements range from petulantly profane to passably pithy to possibly profound, with occasional nodes of nihilistic nonsense. For some participants, the fingers on the keyboard are faster than the mind, and for some, just the reverse is true. Both mismatches represent chat challenges.

To give a touch of the flavor to those who have not been in an online chat room, spiritual or otherwise, here's an excerpt from a **New Age Spirituality** room conversation I entered in progress (speakers' "screen names" are on the left, in bold type. References to other speakers' names, which are often shortened during chats, are also in bold):

BdyMndSprt: Ah, but I do have a foundation. Faith, my own God-given religion, but it seems you are here ...

STANSONELL: Silly, private room "feng shui."

Orion Zen: I don't think SSOOOOOOOOO ...

BdyMndSprt: ... to proselytize, so I will not get into an argument with you.

HolyGhost: No, the mind is the liaison, the soul is the operator!

STANSONELL: Orion, about what?

Orion Zen: Bible.

Sprtljrney: oh ... okay, **Holy** ... my ignorance of souls, maybe. Don't know much about souls.

Meemoe: Religion was god given.

WildHealer: I like that, **Ghost.**

SoulWind2: It is all one, **Holy,** no separations.

Light22: Let's do "LOVE IS"!

SoulWind2: The consciousness is ...

UhOh007: Metaphysics can be argued forever ... but lying can be seen easily.

Faithmom: Wide is the road that leads to destruction.

STANSONELL: Oh, must've missed something.

Silly47787: Thanks ... I need a spiritual interior decorator here ...

Sgusakov: Light ...

Orion Zen: Love is ... all of us.

Light22: Love is ... accepting others.

HolyGhost:Sprtl ... how can that be? Soul is YOU!

UhOh007: Love is ... not Manson.

RBCF Soul: Holy—Yes, SOUL runs the whole show!

Orion Zen: Love is ... you, **Light22.**

HolyGhost: Not something out there!

STANSONELL: Silly, you're telling me!!! My house is a wreck.

Faithmom: Narrow is the path that leads to eternal life.

Sprtljrney: Ghost, then maybe I don't know so much about me.

WildHealer: Love is ... healing.

SoulWind2: This world is made up of the same stuff as the "inner."

CaseCorp11: I have a question for everyone and was wondering if you guys could help me out?

Sprtljrney: Faith ... how many different paths are there?

WildHealer: Love is ... letting go of fear

Light22: Love is ... smiling at the person in the car next to you—and letting them pass.

Orion Zen: Wise words, **Wild**

UhOh007: Love is ... a four letter word.

Brando895: Case, go ahead.

RCBF Soul: Wild—yes, divine love can even heal the physical body.

HolyGhost: Perhaps! But I know how to introduce yourself!

WildHealer: Yep!

Light22: Love is ... knowing that all people long for the same thing—feeling love.

CaseCorp11: Why aren't words like Love or Compassion capitalized? To me those are more powerful than ...

Sgusakov: Love is something you have never seen until you experience it.

Faithmom: One path to heaven, many to hell ...

STANSONELL: Love is ... doing random acts of kindness.

Silly47787: Ha Ha Ha. Give ... love ... and blow the dust as I walk by to sit at the computer.

Orion Zen: Madonna—come on in.

The foregoing represented about two minutes of chat time. Keeping up, following the threads, getting your comments in before the topic changes, and keeping an eye peeled for someone "calling" your name end up being a fairly good workout for the intellect and an even better one for the reflexes.

Not long ago I engaged in a brief chat room conversation with a woman in North Carolina. She had recently gone through a powerful spiritual experience and mentioned that she had written about it. I asked her if she'd send me her writing. She did, via electronic file transfer. After 10 minutes of faceless screen interaction, I was reading an 8,000-word document of ultimate intimacy describing this woman's marital and physical problems, hospitalization, surgery, fear of death, and middle-of-the-night revelation. If we had met in person she probably would have shared none of this.

Face to Face

When all is said and done, what does it mean to substitute screen and keyboard for live humans; to replace bricks-and-mortar meeting places with wire-and-cable connections; to have newsgroup monitors in the spiritual communication loop instead of ordained clergy? Are we seeing the search—and the means—for a new paradigm, one that seeks to distill a pure, solitary spirituality and filter out particles of traditional, organized religion?

Irving Kristol is a fellow of the American Enterprise Institute. In a February 3, 1997 *Wall Street Journal* article on what he believes is a form of spiritual crisis in our nation, he says:

> *... it is not astonishing that the search for spirituality*
> *has become so fashionable. It is what individuals,*
> *liberated from religion, desperately seek as a substitute.*

Spirituality is indeed an integral part of all religions—but a minor part, and it cannot be a substitute for the whole. Religion is not some kind of psychic exercise that occasionally offers a transcendental experience. It either shapes one's life— all of one's life—or it vanishes, leaving behind anxious, empty souls that no psychotherapy can reach. And for religion to shape one's life, it needs to be public and communal; it needs to be connected to the dead and the unborn.

Public. Communal. Connected. We understand the traditional meaning of these words. But maybe they've acquired extended meanings. Perhaps those meanings force us into uncomfortable semantic conflicts. Can we be public without leaving the house? Communal without being in physical proximity to other humans? Connected without ever looking into our discussion partners' eyes?

For a good number of techno-souls in cyberspace, I think the answers are "yes." Further, the pieces are in place to support the argument that this will continue to be a high-growth phenomenon. Based on the number of churches and institutions establishing websites, or trying to figure out how to establish them, it appears many are coming to the same conclusion.

For those who want to see others, be seen, and still not leave the house, current technology provides an alternative to looking into real eyes. It's like a telephone call with video as well as voice. The necessary software runs on many personal computers, and the hardware includes a mini-camera at each end. The camera sends a continuous picture of each participant to the other's screen. Resolution isn't great, and motion is a little jerky. But it will improve, and it does allow credible visual contact without requiring people to get out from behind their keyboards. And behind their keyboards, many will choose to stay.

I don't think most people would say we're at New Jerusalem just yet—perhaps we're closer to the virtual Tower of Babel stage—but that's where some may feel their online pilgrimage is heading. As a matter of fact, at least in one vision, technology-based spirituality may be destined for a startling, infinitely more profound role. Chapter Ten will include a look at the concept of computers being the ultimate tool for achieving immortality and the promise of eternal life.

CHAPTER NINE

᳄

Saying No

Irreligion: The principal one of the great faiths of the world.

Ambrose Bierce, *The Devil's Dictionary*

I ... became an actively practicing intellectual agnostic; one who took pride in explaining to others that because of recently acquired knowledge he now knew too much to be able to know any longer whether there was a God.

Dan Wakefield, *Returning—A Spiritual Journey*

What causes people to reject or leave a spiritual path?

The reasons for saying no to starting or continuing spiritual life appear as varied as 20 years of Chevy models. The purpose of this chapter is to explore some of the underlying thoughts and processes. We'll look at the topic of spiritual rejection through the eyes of some who have made that personal decision, and some who haven't but who have opinions about it. We'll also hear from some clergy why they think people decline their offerings.

In approaching this area, I guessed there were two major categories into which Valley residents without spiritual lives might fit:

❖ Those who found religion or spirituality *irrelevant* to their lives. No hook. No connection. I anticipated that this perspective would spring from a near-complete absence of exposure to spirituality, particularly during early life. Subsequent years would bring neither people nor experiences which would trigger an examination of the area. Silicon Valley life and culture would be seen as de-emphasizing or even marginalizing spirituality. Eventually, spiritual pursuits would become just something that other people did, for reasons known only to them. The topic would lack both reality and interest.

❖ Those who had explored the area, maybe even had a spiritual path at one time, but whose lives included events or experiences or changes in belief that caused them to abandon the path. The end—or the decision not to start—was not passive, not a vacuum, not a default. These people had *thought it out*. And their conclusion was that they and a spiritual life were not going to be an item. The decision represented active rejection, sometimes with a great deal of energy behind it.

Those were my guesses. I was almost, but not quite, right.

First, I discovered that everyone has had enough contact with spirituality and/or religion to have gotten past being a blank slate on which nothing had ever been written. And while some people lack interest in pursuing a spiritual path, everybody I interviewed had an opinion about it.

Second, I discovered that the reasons for rejecting a spiritual path are too varied to fit neatly into just two groups:

❖ Some say no because they see hypocrisy: spiritual values extolled on Sunday, same extollers making decisions which ruin people's lives on Monday; or spending money on frippery on Tuesday, instead of using it to make a better world.

❖ Some, as protesting kids, were dragged to church by parents. They vowed that when they grew up they would never go to such boring places again. It's a vow they've kept.

❖ Some started on a spiritual path at one time and found it enticing. Then their burgeoning beliefs presented an uncomfortable demand, and the most comfortable way to deal with the conflict was to get off the path.

❖ Some fear foolishness. Cynicism and skepticism often play better in the Valley than belief.

❖ Some feel spirituality is isolated, forbidden ground.

❖ Some feel there's an incontrovertible prima facie case against at least the Higher Power version of spirituality: too many bad things happen to too many good people.

❖ Some see rigidity: One True Way. Silicon Valley may be the least likely place on the globe for the One True Way approach to have much appeal.

❖ And the most pragmatic dynamic of all: some are just too drained after the long, demanding days at the office to pursue deep philosophical concepts. The required intellectual capital has been spent elsewhere. This may be a distant kissin' cousin to rejection by default.

There is one view of spiritual life which may make the difference between acceptance and rejection moot. Edward, a priest at a large Roman Catholic church, says, "Spiritual life is what you are and how you live. Spiritual life can't be separated from the rest of life. Your life is one entity. My dad read the racing form in the car while the rest of our family was inside the church at Mass. But he *lived* the highest spiritual life."

Whether spiritual life can exclude spiritual practice is a juicy topic for high-energy debate and highly technical theology. Or, it may hinge on definitions. Is a moral life, an ethical life, the same as a spiritual life? Or do they simply travel a long stretch of the same road side by side, going in the same direction, maybe toward a common destination, but with a different mission?

Regardless of how one lives, Edward thinks the act of rejecting spirituality is painful, always nagging at the people who do it. Jerry, a Valley rabbi, rejects the idea that those rejections really happen. "I don't know any human who isn't searching for meaning and doesn't want to connect to something bigger," he says. "I know some who are misguided in their search, maybe, but none who say 'no spirituality.' They're looking, even if they don't know it consciously."

Sam, a Protestant minister, believes basic personality characteristics affect the decision about spiritual paths. "Thirty-five percent of the population are Myers-Briggs 'Introvert' types, who don't like crowds or socializing. It can be hard to get them to try going to church." He also observes that fiscally conservative types may

---

Some people reject a spiritual path because of the pain in facing themselves. How do you accept your brokenness, your failures, your humanity, in a society that emphasizes perfection?

Victor, a Silicon Valley teacher

be critical of the way churches spend money, and reject spiritual paths on that count. "Some people see the new church building and say, 'Look at that church, just suckin' dough!' "

Among the people interviewed, strong commitment to one's own spiritual journey often went hand in hand with extensive insight into why that journey is rejected by others. Maybe that's because folks remember well the obstacles they faced along their own path.

Colin, the marketing manager for a computer equipment maker, captured several variables. "People looking at churches often see them as hypocritical, controlling, freedom-robbing. Or they see them as superficial social groups without real meaning. Some may confuse spirituality with religion and get turned off to spirituality because of problems with religion."

The issue of control was a recurring theme. Frank, the bank CEO, pointed out that unwillingness or inability to conclude there are things one can't solve oneself deters many from exploring spirituality. Can't go it alone? Need outside help? You're showing weakness. You're vulnerable. Next thing you know, someone's calling in a consultant. Can a reorganization be far behind?

Gerald is the chief financial officer of a laser equipment company. In his view, a frequent factor leading to rejection of a spiritual life is that taking the high road can be tough. It's easier not being spiritual. Commitment requires you to put yourself on the line, and stand up for what you believe. Keeping the faith takes guts. You have to be willing to pay the price. You might also be dealing others into the game, and there's risk that they could suffer for your beliefs. If you have two kids to support and your boss tells you to do something wrong ...

As a journalist for a widely read Valley publication, Duane has an excellent observational perch. "Lots of things turn people in this area off to a spiritual path," he notes. "The sense that every-thing is OK as it is. A sense that religion is silly, that there's a lot of flakes involved and you don't want to be one of them. The flake thing is a big thing.

"You see people presenting themselves as spiritual, then you find out they're bad parents, or on their fourth marriage. Or, work drives spirituality out because there's no time and too much pres-sure.

"Spiritual leaders and clergy can be the problem. Some are good, but some are jerks, screwing around with their parishioners and embezzling money.

"Then, there's TV and the Internet."

Rita is vice president of corporate communications for a pub-licly held environmental technology firm. She's well positioned to observe the challenges that being a corporate officer can offer to spiritual beliefs. (The CEO of her company, commenting on their internal culture, has said, "If you want a friend, get a dog.") She sees the key issue keeping some people from spiritual paths as a primeval one: fear. Fear of not understanding what the path is. Fear of letting go. Fear of self-awareness. Fear of surrendering. Fear of admitting fear. She thinks these last two are much more issues for men than for women.

Rita also believes it's easier for women to let it be known in the business world that they have a religious affiliation. "I've known some men who teach Sunday school who would never admit that fact in their work lives," she says. "I think they're afraid they'd be considered odd by their colleagues."

> *Some are simply afraid to think what it might mean if there was a God.*
>
> Melinda, a Valley therapist

In fact, it may be deeper than just "odd." For some, the fear might be that the "surrender" involved in that area implies the possibility of surrender in other areas. Vulnerability established, the next sound could be fins cutting through the water.

One of the dynamics of spiritual life rejection I asked interviewees to reflect on was the two-opinion household: one partner in the marriage or relationship has a spiritual life, but the other does not.

LARRY AND HELENE

Larry is a residential general contractor. He sees firsthand that the extraordinary runup in property values in the area encourages people to spend copious amounts of money maintaining and improving their houses. It's usually a good investment.

Working with his customers has given Larry ample opportunity to observe Silicon Valley lives and styles. The experience has fueled his conviction that spirituality, at least in this area, is usually synonymous with hypocrisy. "Belief systems in other countries seem to have more meaning," he says. "The only thing we grab onto are our Jeep Cherokees and our gyms. It's hypocritical to say one is spiritual when one can't get on a bicycle without wearing $300 worth of the right clothes. I couldn't do that if I were spiritual.

"Going to church just on Christmas and Easter, as many people do, is also hypocrisy. So are the proclamations of certain well-known spiritual leaders. They tell people to give up affluence, but they certainly enjoy it themselves."

He doesn't rule out all possibility that his opinion could change. But for now, Larry puts himself in the category of having said no for keeps to a spiritual path, at least as normally defined.

"My parents were Protestant. In my teens, my dad was shocked that I didn't believe in God," Larry recalls. "But he never pursued it. We were alienated anyway.

"I went to a church funeral when I was 17, and it was the longest day of my life. The bells and chimes scared me. Now, robes and candles and bells strike me as hokey. Structured religion is a joke, and I think it has little appeal to most people.

"I do have some respect for fanatical believers, though. If you're willing to kill yourself for your belief, the belief system must have something going for it.

"There may be a 'greater power' in the universe, but it's not some old man in white robes. The universe is vast. If God is there, we would be an ant farm, too small for Him to notice.

"I believe something in us does last after death. We don't get white wings or sit on clouds. But I'm interested in this, and without being morbid, death might actually be a welcome experience. It's surprising to me how many people don't like to talk about death."

Larry doesn't believe people with spiritual lives have different moral or ethical codes from those who don't. He tries to treat his customers fairly, and traces the development of his ethical values to "… my parents, and the times in which I grew up. I had no heroes along the way. It's too bad things have changed so much that people now think it's OK to cheat on everything."

Larry's wife, Helene, has a very active spiritual life, so this is an area of sharply defined difference for them. They appear to have worked this difference out well. Both display great respect for and acceptance of the other's views. "I used to tease Helene that I liked to watch Jimmy Swaggart," he says. "I knew he was a big phony, but he seemed to bring something to people."

Helene believes the key to making a relationship work in this situation is to accept the difference: that what refreshes her spirit doesn't refresh his. She knows Larry's spirit is there; he's just not acting on it. It's important for her to affirm that he does have a spiritual side, but it's OK that he doesn't express it the same way she does.

There are challenges, however. Sometimes she feels lonely because he doesn't understand what she's talking about. Having friends and professional colleagues who do is helpful. She also knows that he's very proud of her. In general, she thinks that split opinions on spirituality are a warning sign in a relationship, and it's important for the couple to work it out. "You have to have unconditional acceptance of who each other is," she says.

Larry recalls having one experience he would describe as spiritual. "I was in the bathtub. I had a feeling of total relaxation, followed by total peace. I'm not sure I could convey the feeling exactly, even to Helene. She's tried to get me to meditate, but I'm just too visual a person for meditation. I've never been able to repeat that experience.

There's no such entity as soul. The traditional understanding is that it's something inside the body which continues to exist after death. Jungians postulate that it relates to feelings and emotions. But the individual self is constantly changing, and no individual self, no "essence" of the individual continues after death. Humans have such chutzpah to think that only we, no plants, no animals, nothing else, have something that survives after death. What arrogance! Our coming and going in life is a continuation of something great.

Ari, a Valley Buddhist leader

"My children are like me, only more so. I would rather they believed in something, or were more open, even though I believe only half of what I see and none of what I hear.

"I do believe there's something out there—maybe a 'nothingness.' It has to be experienced, though. No one can convince me with words. But too many people to ignore have had out-of-body experiences that seem to indicate something's there.

"I almost envy people who have the certainty of beliefs. I like to think I'm open to anything that might come along. But I'm not open to easy, clichéd answers."

THREE GUYS

Once there were three guys from New York City: two from Brooklyn, one from Manhattan. Now they're from Silicon Valley, and they're friends. Marvin and Jeremy are lawyers, a fact which Lonnie, a real estate agent, has been willing to overlook in the interest of friendship.

Jeremy is a corporate intellectual property attorney, charged with protecting the patents and trademarks of a major Valley biotechnology company. He is an outspoken social commentator and a sensational chef. It's well known in his circle that dinner at his house will be a gastronomic delight guaranteed to add a pound or two to one's presence.

Marvin has a private legal practice specializing in tax law and estate planning. He has three children successfully launched into adult life, and is a scrappy sports competitor. He was probably the

---

If only God would give me some clear sign! Like making a large deposit in my name at a Swiss bank.

Woody Allen, *Selections from the Allen Notebooks,*
in *The New Yorker,* 5 Nov. 1973

only 145-pound interior lineman in the last 50 years of college football.

Lonnie dukes it out in the wacko Valley residential housing market, which has recently hit new levels of insanity. Driven by an exceptionally low number of homes listed for sale in the more desirable communities, houses are selling for substantial amounts over asking price, usually with multiple offers. Prices are up 15 percent or more (over their already sky-high levels) over the past year.

It's not unheard of for Lonnie's clients to make over-list-price bids on several houses, and still end up not having bought anything because someone else offered more. Telling a client they've lost another one can be—taxing. Maybe the streets of New York helped Lonnie develop the toughness and resilience to deal with this environment, and keep his sense of humor.

In addition to their New York heritage, these three men have other things in common. They are serious about sports, both as spectators and participants (tennis, racquetball, season ticket packages to Warriors basketball and Sharks hockey). They've all gone through more than one divorce and were obliged to become midlife dating drama veterans. (Marvin and Jeremy are happily remarried. Lonnie thinks he'll recognize Ms. Right if he ever meets her.) They were all born into Jewish families. And they've all made the personal decision that pursuit of a spiritual path or practice is not going to be a part of their lives.

JEREMY

Jeremy's parents didn't attend synagogue or have a regular spiritual practice. "My mother lit a candle here and there," he says. His grandfather was "reasonably Orthodox," but he and Jeremy's father became alienated. That led to alienation between his father and most of the family, and ultimately between his father and the religion.

Although religion didn't play much of a role in his early years, Jeremy recalls an experience which might have been a crossroad. When he was 18, his maternal grandfather died, shortly before the Jewish holiday of Yom Kippur. Jeremy felt a rare spiritual urge. He wanted to connect with his grandfather, honor his passing, engage in a traditional ritual of comfort. He decided to go to temple.

Yom Kippur services often fill synagogues, and many synagogues provide tickets to their regular congregation members to make sure they can get in. Jeremy had no ticket. He was not allowed in.

He decided he didn't need to go back.

When it came time to select a place to call his home, he recalls, "I wanted to be as far away from my family as possible while staying in United States territory." California provided a reasonable fit to this uncomplicated specification.

After unpacking and settling in, he did a California thing and attended consciousness-expanding seminars such as est. They didn't expand his spiritual consciousness, but he found them useful for "opening up and looking at new things."

His skeptical views of organized religion ended up being reinforced by his first wife's path. "She became interested in 'psychic churches,'" he remembered. "She started believing what the charlatans were telling her, and was taken advantage of, financially and mentally, by some Elmer Gantry types. It had tragic consequences for her, for me, for our relationship, and for the kids. The ironic part is that she couldn't put her religious beliefs into practice in her own life. She was cruel to the children."

In what might have been a symbolic act of defiance, many years ago Jeremy sent $10 and a completed form to the post office box of the Universal Life Church. In return, he received a certificate ordaining him as a minister.

The Universal Life Church may itself be an act of defiance. Its founder despised all religion, but "wanted to get away with what the other churches got away with." The Church's theology is straightforward: everyone is free to believe whatever they want to. After substantial legal wrangling, despite its in-your-face contrariness toward what might be viewed as the usual religious perspective, the California courts ratified its right to exist.

Jeremy did not state that he joined the Universal Life Church in a mood of defiance. The attraction for him initially was the ability to obtain discounts on airline tickets, and other such benefits. However, as a Universal Life Church minister, he can legally perform marriages. He has officiated at many, and enjoys it. As a matter of fact, on the day we met for our interview, he had joined a couple in matrimony at 10 o'clock that morning.

(He mentioned that he has an idea for a revenue-generating sideline, combining his ministerial and legal training: divorce representation. He had even given some thought to a slogan: "What Jeremy has joined together, Jeremy can put asunder—for $250 up front plus costs." I *think* he was being facetious.)

Absent inputs from any religious doctrine, Jeremy ascribes his moral and ethical codes mostly to upbringing. "I was brought up in a simpler time," he says. "There were things you knew were right, and those you knew were wrong. I didn't always do right.

Question with boldness even the existence of a God; because, if there be one, he must more approve of the homage of reason, than that of blind-folded fear.

Thomas Jefferson, Letter, 10 Aug. 1787

But I expected to pay the consequences if I got caught, and people took personal responsibility for their actions.

"When people reject a spiritual path, it might not always be the result of a decision. It might just be evolution. But many people probably revisit the issue as life changes occur. I'm open to finding that new experience tomorrow that may cause me to take a new path.

"Some people probably lack any real need for a sense of spirituality. I don't believe in the concept of a soul or an afterlife. But I'm satisfied with my relationship with the universe, and I'm not aware of any reason exploring spirituality would make it better.

"But there's a form of spirituality that doesn't focus on religious practice or a deity. Spirituality has to deal with a contemplation of forces and natures that are beyond our experience. We need to recognize we're relatively insignificant entities in a far grander scheme, and we're lucky to be here for a short period of time. The concept of spirituality is the concept of coping with the unknown."

MARVIN

Unlike Jeremy's family, Marvin's practiced what he refers to as "the trappings of Judaism." Although he didn't regard it as a religious experience, he accompanied them to temple for the holidays. "I did it for family peace, mostly," he recalls. "My father liked to have me around on High Holy days so he'd have someone to play cards with. Our family was kosher, but I suspect it was more cultural than religious.

"I was forced to go to Hebrew school, and felt forced to go to temple when there were other things I wanted to do. It took me two years to get through one year of Hebrew school. I was also forced into piano lessons, and that turned me off to music.

"Our school taught language and customs, but not really religion. And I never felt religious there. Even if one had it, belief would not be reinforced by *that* experience. The temples were orthodox, and it was mostly old men chanting in Hebrew and the scene put me off—then and now.

"There's probably less spiritual life in Silicon Valley than elsewhere, because so many people are physically separated from their family and traditions. But it wouldn't be any different for me even if I were still back in New York."

Marvin's view of spirituality is that, by definition, it has a religious context. "Although that might not be true for Buddhism," he adds, "which is more a way of life than a religion."

Asked about his concept of the soul, Marvin replied, "It's not separate from the body. If soul has meaning, it's the character, the personality, the emotional content of the person."

A substantial part of Marvin's law practice involves representation of people who have tax disputes with the IRS. "I see a certain amount of lying, cheating and stealing," he says. "I don't like it, and I try to be careful around people who do it. It's sometimes an ethical conflict when I have to represent clients who really did what the government says they did.

"You get moral and ethical codes from family, from upbringing, from life experience. Lying is a weakness. You can't contend with a situation, so you have to resort to subterfuge to get by. I don't think people with spiritual beliefs are any more honest or ethical than people who don't have them. The worst are the ones

---

I recalled the remark of William F. Buckley, Jr. in a television interview that if you mention God more than once at New York dinner parties you aren't invited back.

Dan Wakefield, *Returning—A Spiritual Journey*

who wear their religion on their sleeve. You know you can't trust those folks.

"What causes people to reject embarking on a spiritual path? *Common sense*. Healthy skepticism. I think it can work out fine if one partner wants to pursue a religion and one doesn't. There's enough problems with relationships without looking for trouble. It doesn't seem to have the same impact as money, sex, children and in-laws.

"My wife doesn't go to church. How much belief she has, I couldn't begin to tell you. It's not a topic of discussion for us.

"I don't believe in any deity, and if there is one, there's no effect on me. The only circumstance I can think of that might launch me on a spiritual path would be if I saw an angel. Absent that, it's very unlikely. By nature, I'm a skeptical person."

LONNIE

Lonnie recalls listening to Old Testament stories at a Jewish summer camp in Pennsylvania, and finding them interesting and enjoyable. Hebrew school was different. "In those days," he recalls, "the biggest problem was that they taught rote memorization, not spiritual concepts. I was happy I was on the streets playing ball while other guys were spending seven years in Hebrew school."

Lonnie's father was religious, "... but he never pushed it on anyone. You wouldn't know." His mother did not practice the religion much.

Early in life he encountered a philosophically baffling circumstance: "Where I grew up, the Jews were noticeably less religious than people of other faiths. But the people of other faiths committed crimes, and their daughters got pregnant, and the Jews did neither. I was perplexed how the crimes and pregnancies played with those people's religion."

Lonnie observes that religion is not as important in Silicon Valley as it seemed in New York. "Is it the area or the age?" he wonders. "Can't answer. But people here would rather be skiing, or on the tennis court, or surfing the Net than sitting in a house of worship.

"I had a neighbor who was searching for the right religion all his life. He ended up joining the Divine Light Mission. But after spending a lot of money on it, he quit the Mission, went into therapy, and decided to have a sex-change operation. He never got it, but I saw him in drag once, looking like a tall Hedda Hopper.

"Many times I've asked myself, 'What's for real?' I have a hard time understanding faith. Faith alone is difficult. I'm analytical. I need to see things. I've met people of so many different faiths in the Valley, and if what they all believe is false, it's confusing. I've read a lot. I've gone full circle. And now I'm back at the starting gate.

"I don't have a clear picture of spiritual things—there's a fog out there. It would be great if there's a life after death. I'm waiting for the spirit to tell me. In the meantime, I try to live my life as best I can, and just let the cards fall. If I get a royal flush, I'll win.

"I feel sorry when I do things I shouldn't have, and that's a change from my younger life. I've always seemed to have friends who were attorneys, or found myself hanging out with attorneys, and maybe that's not so good."

If I could make one change in this area's culture to improve spiritual lives and values, it would be to wipe out bad childhood memories so adults could come to religion with a blank, open mind.

Debra, a Valley minister

(Jeremy and Marvin: is the defense ready?)

"Atrocities like the Holocaust make me wonder, 'Can the world ever be peaceful?' Most people should be forgiven for what they've done if it was a spur-of-the-moment thing, like a bar fight. As long as it wasn't an intentional atrocity.

"A woman I was dating wanted to get into Judaism, and we started going to a temple to take classes. But she wanted to get seriously into the practice, and go through the Friday night candle-lighting ritual, and I just wasn't into that. When I told her that, she made a good point. She said, 'I can't be an ethnic Jew, I can only be a practicing Jew.'

"If something is going to happen to us when we leave this world, it has to be through the soul. It's the essence, the spirit. The soul might go into another physical body, but I have a hard time understanding that. If God exists, no matter what religion you are, there has to be a soul. We're measured by good and bad.

"When striving for success, one usually steps on others and blots someone out. Maybe some haven't. But when it comes to making money, the average businessman will do whatever it takes. My beliefs have probably changed for the better since I was a kid growing up in Brooklyn. Now I'm always up front, always disclose everything. I enjoy getting people into homes they'll like. I point out the negatives because it's the ethical and moral thing to do.

"My father was a bookie, but he was well trusted and well liked anyway. My mother came across as more ethical, but probably had more larceny in her heart. She would probably have been more likely to keep an unearned windfall. New York City was dog-eat-dog. Everyone was scheming. But I sorted things out. Even in Brooklyn, I never enjoyed hurting people. Winning, yes. Hurting, no.

"Some people use the church as a way of saying 'Look how moral I am,' and some of those are the ones you better make sure you cut the cards with. But some are sincere in their beliefs. The bottom line, if you look at a cross-section, is that people in churches might have higher morals and ethics. But then there's the 'God-father' thing: while the women are in church, the men are out killing.

"I'm hearing more and more that religion is joining racquetball and tennis in declining interest. My guess is there's less spirituality than there used to be.

"Could anything get me on a spiritual path? Maybe if I got a message from 'beyond,' saying 'Lonnie, you've been a good person, and we want you to join the pack.' I believe that as you go through life, it's important to treat others as you would want to be treated, whether or not there's someone up there paying attention. You have to feel good about yourself when you go to sleep at night.

"Sometimes I find myself talking to God. I don't know what God I'm talking to—but I talk to God."

ROD

One of Rod's earliest memories regarding matters of the spirit was noticing that his parents dropped him off and picked him up at the church for Sunday school, but never went in themselves. "Hmmm," he remembers thinking. "What am *I* doing here?"

For a while he thought the answer was that he would "matriculate" from Sunday school to church. Finally he went into church. "It wasn't what I had in mind," he recalls. "I also remember being put off by the passing of the plate; the idea that to be there you had to give money."

Rod hails from Southern California, but he's been in Silicon Valley for over 30 years. His entire career has been in the technology world. He's worked for a peripherals provider, a microwave manufacturer and a mainframe computer vendor. He's fought the good fight as a member of management teams in materials, manufacturing and engineering. His bachelor's degree is in engineering. He has an MBA. Recognizing that in the world he's chosen you can't sit still for a moment, he's pursuing another master's degree—this one in computer science—through an evening program.

During his MBA program, Rod took courses which gave him an opportunity to do some serious noodling about the meaning of life. These included "Philosophy of Religion," "Philosophy and Personal Values," and study about "Man and His Gods." He enjoyed the exploration. But it did not end up leading him down a path.

When young love struck, Rod's fiancée wanted to get married in a Protestant church which required nuptial participants to be baptized. He had no problem with that, and went through the appropriate procedures. After the marriage, it turned out neither of them had any interest in continuing the relationship with the church, and the connection lapsed. Eventually, so did the marriage.

Throughout much of his life, Rod recalls being around people who practiced religions. It's made him want to explore, to ask questions. His engineering-oriented mind doesn't like blank areas: "I don't know, so I need to find out."

But exploration failed to uncover anything he felt would lead him to ultimate truth. "It always got to the point where it took a leap of faith," he says. "Maybe I'm too independent. Maybe I'm too technical. Maybe I'm just too stubborn. But I just couldn't make that leap of faith."

Death is an area Rod has thought about a lot. Not brooding, morbid thought. Philosophical thought. Perhaps an engineer's thought. "What has happened?" he wants to know. Has the person assumed a spiritual form? When his father died of cancer, he remembers looking at the body in the coffin and puzzling, "His body is here; where is his essence?"

During the final days of his father's illness, Rod was deeply touched by the way one of the nurses in the hospice helped his father. He was clearly in pain, and approaching the end. "She kept saying, 'It's OK, you can let go,' over and over, and finally he did. Maybe he made that leap of faith.

"But if I believe in these things, how do I test them? Are there answers or directions, or is it all fluff?"

Part of Rod's thinking about death, and the concept of soul, relates to his awareness of humans as energy producers and containers. He thinks there's a possibility that we contain energy that's separate from mind and body, that can be talked to and heard. Maybe that's soul.

If it is, everyone has one, Rod believes, and not just those who have had some form of spiritual awakening. "On a judgment basis, we may not like the form some people's souls have taken," he says, "but they have one.

"If I had to guess about life after death I'd say no, but maybe we get hung up on the terms. Does it mean we exist with no bodies? Is there a North Pole/South Pole electromagnetic implementation?"

Spirituality involves gratitude, and disbelief is the greatest form of ingratitude.

Kamal, a Valley software engineer

A recent movie named *Powder* told the story of a bald, albino mutant with the power to mentally control electromagnetic force. He was shy and sensitive, as most of us might be if we were bald, albino mutants. He was, of course, rejected and attacked by most of the people in his town. A line from this movie struck Rod and stayed with him: *Hopefully, some day our humanity will catch up with our technology.*

Rod traces the development of his moral and ethical codes to his parents and his study of existentialism in college. He believes *strongly* in the precept that individuals have sole responsibility for themselves and their actions. He tries hard to stay true to his codes, but understands the conflicts. "In philosophy," he says, "you wrestle with 'is mankind good or evil?' and it's both. We're born with both.

"It seems you can't treat people directly, honestly and openly and still move forward professionally. You have to make sacrifices, tradeoffs. Do I stay consistent with my beliefs, or do I do what advances my career and salary, and argue that I'm doing it to take care of my family? We all face that, and maybe the only person who always stays with their beliefs is Mother Teresa."

Having to lay off several people in his group presented a tough conflict to his ethical values. "But sometimes you can't avoid it. I was honest with them. I gave them a chance to share their feelings of rejection, and their pain, and their concerns for their future. Then I went home that night and cried."

Rod believes that those who adhere to a religious practice may have somewhat different moral and ethical codes from those who don't, because of their commitment to doctrines. He has a

---

I pray, even for the people I want to see fired, who should be fired, and who are going to be fired.

Celeste, a Silicon Valley attorney

serious beef with doctrines that teach that only *their* believers go to heaven. "What about believers in other religions?" he asks. "What about those who live good and upstanding lives? Not that I believe in heaven, but when someone says good people aren't going to heaven because they don't have the right belief, I think that's revolting.

"People may not have religious or spiritual beliefs, but that doesn't mean they might not at some time in the future. Humans are thinking beings. They don't take areas and set them aside and say, 'I never need to think about this again.' Particularly not in Silicon Valley. This is a thinking area.

"But some people might turn to religion for the wrong reason. They may get 'born again' because they've hit a crisis point, or an event where they feel inadequate or incapable, and they embrace a religion, unquestioningly, more from needing something than from true belief. But then they might hit some part of the doctrine they just can't accept, and leave again.

"Let me tell you what's really in my heart about this. I think some people embrace religion because everyone wants to experience a true love, and many don't get the chance to experience that in a relationship. I've been fortunate to have the experience, the opportunity, the ability to truly love another person for what they are. Every human wants that. But if they don't get it, they might find that tug takes the form of a religious or spiritual call.

"Technology is making people more isolated in Silicon Valley, and that might mean spiritual involvement will become greater. People might *need* to get together once a week to do some real touching and community and friends, and church might be where that happens.

"Religion on the Internet is an area of potential impact. It allows those who don't need that gathering to pursue their religious path without leaving their keyboard. But that might be the spiritual equivalent of just watching pornography: if you don't get real sex for too long, you may become very disturbed.

"I can see every opportunity for something to happen that would affect me emotionally and cause me to consider a spiritual path. I'm not so independent and strong that I feel I could never need something or someone to help me through my troubles, or deficiencies, or needs. But given that my life stays on a stable emotional base, I don't see any need to start on such a path."

WHAT WENT WRONG?

Roland, a Silicon Valley pastor, has been very affected by the experience of one of his parishioners. He believes the situation reflects the vulnerability of spiritual paths to failure and disappointment.

"Dale has always succeeded and done better than others around him," Roland recounted. "He had a 20-year track record of executive success. He became CEO of his company. He had *never* failed.

"But this is Silicon Valley, and things change. The company started to stumble. The board of directors decided Dale just didn't have the ability to move the company forward anymore. They voted to take him out. The unthinkable happened. He got a pink slip.

"His professional crisis caused a spiritual crisis. He couldn't accept the situation. He kept asking, 'God, what's this about? What's happening? I've been a God-honoring man. What do You want?'

"He managed to persuade the board to give him a six-month extension on the job: a trial period, to let him demonstrate he

---

When I was growing up, I had no idea what the men in our church did for a living. I just looked up to them as spiritual leaders. Now it bothers me if someone wants to know what I do for a living before they've figured out if what I have to say is worthwhile.

Trent, president of a Valley telecommunications company

could deliver what the company needed. At the end of six months they did the evaluation. It was unanimous: no, he hadn't done what they wanted. He should leave.

"He resigned, feeling abused and taken advantage of. Seventeen months later he's still unemployed. He doesn't necessarily blame God. But he has a feeling that God fell short of his expectations. He can't believe God allowed this to happen. So he's moved off his path, and is floundering in his faith. He has formally left the church."

Roland and I also discussed a more secular, less spiritual dynamic that can plague a high achiever in situations like these. For years, Dale greeted his fellow parishioners as a successful and powerful executive. It's possible that without that standing, his identity became subject to inner doubt. Image is big in the Valley. Perhaps he no longer knew how to present himself, or how his greetings would be received.

A fact of the human psyche: people can get caught up in excruciating concerns over issues that are nonexistent outside themselves. Those concerns may have caused Dale to leave his community just when he needed it most, and when it might have been able to show him its best colors. People there might never have known or cared that he was a successful executive.

For engineers, scientific or executive types, losing responsibility in their jobs is an existential crisis. They don't know who they are because they can no longer lead. They feel lost. And often they don't turn to their mates for solace, because they don't think their mates will understand.

Rochelle, CEO of a Valley counseling group

KEN

On an early summer evening, Ken and I relaxed on the patio. Warm-weather fragrances abounded, led by the gardenias my wife tenaciously nursed back to health from a freeze-induced, near-death experience a few years ago. The 6 o'clock sun slanted through laurels and pines to glint brightly off half the pool; the other half serenely captured the reflection of the trees on the shady side.

Ken came by after his work day as telecommunications manager for a computer networking company. He's a Northern California native, and has lived in Silicon Valley for 14 years. I had invited him over to talk about the reasons he's decided not to pursue a spiritual practice.

We started with a little history. His parents had introduced him to their religion, but left the decision whether or not to pursue it to him. He knew what he wanted to do by his early teens. "I bailed," he recalls.

Since bailing, he has not felt the urge to go back. I asked him to reflect on his accumulated impressions of spiritual matters, and his current philosophical perspective.

"I don't feel that I'm missing anything," he began. "For one thing, our local, fast-paced lifestyle seems more geared to consumerism and materialism. It doesn't make it easy to find time for spiritual exploration, even if one were so inclined.

"For another thing, so much spiritual stuff seems hokey: something else for people to blame instead of taking responsibility for themselves. For a while I saw a therapist to work on a problem I'm dealing with. When she started talking about a 'higher power,' I got really turned off. I thought it was a cop-out. I know I have the ability to deal with the problem, and the idea that I required a higher power to do so seemed like flaming BS.

"I'm actually an agnostic, not an atheist. Agnostics believe 'something' may have created the earth and the universe, but don't know what that something was. But believing that something had a hand in getting things started doesn't mean it is something I would worship.

"I could be convinced that such a thing as a soul exists while a person lives. But as something that continues in an 'afterlife,' I don't believe it for a moment. If the soul is what helps you make decisions and function as a person, then maybe it's there. I do have a hard time believing that all we are is electrical impulses and synapses firing.

"My moral and ethical codes come from my parents, from home-town values, and from having a great circle of friends while I was in school. We knew what was right and wrong. My ethics and morals are probably very similar to those who have spiritual lives. Much of it comes from common sense. I don't need spiritual beliefs to do right things.

"Many things can turn people off to religion. Bad, early experiences. No results from prayer. No time. Achieving success and getting to a good place in life without having had a relationship with a higher power.

"My wife is Catholic and has strong beliefs. This issue could become hard. It's something we'll probably have to address. We weren't married in the Catholic Church. I'd be willing to formalize the marriage in a Catholic ceremony, but I would not be willing to become a practicing Catholic.

"It can actually be interesting having one partner who has faith and one who doesn't. There are more important things in a relationship than views on faith. Communion is both fascinating and silly. Not in a million years could I truly believe that. But I'm willing to love my neighbor without a church telling me to.

"The race in Silicon Valley keeps getting more and more accelerated. I don't know if there's a practical limit to the stress people can take. But we're creating a lot of stressed-out individuals who are keeping it together because they have to, and they're cruising for a breakdown. Many may come to a point where they need to stop and ask where they're going, and why. They may be candidates for developing or rediscovering faith. I suspect that folks who live the good Silicon Valley life will someday come to a point where they say, 'What did I do all this for?' and want to give something back, and develop their insides as well as their outsides.

"I don't think anything would vault me onto a spiritual path, but maybe it's not that black and white. There are certain things I could never believe, such as Christ being the son of God, or maybe even that there is a God. But there are some things I need to change about myself, and I don't seem to be able to make those changes. I won't reject any discoveries I make, and that might take me down any road. I have some end results I want to accomplish. I don't know that I could put a hundred percent into any faith, but if some aspect of spirituality could help me get to my objectives, I'd consider it."

In *Roads Home—Seven Pathways to Midlife Wisdom*, Kathryn Cramer discusses "Midlife Readiness Signals for Spiritual Serenity." These include increased reflection time; consciousness of world problems; confronting the prospect of death; seeking a more satisfying philosophy; and yearning for more solitude and silence.

There's an intuitive sensibility here. Spirituality and serenity are different concepts. They can and do exist independently. But it does not require a boundless leap of imagination to picture them getting into an individual's psyche at about the same time, and finding they have a lot to talk about. Nor is it difficult to see the signals Cramer mentions emanating from many overly challenged Valley residents.

The "I've-said-no-but-I'm-open" group will stride in a different direction from the "I've-said-no-and-I-can't-conceive-of-that-changing" crowd. But the stage may be set for Silicon Valley to produce a plethora of ultimately iconoclastic new path-walkers, blazing intriguing trails and asking provocative questions.

Here are some comments nonclergy interviewees offered regarding relationships with yes/no splits on spirituality:

Pretty uniformly, the marriage will break down. With most couples it's not likely that both parties will be on the same path with the same intensity at the same time. But where one has strong spirituality and the other has none, or purely a social involvement, the marriage dies even if they stay together for economic reasons.

It can be resolved, but it's difficult. At one point I was dating a man who didn't share my beliefs, and it was always in the back of my mind. How do you address that when it's so much a part of you? Spirituality is not just the structure of religion, so maybe it can be dealt with in the realm of spirituality instead of religion.

If my husband doesn't share my spiritual life, that's between him and his God and not for me to judge, although it's very slippery for me not to judge what someone else does—particularly him. I wouldn't like it if he finally declared for no faith. It would make me sad. It would be crumbs when he could have a banquet.

My husband has a belief in God, and some spiritual life, but not on a daily focus basis. It's not something he wrestles with. We're very different, but he's very content with who he is. It would be precarious for me to judge him. That's God's job. If you have a strong spiritual life, you need to marry someone who also has one. Sometimes I think that maybe my husband wouldn't have been God's first choice for me, but he was brought into my life for some reason.

It's very common for women to be in church alone, with their husbands not sharing their beliefs. These women pray for their husbands and want the relationship to work. One of the reasons I like my current church is there's a lot of men there. The main word where one doesn't share the other's spiritual life is lonely.

I know two such instances and they both work OK. I think the issue is mostly one of personal dynamics.

The situation often brings tension. It's sad that their souls can't share.

There might be tension, but it can become a creative influence and a source of good.

My spiritual life is more important to me than my boyfriend's is to him. But he flies a small airplane, and I believe his spirituality happens in the plane. He feels it's magical and wonderful to be up in the sky, even though he's a scientist and knows exactly how a plane works. When he flies over the desert at night and sees just a few lights, he might not admit it, but it sounds to me like he's having a spiritual experience.

Sometimes a spiritual life helps women accept their partner even if he's a lyin', cheatin', drinkin', no-work guy. God bless 'em if it helps 'em get through the day. I myself wouldn't want to go through life plagued with misfits and miscreants.

It usually works OK. But it would be so nice not to have a "silent zone" between us.

Sometimes people are just in different phases of what will eventually be the same journey.

It's a struggle. Women are usually more spiritual, maybe because we men tend to be more competitive. Often men are more involved with work and women more involved with family and relationships, including the relationship with God.

Following are some responses to the same question from clergy and spiritual professionals:

If spirituality is not shared, for the friendship or marriage to work each must be mutually supportive. Both must be aware of the common good, and in supporting someone, you're being spiritual.

If one believes and one's an atheist, a basic disrespect is likely to creep in and hurt the marriage. It could probably work with an agnostic rather than an atheist, though.

What doesn't work is trying to drag someone kicking and screaming to something they don't want. If one partner manifests good stuff, the other partner may be attracted to it.

It's helpful if the spouse who doesn't have a spiritual life is at least respectful of the one who does, and doesn't deride their faith. The believing spouse should feel free to pursue the journey without feeling the need to convert the nonbeliever. Theology is important here. It doesn't work too well if you believe your spouse is going to roast in hell forever.

It can confuse the kids and be an area of constant disagreement, but if the relationship is strong it can work. Sometimes the believer has church mail sent to the office instead of home. Faith is close to the heart, and to deal it out is a huge challenge. This is a gender-equal phenomenon.

It can be delicate, but I've never seen it cause a divorce. It's actually rare when a couple shares precisely the same path.

In general, *religious differences are irreconcilable, but it can work if both people have great maturity.*

It's not a balanced, harmonic situation. The seeker gravitates to other seekers, and the nonseeker says "uh-oh."

The "different faith" scenario is easier than the "faith/no faith" scenario.

It drives the spiritual spouse crazy, because they're going someplace that their chosen mate is not.

The believers pray that some day the nonbelievers will believe.

If spiritual spouses believe they have a responsibility to convert nonspiritual spouses, the tension falls on the nonspiritual ones because they're the focus of an effort. If spiritual spouses keep it inside and hope conversion just happens, perhaps because they're setting a good example, the tension falls on them.

Worked fine for my folks. They agreed the children would be raised Catholic, and my father said, "Just don't bug me about going to Mass."

CHAPTER TEN

✥

The Path Forward

Legends of prediction are common throughout the whole Household of Man. Gods speak, spirits speak, computers speak. Oracular ambiguity or statistical probability provides loopholes, and discrepancies are expunged by Faith.

Ursula K. LeGuin, *The Left Hand of Darkness*

It is possible to believe that all the past is but the beginning of a beginning, and that all that is and has been is but the twilight of the dawn. It is possible to believe that all the human mind has ever accomplished is but the dream before the awakening.

H. G. Wells, *The Discovery of the Future,* lecture,
24 Jan. 1902, at the Royal Institute, London
(published in *Nature,* no. 65, 1902)

vi·sion quest (*n.*). A period of spiritual seeking among
certain Native American peoples, often undertaken as a
puberty rite, that typically involves isolation, fasting,
and the inducement of a trance state for the purpose of
attaining guidance or knowledge from supernatural
forces

American Heritage Dictionary, Third Edition

A frequent event on Silicon Valley calendars is the
offsite planning meeting. This function is by no means unique to
the Valley. What is unusual here is the frequency with which these
meetings are held, and the comprehensiveness of the list of participants.

The purpose of going offsite is to get people out of the daily
operating environment, clear their input buffers, free up memory
and processing cycles, and invite creative thought about the
company's destiny. Strategic issues may be dealt with in depth, and
new directions charted. Agendas for these events often indicate a
time slot for a company "vision quest." Former president George
Bush inelegantly referred to "the vision thing," but people knew
roughly what he meant.

Many Valley workers might say that trance states and hope
for guidance from supernatural forces sound like business as usual
to them. It isn't easy to coax glimpses of what's around the next
corner from a universe whose physical laws seem hostile to even
the most modest time travel. The smart mind stays open to anything that might work, no matter how unorthodox, because prog-
nostication needs all the help it can get.

The questions on the table for this concluding chapter are:
Where is the Valley going, spiritually speaking? Where do people
see their individual paths leading them? And if spiritual leaders

could wave their magic wands and evoke changes in the area's culture to improve spiritual life and values, what changes would they bring?

"Two Roads Diverged in a Wood ..."

As with most matters of opinion, interviewees' projections of the Valley's spiritual direction and destiny range across a wide spectrum. At one end are those who believe the Valley is headed for a spiritual renaissance. Borrowing from the Crimestoppers' 1A textbook, they perceive the basics of motive, method and opportunity:

❖ **Motive**. People are becoming aware of the missing pieces in their lives. Pursuit of affluence isn't filling their inner tanks, even when the hunt is successful and the affluence is captured. Technological mastery is an infinite loop of short-term illusion, because the technology mutates, divides, recombines, and grows into shocking new forms. The fight to conquer it must be re-booted, re-run, and re-won, without end. Time demands, stressful conditions, and drums constantly pounding out a ramming-speed pace are grinding people down, and creating space which needs to be filled with true values, true meaning.

❖ **Method**. Tried-and-true methods of spiritual pursuit are morphing into new forms. Limitations are crumbling. New methodology, new pathways, and custom-tailored approaches

---

I'd reduce the power of money, put a limit on CEO salaries, give every citizen a right to shelter and health care, reduce the impact of superficial material things, and make humans our number one value.

Helene, a Valley minister

to spiritual life are available in abundance. Even among the old established religions, energy is being allocated to understanding what is needed, what will appeal, and how to provide it. Valley culture features a high level of acceptance of individuality, and a low level of requirement for conformance to tradition.

❖ **Opportunity.** The diversity of spiritual offerings, belief, and leadership in the area is remarkable, particularly considering that the Valley is not really a big-city urban setting. A cornucopia of opportunities for exploration can be identified by a few moments' intimate contemplation of the *Yellow Pages*. Assuming you don't go during commute hours, you can be in the right spot to pursue virtually any spiritual path you ever heard of, and plenty you never heard of, in 20 minutes.

At the other end of the spectrum are those who anticipate a *decline* in the role of spirituality in Valley lives. In most cases, people with this perspective see the decline as continuing a trend which is already well launched. Factors cited by these people include:

❖ **Economic theory.** Those who stayed awake during their college microeconomics courses may recall a concept called "local nonsatiation." Basically, this says that consumers can't get enough: there is no point at which the demand function for goods and services flattens out. Many people see the Valley culture driven by that concept. They believe that materialism here, if not all-consuming, is close enough to declare it a religion in its own right. In this view, material pursuit will not only preclude growth in spirituality, it will continuously drive out some which already exists.

❖ **Generation X and Generation Y.** In reviewing the chronological pattern of their own lives, many of the people interviewed recalled a gap in their spiritual development. It often started in their teens and ran through thirtysomething. The nature of the gap ranged from lack of interest to active hostility. It may be endemic to young adulthood.

Technology is a youth magnet. Over the past few years, corporations throughout the country have been increasingly precarious places for older workers. But that's not news here. The Valley has always had a youthful corporate orientation. New graduates with degrees in computer science will be slavered over and fought for with increasing ferocity. More people in their 20s and early 30s will arrive (assuming they can find someplace to live). And ready or not, here they come: there's even a teenage CEO or two on the scene. These young hard-chargers will be interested in their careers, not spiritual matters.

It's true that many religious institutions in the area are acutely aware of the graying of their congregations and their failure to broadly appeal to younger adults, and they are working on the problem. But many people feel this issue won't be easy to address. They are concerned that youthful Valley trendsetters will not be attracted to spiritual paths.

❖ **Inherent rational secularism.** In the perennial tension between search for truth via science/technology and search for

> *There won't be any change in spirituality in the Valley unless an earthquake or two comes along. And even then, the change will be temporary.*
>
> Chuck, president of a computer printer accessories manufacturing firm

truth via spirituality/religion, this area's vote is hard-coded for the former. In addition to this regional predilection, there's an edge of derision toward faith followers that will discourage many people on the fence from climbing down on the spiritual side.

❖ **Time.** No one has any, and that will never change.

Quo Vadis?

Between these two extremes, interviewees saw possibilities containing elements of both visions. Celeste, a partner in a large law firm, doesn't think youth and technology are knockout blows to spiritual growth in the area. "This place is full of young, scientifically oriented people," she says, "and I think they'll have a growing spiritual awareness. Eventually it may awaken into a full hunger. Lots of spin-off interest in education and the arts in this area is a ripple effect from the technology business. This is an amazing, high-energy environment, and it may someday turn its attention to spirituality."

Stacy, the software company field marketing director, sees a similar possibility. "A lot of people talk about balance, although not many do anything about it," she says. "But there's tremendous breadth: all kinds of people trying all kinds of things. That won't change. It'll always be part of the Silicon Valley culture. We're explorers and seekers."

Many mentioned a possible change on the horizon: spirituality coming out of the closet and becoming more open and shared. Maturity and security play a role in this trend. Melinda, the therapist, thinks increased maturity yields spiritual benefits even if it's a drawback in the Valley's youth-happy professional world. "People are embarrassed to talk about their spiritual lives," she observes, "partly because they're out of balance. But one day they get jolted by a message: 'you're obsolete; if you're over 35, you're not young anymore; get out.' Maybe that gives them the chance to let something else in. I'm over 35, and my spiritual life is better than ever."

Melinda joined many of the women interviewed in expressing a desire to see the role of women in religion changed and enhanced. "I like Mary as an image in Catholicism," she says, "and I would like to see more femininity, more 'Mary' in spiritual approaches. Computers are masculine. I'd like to see inclusive, rather than exclusive, cooperative rather than competing. I hope the Valley triggers the beginning of a worldwide spiritual revolution."

Kamal, the software company curriculum developer, believes there will be strong growth in Islam in the Valley. "But it's not likely to be the people with the high standard of living," he says. "They're too caught up in their mansions and racing boats. Most converts will come from women, youth, African-Americans and Hispanics. The intelligent and the poor will enter Islam. And we'll need more Islamic educational structure to support them."

This observation touches on an important point. A key variable for the Valley is how the extraordinary increase in diversity plays out. No one doubts that the area's attractiveness and tolerance will cause it to continue as one of the most culturally and

---

I would like to say we'll see better understanding among people, but knowing people, we probably won't. The different cultures and different spiritual beliefs have the potential of leading to conflict. I hope understanding prevails. There's a trend toward smaller, less-organized churches, and an overall trend toward smaller spiritual groups. This is partly due to schism prevailing over reconciliation— a sad fact of human nature. I think we'll have a resurgence in secular humanism.

Eric, a Valley software company documentation manager

spiritually diverse locales in the world. This can happen in an atmosphere of separation or unity. Regarding matters of spirit, some think we're right on the cusp.

Stan, the technology consultant, doesn't think churches are responding well to the challenges of either youth or multiculturalism. "The group coming up now wants to be entertained," he observes. "They want multimedia approaches to functions and worship. On the other hand, I don't want to see established institutions chasing trends and abandoning tradition." He has put his finger squarely on the troubling paradox with which those institutions are wrestling: please some and you'll displease others. Or, perhaps the question is whether religious institutions should be *pleasing* people at all. Maybe that's not their mission.

Stella thinks it's possible that the area's extraordinary material affluence could blend into spiritual pursuits. She's senior public relations manager for a company which correctly read network architecture and Internet growth directions. From a standing start in the '80s, the company blew by the several billion dollar sales mark in the '90s, and made it look easy. No one knows for sure how many newly made "stock option millionaires" roam its corridors. But there's a bunch.

I'd bet that Bill Hewlett and David Packard had strong spiritual lives. I would not make that guess about many of today's CEOs. We seem to be in the age of "soulless technocrats," and I'm not sure there's a spiritual renaissance waiting around the corner. But people are unhappy with the decision to define their success by the titles they hold and the money they make. They're concerned about the fact that kids develop sex lives before spiritual lives. There's yearning, and there's a lot of individual searching going on.

Stuart, corporate general counsel for
a Valley electronics company

"I look around the parking lot at work and I see $90,000 cars all over the place, and they don't all belong to the executives," she says. "One guy I work with sits in his cubicle and plays the options market. He lost $300K one day, then made $350K the next day. This is the kind of thing that makes me have to go to Idaho periodically and water my roots.

"But these young professionals often had some spiritual life in their youth, and now they're having children. Some of them seem to want to return to spirituality so their children will have it."

KATE

Kate counts herself among those who do not believe spiritual life in the Valley is on a roll. That hasn't stopped her from motoring briskly along on her own journey, however.

For 17 years, Kate worked for one of the Valley's largest defense electronics contractors, ending up as manager of a proposal group. The money was excellent. "But it wasn't conducive to a harmonious life," she recalls.

She focused on figuring out what else she'd like to do. Her program included a midcareer assessment workshop and an unpaid leave of absence to read, think, and cast about for meaningful work.

She found it. She's now the office administrator for a medium-sized Protestant church, making less than half her former salary. This experience has provided her with a fine study in contrast.

"My sense is that Silicon Valley is one of the strongest areas for exploring spirituality, but one of the worst areas for organized religions," she observes. "Alternatives are so abundant. Some people explore, but never find satisfaction. They talk about spirituality, but at a very naïve level. They're looking for something. They don't know what, but they know it's not organized religion.

"One of the most interesting aspects of this job has been dealing with the variety of people. The county inspector who comes out to inspect the church kitchen is a Muslim. I enjoy conversations with him where we swap ideas about our different beliefs. Lots of people call the church, and ask what we stand for and what we believe in. I've had ashes spend the day with me in the office before going to the columbarium.

"I was probably making too much money before. I could go anywhere I wanted, do everything I wanted. But it closed me off spiritually. It was too easy to write large checks to the church, but not do anything else. Now, the problem is at the other extreme. I'm barely making a living wage, and I've had to ask, 'Does God want me to lose my house? Is that where this is going?'

"But I can't forget the philosophical and spiritual tension I had when I was working in the defense business. I kept asking myself, 'Why are we putting billions into military hardware when people are dying from hunger and need our help?'

"When I left the company people told me privately they really admired what I was doing, but they would have too much fear of losing what they had attained to do it themselves.

"I hate to sound dismal, but I have bad vibes about where spiritual life is going in this area. I've been here 17 years, and most of the problems seem to have gotten worse. More and more, people

---

One of the most pronounced trends is the growth of experiential *religion. People want to emphasize meaningful personal experience in their spirituality, not just doctrinal understanding.*

Jesse, a Bay Area journalist

are getting sucked into the 'work is life, and there is no life outside of work' syndrome.

"I've reached a plateau. I'm not growing spiritually right now. But my spiritual life is really going to take off in the next few years. I'll have more time for meditating, for reading, for quiet. I might even sponge off my boyfriend for a while, and without all the distractions, I can see my spirituality getting deeper and richer."

GROWING SMALL

A trend which may have great impact is the movement to small groups for exploring and sharing spirituality. Many people are finding that small groups are much more open and inviting to individual needs, beliefs and search methods than larger groups tied to institutions. Small groups doing their own thing plays very well with Valley startup culture. We might see lots of them.

Marie, the former telecom marketing analyst, notices another benefit in small groups: people learn to talk about spirituality without getting "churchy," a style that can quickly turn people off.

Marty, the minister-turned-car-salesman, says, "The red meat of Valley spirituality will come from small groups, and the most successful churches will emphasize and support small group formation.

"Churches must adapt to the way we live. Sunday services are just not for everyone. We must develop an acceptance of people's absences, make sure people don't feel they have to be perfect to be there, and make sure they feel OK showing up whenever they want to. The Bible should be seen and taught as a love letter from God.

"I'd like to establish an informal, accessible urban ministry for everyone. Maybe the right way would be to just set up a table at Starbuck's. Then let everyone in the community know the minister is on duty and available whenever they want to quaff some java and talk about something."

Theresa, the human resources manager, sees the small group dynamic intersecting with the drive for increased community. "I know and meet many people who are becoming small church or community ministers in some way," she notes. "If you ask them what they do, they say, 'I'm a hair stylist during the day, but at night I work with teenage drug addicts.' When layoffs hit the Valley a couple of years ago and dollar contributions went down at United Way, time contributions went way up. People want to feel there's a reason, a purpose, a point to their being alive."

GHOST IN THE MACHINE

A wry thought: how long before we start seeing "Divinity in the Net," or "Spirituality in the Machine?"

> Eric, a Valley software company
> documentation manager

The answer to Eric's wry thought: as a theory, not long at all. At least one projection—a sweeping, staggering vision—closely ties human spiritual destiny to the distant descendants of the very technology being developed in the Valley today. It is a vision of the ultimate, intimate, eternal marriage of soul and silicon.

The vision is that of Dr. Frank Tipler, a physicist at Tulane University, in his book, *The Physics of Immortality—Modern Cosmology, God, and the Resurrection of the Dead.* Tipler's concept is that God, heaven, resurrection and eternal life are provable, demonstrable features of our physical universe. At the moment just before the end of time, everyone who ever lived will be resurrected into eternal life—*as a computer program emulation*. The emulation's operating system will include individually customized implementations of heaven.

Technical types might ask: how can life be eternal if it starts a fraction of a second before the end of time, and then, by definition, ends with the end of time? The answer is that time passage is subjective. Within the computer emulation, it will *seem* to the resurrected souls that they are living never-ending lives. (Technical *and* nontechnical types may not receive this message with joy. When I presented this concept at a recent "Science and Theology" seminar, the people there were absolutely horrified.)

Tipler's chronicle of how the computing power and related technology for this vision will be developed is far beyond the scope of this book, as is most of the associated theology. The time frame involved is a few quintillion years, so don't look for this in the next software release you buy at Fry's. But the striking point is that his eschatological monument, with its God of love and near-universal salvation, constructs a view of resurrection, eternal life, and heaven which seems similar to, and consistent with, that taught by many major religions. They have simply never gotten into the implementation details. Now someone has. The Valley's computer development work may now have to be considered in an entirely new light ...

In the Meantime

Olivia, the Southern transplant, thinks that meditation and spiritual retreat centers may find business booming, particularly for the 40-plus crowd. "With age comes wisdom, and part of wisdom is

> *It's not enough to just offer Sunday morning worship. Those days are gone. Our offerings must be as broad and diverse as the Silicon Valley community. I'd shift our service to Saturday night if it would help.*
>
> Audrey, a Silicon Valley minister

looking back over your life, and then at what's left, and trying to make sense of it. When sex, exercise, food and material things lose their appeal, what's left is the mind (and, presumably, the spirit). There will be a lot of 'what's it all about?' thinking." Who knows, perhaps the hot IPOs of 1999 will include retreat chains for spiritually revived techno-boomers.

Richard, the software company business development vice president, speculated along similar lines. "The '70s were the times of trying new things and changing everything, following the tumultuous '60s," he said. "In the '80s, everyone buckled down to careers and economic endeavors. Nineties people are trying to lead more balanced lives.

"We need more of a community feeling. This Valley has lots of ambivalence about distribution of wealth, but we're skeptical about the ability of government to solve much. We're starting to have doubts about the efficacy of large organizations or institutions.

"We believe in merit, but there's still compassion for the havenots. We believe in enterprise, and performance-based awards. Some people never need help, no matter what; some people always need help, no matter what. And some people, if you can help them a little, it makes a huge difference. I think we're trying to find the Aristotelian 'Golden Mean.'

"We're doing what we can to manage tough tradeoffs in our lives. I hear more spiritual voices around, I see more spiritual books

> *Valley people seeking religious experiences want personal attention, a personal manifestation or revelation, from God. They reject "the Book." They tell me, "You're the minister, the Book is for you."*
>
> Roland, a Valley pastor

in stores. We're starting to ask what's important, and what's going to happen when we die. Spirituality will continue to emerge, but we also know we have to stay competitive. We have to provide for good family life, both economically and otherwise."

Some additional crystal-ball revelations people saw in the Valley's future:

❖ increased spirituality leading affluent Valley residents to do more for the disadvantaged as government downsizes

❖ growing acceptance of unconventional families

❖ increased recognition that spirituality involves a reconnection with nature

❖ an uptick in the influence of non-Western religions

At the personal level, the predominant theme might be summed up as a longing for the luxury of *time* to let spiritual exploration move far up life's priority list. Would enough affluence make this luxury widely available? Would it enable Silicon Valley to be the leader in the American Spiritual Revolution?

CLERGY PONDER THE FUTURE

Jerry, the rabbi of a large synagogue, thinks more people are making spirituality part of what they're looking for. "The question is: is it a fad, or is it lasting?" He also sees a good side to a trend

> *Shopping malls are the temples of our society. That's what people worship. I'd like to turn them all into real temples.*
>
> Jesse, a Bay Area journalist

toward less reverence for established religions. "One of the benefits of pop, idolatrous, pagan religious emergence is that some now feel it's easier to talk about religion."

Regarding the Valley's economic picture, Jerry says, "It's profoundly positive when people take risks and do entrepreneurial adventures. But telecommuting brings feelings of disconnection, which may spur more desire to pursue spirituality, meaning and community."

Justin, the pastor of a medium-sized Protestant church, sees population and consciousness change as the lead stories in the Valley's future. "Overwork will be seen as increasingly nonfulfilling," he projects. "There will be a renewal of what it means to be a parent.

"The biggest change will be in demographics, more than in belief sets. Older people are dying or moving to retirement communities, to be replaced by young families, and we need to find them and find ways to support them."

Michael, the Roman Catholic priest from Ireland by way of Kenya, has been struck by the impact of technology on the spiritual realm. "Everything is happening via e-mail," he says. "Multimedia will be used more and more for getting across the messages. Even our diocese has a Web page.

"I hope the technology will be used to address meaningful questions. For example, is the church fundamentally an institution, or fundamentally a community of believers?

The world would be so much more peaceful if people could integrate a spiritual practice into their workplace, or even their trips to the market. Maybe we have to go farther into the dark night first.

Victor, a Silicon Valley teacher

In discussing the spiritual future of Silicon Valley with clergy of various persuasions, I invited them to add another dimension. Leaving reality aside, if they could make one change in this area's culture to improve spiritual lives and values, what would it be?

Jerry: The change I would make would be that the cultural message the Valley puts out would send people more toward shared responsibility for each other, and less toward individual consumption.

Justin: An appreciation for quality over quantity. A definition of quality that says quality products *help people, they don't just make money. A definition of quality that says* quality people *contribute to the community, they don't just make money.*

Michael: My first thought about the one change I would make was to put up a catchy billboard. I'd like to see the leaders from all the different churches come together for a weekend and say, "We can't do this on our own, why can't we get together?" Maybe we ought to get some sales trainers in to show us how to get the message across, and get some of the big companies to fund the training. We need to show everyone, "We're working with you, not against you."

Erica: If I could make one change in Silicon Valley, everyone would truly take a Sabbath: a day of rest and reflection, a day to look back on the past week, and look forward to the coming week and how they want to shape it. We need to be more reflective on what we do.

Roland: My one change in the area's culture would be for people to be more committed, and more faithful to their commitments. If you make commitments, keep your promises. Too many people today nod commitment, then blow you off. Solid commitments and kept promises would improve spirituality, and honor the Supreme Being's design for us.

Ian: If I could make one change, it would be to create a strongly backed organization to bring all the diverse charitable and spiritual groups into meaningful dialogue and coordinated efforts. Every nonprofit nibbles at people's pockets. There's so many letters soliciting donations.

In my former parish in Taiwan, when it came to pledging, the congregation had no trouble giving everything they could to the church, and letting the church decide how to donate. Americans want to be involved in those decisions, in itemizing the expenditures and donations, and not just give the church carte blanche. Looking at how many solicitations people get, I can understand why. But there's not enough coming together of resources, of coordinating good work. Some really valuable efforts don't get funded, and I'd like to see us have a better way of channeling resources.

Rob: The one thing I would change would be our understanding of time. [Rock musician] Sting has gotten into Buddhism, and meditates two hours a day. He says when he does it, he has time. When he doesn't take the two hours a day, he has no time. We have to break the perception that there's not enough time, that we must always do more, that everything must be faster.

"I see growth in smaller communities of prayer and Scripture study, and I think the teachings will have more meaning in smaller groups. We'll see increased use of specialized retreats for affinity groups: mother-daughter retreats, substance-abuser retreats, businessperson retreats. There seems to be a thirst for God, and maybe more evangelization is in the cards. Cross-pollination and reaching across church boundaries might happen more. We Catholics can learn a lot from, say, the zeal of the Baptists."

Aaron's vision, from his position as rabbi of a small synagogue, echoes the cross-boundary theme. "I'd love to hire 10 more rabbis and disperse them through the area," he says. "But what I really care about is how many people are being served, not where they're being served. I'd like to see Valley spiritual leaders focus less on filling their individual houses of worship, and more on just reaching people. Why do we care where they go, as long as they go?"

Erica, pastor of a small Protestant congregation, sees Christian practice in the area opening up, being more comfortable with the idea that "… there are many pathways to God, and ours is one. Maybe we're starting to understand that God works *through us*, rather than coming down as lightning bolts. There's a sense that the inclusiveness of God's spirit is at work in the land. But there's also a rise in the more fundamentalist churches, because changes

---

We'll come to a point where people will move inward. This may manifest itself through churches, retreats, Heaven's Gate groups, Deep Space Nine groups, Hale-Bopp comet groups, more labyrinth walking, spiritual song and dance, or all of the above. You can't process the overwhelming amount of information and complexity out there. We'll need simple things.

Victor, a Silicon Valley teacher

and new ideas can make people uncomfortable, and sometimes change causes backlash."

Roland, pastor in a large Protestant congregation, has seen significant change in the 12 years he's been in his current job. "When I first started as a minister in this area," he remembered with a chuckle, "and told people what I did for a living, they often said things like, 'My goodness! What about money? What about achievement? What about success?' Even recently, I told a woman at my son's Little League game that I'm a minister and she said, 'Really! They actually pay you for that? I didn't know they did that anymore!'

"But I think spirituality in this area is becoming more accepted, as long as you don't try to force beliefs down anyone's throat. It used to be that when I started to talk about religion to someone I didn't know well, the response was along the lines of 'get out of my face.' Now I'm more likely to hear, 'You have some spiritual beliefs? That's cool.'

"I think the Valley will get more spiritual dimension over the next few years, but a conflict is coming. Some people won't be comfortable with the hang-loose, anything-goes brand of spirituality, and we might have some fundamentalist backlash. But it's easier for me to walk through the community than it used to be."

IAN

Ian was born in Singapore, and began his career as a Protestant minister in Taiwan. He's taken on a role which puts him front and center in an effort to meet the Valley's increasing need for diverse, multicultural spiritual offerings.

Ian moved to the San Francisco Bay Area five years ago, motivated largely by issues relating to his children's upcoming college careers. "In the U.S.," he points out, "higher education makes coaching available: English as a second language, all the help you need. Higher education in Singapore is harsh. They screen. If you don't do well, you're out."

Initially, he tried the "astronaut" approach. His wife and children relocated to the United States, while he continued his ministry in Taiwan, flying over for visits whenever he could: a commute that would make even the most hardened Bay Area freeway trekker blanch. He hung in for two years. His Taiwan parish had made him a "fat offer" to stay. But eventually he got to a point where he couldn't stand the separation. A Bay Area work opportunity arose, and he took it.

Through this period of decision and change, his prayer was, "… for God to tell me that my time in Taiwan was ended; that my mission there was over." I asked him if he had heard that. "More yes than no," he responded, "but there's still some pain."

Ian's new job was to function as "Chinese missioner," working for his church's regional organization. The post was created in recognition of the growing size and importance of the Chinese population in the Bay Area, and the need to have available bilingual, bicultural spiritual support. This was considered to be particularly important for recent immigrants.

In 1993, the head of the church's regional body asked Ian and a parish in the heart of Silicon Valley to partner on a new project: formation of a Mandarin-speaking congregation to be affiliated with the parish. By Silicon Valley standards, this particular church is a time-hallowed institution, over 80 years old. Institutions that

> *I don't find it wrong or offensive that there are spiritual absolutes. In fact, it's appealing.*
>
> Frank, a Valley bank executive

old can get conservative and often have doubts about change. No one was sure how this was going to work.

"I was willing to take it on as an experiment," Ian recalls, "and I don't like experiments to fail." He felt an affinity for the vision of a multicultural congregation. It offered him a chance to creatively address an important issue. "Churches lag society," he observes. "They pick up what society is doing later, and try to make sense out of it. But they don't lead. I felt the church should take a lead position in working toward racial harmony, and be an example to society, a living witness where people come together."

In addition to his Silicon Valley work, Ian is building and ministering to two other Mandarin-speaking congregation-within-congregations in the Bay Area. It has not been an easy task, even excluding the insane number of miles he drives each week. "You have to learn to temper the vision with the realities," he says. (I think that's a call for patience.) "There are many models of churches. In Silicon Valley, we're working to have the two congregations close together. In east Contra Costa County, there's complete separation from the Caucasian congregation. At our third location, I hope we can eventually bring the Mandarin-speaking congregation fully into the parish. Sometimes I feel there's no real understanding between the Caucasian and Chinese constituents, but we're slowly moving and learning together.

"In the '70s and '80s, churches may have been more important to the Chinese community. They were places to find help and identity. It was almost a 'golden age of conversion.'

I'd wipe out all the fundamentalists—Christian, Jewish or Islamic—who say there's only one right way to do it and everyone else is wrong.

Debra, a Valley minister

"But the Chinese community has broadened enormously, and there are many different parts of the community. Terminology which is sometimes used within the community to describe people's background is the '1.0 generation' for those born and raised elsewhere; the '1.5 generation' for those born elsewhere but raised here; and the '2.0' generation for those born and raised here. Each of these groups has its own needs."

We then talked about some of Ian's observations about his bicultural world. "There's a difference in the way Americans and Chinese see spiritual leaders," he pointed out. "If you meet an American and say you're a priest or minister, the image he has is mostly of you, of a person in a particular profession, which just happens to be religion. But to Chinese, the image of a Buddhist or Taoist or Christian priest is truly that of a holy man.

"Chinese Christians tend to not be philosophical about who and what God is. More experiential. Confucianism is a deep humanism, and many Chinese are humanists. So are many Christians, whether they realize it or not. You can be both deeply humanist and deeply spiritual.

"Many Chinese believe in God but not in a religion. In this area, I see the Chinese community turning more toward a religion of the heart than a religion of institution."

I asked him to comment on his community's vision of the human soul. "The Chinese tend to see a dualistic element in the soul," he offered. "It's a continuity of the ego. There's lots of stories in Chinese culture about souls, dreams and spirits. All people

It's not politically correct to be a conservative evangelical in this area, but some evangelicals might like that.

Jesse, a Bay Area journalist

have souls, but Buddhists, for example, believe that enlightened souls go on a different path from the unenlightened.

"The Chinese culture has always been able to be very dichotomous between secular and spiritual issues. Belief in spirits and souls is so ingrained that technology and modern developments don't affect their spiritual beliefs. But the Western mind will reorganize beliefs around new parameters such as technology."

Finally, I asked him where he thought our path was leading us. "As a Christian in Chinese culture," he said, "you always face a test of faith. In the American culture, it's more an exercise in reinterpretation. Silicon Valley will stay very pluralistic because of the diversity of the culture. I don't think the different spiritual traditions and searchers will come together."

ROB

Rob is pastor of one of the most affluent Protestant congregations in the Valley. Something one of his parishioners told him shortly after he joined this church stuck with him: "The gods of this area are excellence, creativity, and connections."

The financial solidity of his church is no illusion. In the last five years, they have raised $3 million for their building fund. (Rob says he has to continually remind himself it's for God's work.) However, a dilemma he sees in Valley culture is what he calls "the illusion of control": if you have enough money, and/or enough power, you're in control of your environment and destiny. A very Valley perspective. "It's smoke," he says. "And those very things

> If every church would adopt and find ways to support an at-risk school, we would change the future.
>
> Pat, a Valley pastor

are what can push you away from your community. But it can be seductive to be among the movers and shakers.

"One of my parishioners just sold his company, and he's gonna be rich. He's 38. He wants counseling on how to be responsible with his wealth. That's refreshing. The usual response to this situation is a new house and a new Ferrari. After an IPO, another one of our locals bought three new cars.

"But despite the distractions of money, the Silicon Valley world view of cooperation, visioning, and comfort with change could end up making us world leaders in spirituality. People here do have reverence and a sense of mystery, although it's usually the mystery of designing complex products. People here also have energy and passion!

"I'd like our church to be a spiritual resource for all of Silicon Valley. A safe place where people can be listened to, not judged. Where mystery is seen as reality. There's the potential for a new wave of spirituality throughout the country, and it just might start right here. I'd like to be a part of that."

A new wave of spirituality.

If it comes, its package might include entrepreneurial creativity; cross-cultural perspective; willingness to take risks; and new models of personal involvement. Fatima's journey seems destined to include all these elements.

FATIMA

Fatima has come full circle. She left her spiritual path—forcefully. Now she's back on it—forcefully.

Born in Egypt, her parents moved to the United States when she was 7. "My father was a pro-Western, anti-Socialist psychiatrist," she recalls, "and very critical of [then-Egyptian ruler] Nasser. We were 'escorted' out of the country."

Fatima's Turkish grandmother was a devout Muslim, but her parents practiced no religion. She attended a Catholic girls' school in Egypt. After moving to America, she became increasingly conscious of restrictions on women in her culture.

"I couldn't drink, couldn't make dates, couldn't stay out late," she says. "My mother interpreted Islam and the Koran in a very dogmatic way. I ran away from being Egyptian, being Arab, being Muslim. I married an Episcopalian who converted to Islam, and my family rejected him. I remember him saying, 'If this is the God you're worshipping, it's not the God I want to worship. Not if He separates people in love just because they're not born into the same culture.'

"I defied Islam. I ate pork and clam chowder, and drank alcohol. My parents disinherited me. My marriage didn't last."

In contrast to the tumult in her spiritual and personal life, Fatima's professional life was a fast track. She got a job as a sales clerk, worked her way up to store manager, jump-shifted to insurance industry marketing analyst, then became a manager with an equity interest in a small telecommunications firm. "I was materially successful, but I felt a vacuum," she recalls. "I woke up to the fact that there was no God in me. That feeling grew for three years. I got scared."

If I could make one change, everyone would work eight minutes from their house.

Sam, a Valley pastor

She was also troubled by what she saw at her company. "Each executive had his own territory and succeeded at the expense of someone else. For someone to win, someone had to lose. I saw corruption. I saw sexual harassment. The higher up you go the more you have to satisfy your boss, and the less personal power you really have. I was losing my spirit—becoming a robot.

"I remember going into the lunchroom one day, and everyone there looked dead. The life had been sucked out of them.

"I started reading a lot of spiritual stuff: New Age, the Bible, the Koran, the Torah. I went to synagogue. I went to Catholic church. But I felt a separation between the clergy and the people. It was as if God was the clergy's, not ours. We were an audience, just observing. I couldn't feel a connection with God."

Then she completed her circle. "As I read the Koran, I started to feel it was tying everything together. God was talking to me directly. It was reflecting my heart. It also affirmed my views about the need to fight corruption and lack of justice in society. I could relate to the trials of the prophets.

"One day I woke up and started crying. I cried for half the day. Then I prayed for the other half. Then I decided to start doing volunteer work in the Islamic community.

"All my friends at the time were practicing Jews and Christians. I was totally corporate. I never wore the traditional Muslim garb. I had some savings. I did volunteer work, and lived on my savings, and had a blast. I got to see how many subcultures we have here in America. Just in this area, there are about 35 Islamic centers, each with its own function and character. I decided to take my corporate skills and apply them to supporting this community."

Fatima was instrumental in founding an organization which has become a focal point for Valley Muslims. Her group provides organization, coordination and communication tools for the

Islamic community. She is a spokesperson and an activist. "I used to make a $100,000 a year," she says. "Now I make $7,000. I don't buy clothes anymore. But I have found God."

The God she has found is a companion: always present. Although she uses the pronoun "Him" when she thinks of God, she points out that in Islam, God is not male, but genderless.

Fatima's path forward is heavily influenced by what attracted her when she finished her circle and revisited the Koran: justice; clearly defined right and wrong; the forbidding of evil; and the need to fight against evil. She has dealt herself completely into the fray. "You have to have the community to practice Islam," she says. "There are too many temptations to be able to fight them alone.

"When I was in the corporate world my idea of success was being smarter than others, more cunning. My mother still says, 'It's great that she's an activist; how much does she make?' The corporate world trains you for 'me-me-me.' Now the competition I'm trying to beat out is evil, not other humans.

"What I'm trying to accomplish with our organization is to influence society toward Islamic ideas of social justice, which should also be appealing to Christians and Jews. There's tension between the Muslim community and other faiths, and we want to educate, be known, be respected. We're working to obtain equal treatment and coverage in the media. And we'll exemplify Islam in the best way possible. Before we can do justice to the rest of the world, we need to do justice to ourselves.

Churches must create an alternative to Sunday morning worship. All the two-career households do chores and projects on Saturday. Sunday is their only day of rest. Most of them are too tired to make love, much less go to church.

Rochelle, CEO of a Valley counseling group

"I want to get us involved in welfare issues, maybe help with implementation of the new programs, and be a service to the poor and the needy. I can see myself ending up in prison someday, standing up for what is right. I don't think you can make change without going up against major forces. But it's not the people we're up against. It's the devil.

"We've gotten involved in coalitions when events require Muslim issues to be jointly addressed. We've also participated in presenting diversity training programs. Sometimes the people taking the training don't like it, and they ask, 'Why can't you guys just fit in?' My response is, 'What is it to be an American?'

"But I never permit myself to think of us as victims. If I ever perceive myself as a victim, then I have a problem. Back in school I hated my name because kids made fun of it and teachers didn't know how to pronounce it. That's over. You can't be a practicing worshiper of God and be a victim."

DUANE

Duane is a Silicon Valley journalist whose writing focus is issues of spirit and philosophy. He's an East Coast transplant, and enjoys covering the Valley's spiritual scene. "It's not like writing about transportation," he says. "Writing about religion opens me up, makes me reflect on life."

Duane's family is Jewish, and he grew up going to a Reform synagogue. "I felt it had an antiseptic quality," he recalls, "but I loved the communal aspect, the 'lifted-up' spirits, and the emotional connectedness and richness."

As many do, Duane fell away from his religion in early adulthood. Music became the most prominent spiritual element in his life. Now he's come most of the way back: religion and music synergistically coexist as inspirations for his spirit. "I'm consciously

Jewish," he says. "I'm a respectful Jew, but not always an observant Jew."

His professional pursuits give Duane the opportunity to probe and profile the full gamut of Valley spirituality. I asked for his observations on the area's spiritual environment and future directions.

"Silicon Valley is everything from conservative Christian churches to computer company pagans," he responded. "There's a major interfaith thrust, and there's a conservative backlash against that thrust. People come here and feel empowered to pursue whatever path they want. The area seems to enable that.

"A lot of denomination-shopping happens. It's like the age of free agency in religion. There seems to be growth happening at both ends of the style spectrum. At one end, contemplative practices are becoming important to more and more people: small groups and emphasis on quiet discussion. At the other end, there's the enormous charismatic thing. Tremendous bonding occurs during charismatic Christian services and events. There's an amazing sense of community that cuts across races and classes in conservative Christian functions. The liberals would be jealous if they knew about it!

"There's a spawning of new churches and denominations. Some of them are very conscious of the need to be 'marketing-oriented.' Many of them are most assuredly not into cross-pollination with others, and have their guard up. But they can be good neighbors with each other even if the tendency is for people to stick with their own.

I'd be happy if we could just get the Y to stop scheduling swim classes on Sunday.

Audrey, a Silicon Valley minister

"Many people here return to the fold of religion because they don't want their children embracing the valueless, materialistic, 'anything goes' California culture that can suck them in. Some people are desperate to protect their kids from the garbage, and religion can be that protection. Other people turn to religion because driving over the mountain to work every day at 5 AM with their lights on and all the nuts on the road is just wearing them out. Or someone they know dies, and they start to ask, 'Why are we alive?'

"In some ways, we're without community here, in the wide open spaces.

"If I could make one change to improve the area's spiritual values, I'd have us back off from a work ethic that's gone bananas. Your kids never see you, you never see your spouse, and you're escaping into a world that doesn't include the people most important to you. There's so much data and information available that no one can remember anything. There's too much negative, jarring, frightening stuff. The complete immersion in e-culture is not good. People should turn off their TVs, get off the Internet, slow down, and get back to other people."

Everyone figures it out sooner or later, on one side of the grave or the other. I'm sometimes concerned about people with no spiritual resources, but that's more compassionate worry than existential worry. No one is going to miss the bus. Some might even come to church.

Anita, a Valley minister

THE PATH FORWARD

So, what's it to be?

Will the technology chase and the cyberculture be crippling blows to the spirit, or the source of new inspiration? Will the invasion of massively powerful computers into the nooks and crannies of life be the death knell of faith, or the door to renewal? Will the manic pursuit of technological mastery and market share mix with new-wave, leading-edge sociodynamics and extraordinary economic success to produce spiritual nihilism, or spiritual nirvana?

Call me a cockeyed optimist if you will. I find myself coming down on the side that says this area will blaze new trails to spiritual understanding and fulfillment. The partnership of soul and silicon may be uneasy, suspicious, stormy, and thoroughly counterintuitive. But I believe the group of intrepid pioneers who have chosen to call this place home will find a way to make the marriage work, and show others how it's done.

Many of the people I've encountered in writing this book find themselves in the "dark wood where the straight way [is] lost" of Dante's *Divine Comedy*. But they are bringing to the age-old questions shared by all humankind the same drive, curiosity, intellectual firepower, creativity and energy that they have used to transform the world in the past 20 years.

And who knows? Maybe Tipler is right. Maybe our road to eternal life will indeed happen via some sort of cosmic computer emulation. If it does happen, it's a good bet that the technology involved will trace its soul-preserving origins to foundations laid on a legendary, long-vanished planet, by amusingly primitive, short-lived, easily distracted biological beings, in a hallowed, ancient enclave called Silicon Valley.

Epilogue

The idea for this book popped into mind out of nowhere as I was driving down Foothill Expressway from Palo Alto to Sunnyvale at the usual 5 miles per hour over the speed limit. I was resisting the usual temptation to make it 15.

At one time, undertaking a project like this would have been about as likely as my running a three-minute mile. Most of my life was lived without spiritual content. My parents practiced no religion. Neither did their friends. Neither did my friends. I went through some exploration in my early 20s and found nothing calling, or even interesting. I placed the topic in the file-and-forget pile. Many years later, two conversations plucked it back out.

The first conversation was with my long-time girlfriend. We had been together seven years. Our many compatibilities included a comfortable, shared lack of interest in matters of the spirit—or so I thought. Therefore, I was both surprised and irritated when we sat down for dinner on a peaceful Saturday night and, after I had made play with the wine and the glasses, she asked, "Do you ever think about your spiritual life?"

We were both hard-working, hard-charging Valley technology company professionals, putting in routine 60-hour weeks. By the time Saturday night rolled around, we were drained. It was a house rule that Saturday dinner discussion topics should never be weightier than the latest *Doonesbury* episode. Her question violated the rule. I also felt that after seven years she knew, or should have known, that the answer was not just "No," but "*Hell* no." I was not pleased.

I grunted a monosyllabic negative. The Saturday mood had been soured. She proceeded to make it worse by launching into substantial detail about the sudden resurgence she felt in her own spiritual life. I did not like the sound of this at all. It seemed out of place, and a violation of my contract, that this brand of ambush was happening to me in Silicon Valley. I gloomily drank cabernet and wondered what was going on.

The second conversation took place not long after the first. On our way to a software expo in Chicago, a business colleague told me about some dreadful things going on in his personal life, and the way his faith was helping him to cope. It was a wonderfully articulate expression of the interleaving of a person's life with his spirituality. I remember having the curious feeling that our intellectual centers were being bypassed, that his heart was talking directly to my heart.

These two conversations started what we call in the computer biz a "background process." It chugged away without my giving it the slightest conscious encouragement or participation. Eventually, it surfaced and expressed itself in a form I could recognize: it asked for data.

I gathered data from reading, from people, from observation, from reflection. I attended a few worship services. I took an "inquirer's" class. The process was leisurely. I had gone over 40 years without this spiritual stuff. No need to rush now.

It took five years for the background process to chomp on the data stream, complete its processing, come to a conclusion and report back. And the conclusion was that a faith had been born.

It seemed improbable. As a matter of fact, it was a little identity-threatening. I knew myself well. And what I had always known was that I was a person who did not have spiritual beliefs. But probability and identity were irrelevant issues, glitches to be worked out. The fact of faith superseded them.

In 1989, at age 46, I was baptized, and am now a member of the Episcopal Church. My burgeoning belief was not driven by any crisis, tragedy, incipient need, internal angst, external events or sudden revelation. It was the result of a gradual process as real as my feet, but more difficult to grasp. I really can't say I understand it yet.

In 1993, I married the girlfriend who started the background process. By that time, as those who are arithmetically quick may have calculated, we had been together for 16 years. No need to rush. I have forgiven her for the stick of dynamite she added to the menu on that long-ago Saturday night dinner. And I have thanked her.

In 1995, a variety of circumstances came together to make a midlife career change inviting and feasible. I had previously written a book on computers for the nontechnical, and enjoyed it. That memory teamed up with the urge to do something different, and the recent start of my spiritual path, to give birth to this book. Why conception happened on Foothill Expressway is still a mystery.

Let me conclude by summarizing what my personal reaction was after spending almost two years writing this book, and by passing on one of the key messages I heard from the people I interviewed.

This project gave me a sense of belonging to an entirely different faith community from that represented by my church. It's not *instead of* my church; it's *in addition to*. It's the community of those who have taken widely diverse paths and perhaps selected completely different approaches to their faith. But it's a community connected by the search for truth, for righteousness, for God (however defined), and for meaningful life in a culture where the rules are new, and change before anyone can write them down.

To a great degree, clergy and spiritual leaders in Silicon Valley are aware of, and comfortable with, this "changing rules" dynamic. During interviews with them, I received a few answers which might be considered "by the book." But the vast majority of the discussions centered on the search for truth, even if the search led to places hostile to their long-established doctrines. I actually detected more than *comfort* with the free-spirited, iconoclastic, Silicon Valley mavericks among whom these people work and minister: I sensed *enjoyment* of the challenge. The doors were open, the welcome mats out.

Perhaps the single predominant theme individuals communicated about themselves in this hectic environment is captured by a term used by members of the Baha'i faith: a desire for *deepening*. In many conversations I sensed a wish, a yen, a plan, a determination that a time would arrive when spiritual pursuit, philosophical commitment, inner knowledge, and food for the soul would move far, far up the priority list. For some, it might await financial security or the fulfillment of career objectives. For others, the gating item might be the successful completion of child rearing. But for many people, the ultimate goal—in a sense the ultimate *luxury*—is to someday, some way, have the time and space to dive deep, and

fully explore their hearts and souls, the meaning of their existence, and their relationship with their God. It is my profound
hope that every one of them achieves this objective.

The author welcomes your comments about this book. You may e-mail him at CAGoldman@aol.com, or write to the publisher:

Rising Star Press
P.O. Box BB
Los Altos, CA 94023
Fax 650/968-2658
e-mail: HiStar@aol.com
website: http://members.aol.com/HiStar/index.htm

❦

References and Suggested Reading

Armstrong, Karen. *A History of God: The 4,000 Year Quest of Judaism, Christianity and Islam,* New York: Alfred A. Knopf, 1994

Bellah, Robert N. et al. *Habits of the Heart—Individualism and Commitment in American Life*, Berkeley: University of California Press, 1985

Brady, Joan. *God on A Harley—A Spiritual Fable*, New York: Pocket Books Division of Simon and Schuster, Inc., 1995

Carter, Stephen L. *The Culture of Disbelief: How American Law and Politics Trivialize Religious Devotion,* New York: Anchor Books, 1994 (originally published: New York: Basic Books, 1993)

Cramer, Kathryn D. *Roads Home—Seven Pathways to Midlife Wisdom*, New York: William Morrow and Company, Inc. 1995

Cringely, Robert X. *Accidental Empires—How The Boys of Silicon Valley Make Their Millions, Battle Foreign Competition, and Still Can't Get A Date,* New York: Addison-Wesley Publishing Company, 1992

Frankl, Victor E. *Man's Search for Meaning*, New York: Washington Square Press, 1984

Friedman, Richard Elliott. *The Disappearance of God*, New York: Little Brown and Company, 1995

Hawking, Stephen W. *Black Holes and Baby Universes and Other Essays,* New York: Bantam Books, 1993

Kaplan, Jerry. *Startup—A Silicon Valley Adventure*, New York: Houghton Mifflin Company, 1995

Keen, Sam. *Hymns To An Unknown God*, New York: Bantam Books, 1994

LeGuin, Ursula K. *The Left Hand of Darkness*, New York: Walker and Company, 1969

Norris, Kathleen. *The Cloister Walk*, New York: Riverhead Books, 1996

Peck, Scott M., M.D. *The Road Less Traveled and Beyond—Spiritual Growth in an Age of Anxiety,* New York: Simon & Schuster, 1997

Saltzman, Amy. *Downshifting—Reinventing Success on a Slower Track*, New York: HarperCollins Publishers, 1991

Schwartz, Tony. *What Really Matters—Searching for Wisdom in America*, New York: Bantam Books, 1995

Sheehy, Gail. *New Passages*, New York: Random House, Inc., 1995

Talbott, Stephen L. *The Future Does Not Compute: Transcending the Machines in Our Midst*, Sebastopol, CA: O'Reilly & Associates, Inc., 1995

Tipler, Frank J., Ph.D. *The Physics of Immortality—Modern Cosmology, God, and the Resurrection of the Dead*, New York: Doubleday, 1994

Wakefield, Dan. *Returning—A Spiritual Journey*, New York: Doubleday, 1988

Whyte, David. *The Heart Aroused—Poetry and the Preservation of the Soul in Corporate America*, New York: Doubleday, 1994

Winslow, Ward, Editor: *The Making of Silicon Valley—A One Hundred Year Renaissance*, Palo Alto: Santa Clara Valley Historical Association, 1995

Wolf, Fred Alan, Ph.D. *The Spiritual Universe—How Quantum Physics Proves the Existence of the Soul*, New York: Simon & Schuster, 1996

Unpublished lecture notes for *Putting It All Together: Seven Patterns for Relating Science and Christian Faith,* a 1996 seminar series led by Richard H. Bube, Professor Emeritus of Materials Science and Electrical Engineering, Stanford University